# OCCUPATIONAL SAFETY AND MANAGEMENT OF RISKS IN HEALTH CARE INDUSTRY

## About the Authors

**Dr. Indu Karki** is currently working as scientist at Central Institute of Post Harvest Engineering and Technology, Ludhiana, one of the institutes of Indian Council of Agriculture Research, Ministry of Agriculture. She has work experience in consumer science and behaviour, ergonomics. She has guided 7 M.Sc. and B.Tech students. She has authored 7 research papers, 8 popular articles, 2 book chapters and I technical bulletin. She has also participated in 5 National and International Conferences and has life membership of 2 national scientific/professional societies. She got Reliance award in 2010 for best scientific paper presentation during national conference of Indian Association of Occupational Health, Mumbai.

**Dr. Promila Sharma,** is Professor in the discipline of Family Resource Management, G.B.P. U. of Agr. & Tech., Pantnagar. She is having vast experience of research in Ergonomics field.

**Dr. Sunil Kumar Rastogi** is an eminent Veterinary Physiologist of National standing. He is holding position of Head of the Department of Veterinary Physiology and Biochemistry at G.B. Pant University of Agriculture and Technology, Pantnagar, Uttarakhand since 2004. He graduated and post graduated in Veterinary Sciences from Haryana Agricultural University, Hisar, Haryana and obtained Ph.D. degree from G.B. Pant University of Agriculture and Technology, Pantnagar. His illustrious professional carrier comprised Veterinary Surgeon with Government of Haryana for three years, Assistant Professor at CSK HP Krishi Vishwavidyalaya, Palampur, H.P. for five years and more than 21 years of teaching and research assignments at G.B. Pant University of Agriculture and Technology, Pantnagar. He has authored 56 research publications, seven laboratory manuals, 10 popular articles, five book chapters and few semi-technical articles. He has also participated in 17 National and International Conferences besides member of several National Level committees for designing post-graduate curricula, review of research projects, selection of scientists and teachers. He is also life member of five national scientific/professional societies.

# Occupational Safety and Management of Risks in Health Care Industry

*By*

Indu Karki
Promila Sharma
and
Sunil Kumar Rastogi

CONCEPT PUBLISHING COMPANY PVT. LTD.
NEW DELHI-110 059

**ISBN-13 : 978-81-8069-911-5**

First Published 2014

*Published and Printed by*

Concept Since 1974

**Concept Publishing Company Pvt. Ltd.**
A/15-16, Commercial Block, Mohan Garden
New Delhi-110059 (India)
*T*: 25351460, 25351794, *F*: 091-11-25357109
E: publishing@conceptpub.com, W: www.conceptpub.com
**Editorial Office:** H-13, Bali Nagar, New Delhi-110 015, India.

Cataloging in Publication Data--*Courtesy:* D.K. Agencies (P) Ltd. <docinfo@dkagencies.com>

**Karki, Indu.**

Occupational safety and management of risks in health care industry / by Indu Karki, Promila Sharma and Sunil Kumar Rastogi.

p. cm.

Includes bibliographical references (p. ) and index.

ISBN 9788180699115

1. Nurses--Health and hygiene--India--Uttarakhand. 2. Nursing--India--Uttarakhand -Safety measures. 3. Nurses--Job Satisfaction--India--Uttarakhand. 4. Nursing services -India--Uttarakhand--Management. 5. Risk management--India--Uttarakhand. I. Sharma, Promila, 1955-, joint author. II. Rastogi, Sunil Kumar, joint author. III. Title.

DDC 610.73095451 23

**G.B. Pant University of Agriculture and Technology**
**Pantnagar-263145, Distt. Udham Singh Nagar**
**(Uttarakhand) INDIA**

# Foreword

Nursing, the profession of caring for the sick and the convalescent, the disabled and the helpless, is one of the noblest professions throughout the world. Nursing covers a range of functions that vary with levels of qualifications and the working environment. Twenty-four hours of operation in health industry is an old history of work pattern in the world since ages and it inevitably involves working the night shift. An important aspect of work environment of nurses is that they are required to work at any point in the 24 hour day. Therefore, stress in the nursing profession is an ongoing worldwide problem, where nurses have high levels of stress.

Better nursing practice environments and higher nurse staffing levels in hospitals have been associated with better nurse and patient outcomes. Amidst a worsening nursing shortage, national attention has focused on improving the nursing practice environment as a strategy to make the profession more attractive and to retain nurses at the bedside. Satisfactory work ability is sustained and promoted by good physical and mental health and by favourable working conditions. Several trends in hospital use and staffing patterns have converged to create potentially hazardous conditions for patient safety.

The purposes of this study has been to compare the nursing practice environments of a broad set of hospitals, with a better known hospital. It was also to suggest ergonomically suitable work schedule and strategies for nursing work.

I compliment Dr. Indu Karki, Scientist, Promila Sharma, Professor and Dr. S.K. Rastogi, Professor and Head for their efforts in publication of this important book. I am sure that the scientific information contained in the form of various chapters on different aspects will be useful for the nurses, hospital management, policy-makers, researchers and all those who are concerned with health and related sectors. The valuable information in the book can also be used as a reference for students as well as for scientists and executives involved in the area of health and safety.

**B.S. Bisht**
Vice-Chancellor

# Acknowledgements

This book is the result of a collective effort of investigator, teachers and the medical staff. Each chapter has been written, discussed and revised several times. We would like to acknowledge all those who have participated in these discussions.

First of all, we express our deep sense of gratitude to God, the Almighty with whose grace, blessings and kindness, we have been able to light this humble piece of work.

With profound reverence, we express heartfelt thanks to Dr. S.K. Rastogi, Professor and Head, Department of Veterinary Physiology, Dr. A.K. Shukla, Professor and Head, Department of Maths, Stat. and Computers, Dr. S.D. Samantaray, Professor and Head, Department of Computer Engineering, Dr. Gyanendra Sharma, Professor, Department of Agriculture Communication and Dr. Seema Kwatra, Senior Research Officer, Department of Family Resource Management for their constant inspiration, valuable suggestions, expert guidance and sustained interest during the course of investigation and preparation of manuscript. We are highly grateful to Dr. T.C. Thakur, National Professor, Indian Council of Agriculture Research, and Professor, Department of Farm Power and Machinery for making the foundation of the study and for giving his continuous guidance from the very beginning of this research till its compilation.

We extend our gratefulness to Dean, College of Post Graduate Studies, and Dean College of Home Science for providing the necessary facilities for conducting the research. We duly acknowledge our sincere thanks to Dr. R. Chandra, Medical Officer, University Hospital, G.B. Pant University of Ag. and Tech., Pantnagar, Dr. Ganeshraj Shivnani, Chairman,

Department of Cardiac Surgery, Sir Ganga Ram Hospital, New Delhi, Dr. R.C. Handa, Medical Superintendent, Sri Ram Murti Medical College and Hospital, Bareilly for granting permission and render their cooperation and support to obtain information.

We would fail in our duties if we do not mention our heartiest thanks to the nurses of University Hospital, G.B. Pant University of Ag. and Tech., Pantnagar, Sir Ganga Ram Hospital, New Delhi, Sri Ram Murti Medical Hospital, Bareilly, private and government hospitals of Haldwani, Rudrapur and Kichha for giving their valuable time to supply constructive and useful information for this research work. Though all others cannot be mentioned but none is forgotten.

Pantnagar
April, 2010

**Indu Karki**
**Promila Sharma**
**S.K. Rastogi**

# Contents

*Foreword by* ***B.S. Bisht*** 5
*Acknowledgements* 7
*List of Tables* 12
*List of Figures* 14
*List of Plates* 15

1. **Introduction** **17**
    - Rationale for the Study 23
    - Objectives 24
    - Hypothesis 24
    - Assumption 24
    - Limitation 25

2. **Review of Literature** **26**
    2.1 Studies Related to Anthropometric Measurements 26
    2.2 Physical Features of the Work Environment 29
    2.3 Occupational Hazards/Accidents/Risks/Injuries in Nursing Occupation 31
    2.4 Sleep Problems Associated with Shift Pattern in Nursing Job 35
    2.5 Studies Related to Psychological Problems Related with Nursing 39
    2.6 Studies Related to Job Satisfaction Level of Nurses 41
    2.7 Physiological Changes Due to Shift Pattern in Nursing 44
    2.8 Studies Related with Nap in Nursing Job 49
    - Salient Findings for Review 52

3. **Methodology** **53**
    3.1 Research Design 53
    3.2 Conceptual Framework 54

3.3 Selection of Variables 54
3.4 Operational Definitions 64
3.5 Selection, Construction and Description of Tools 71
3.6 Sampling Design 78
3.7 Method of Data Collection 80
3.8 Analysis of the Data 82

**4. Results and Discussion 86**
4.1 Personal Profile of Nurses 87
4.2 Family Profile of Nurses 90
4.3 Medical History of Nurses 92
4.4 Detail About Ailments of Nurses 99
4.5 Caffeine Consumption 101
4.6 Physical Exercise Performed by Nurses 102
4.7 Nutritional Status of Nurses 102
4.8 Occupational Details of Nurses 103
4.9 Tips to Reduce Work Stress 108
4.10 Opinion of Nurses About Themselves 109
4.11 Type of Activities Performed by Nurses 111
4.12 Handling of Medical Equipment/Scientific Gadgets/Medical Accessories/Furniture 111
4.13 Comfort/Discomfort from the Use of Furniture 123
4.14 Experience in Handling of Medical Equipments/ Scientific Gadgets/Medical Accessories/ Furniture 125
4.15 Occupational Hazards, Accidents, Risks, Injuries at Workplace 128
4.16 Environmental Parameters at Workplace 134
4.17 Psycho-Social Parameters 137
4.18 Physiological Parameters 150
4.19 Testing of Hypothesis 168
4.20 Ergonomically Suitable Work Schedule Approaches and Strategies for Nursing Work 174

**5. Summary and Conclusions 200**
5.1 Results of the Study 203
5.2 Conclusions 212
5.3 Implications of the Study 217

5.4 Recommendations to Fill the Research Gaps on Nurses in Night Shift System 218

*Annexures*

1. Interview Schedule 220
2. Chi-Square Value for Action Categories of REBA Postural Analysis 238
3. Analysis of Variance for B.P., H.R. and E.E.R. 239
4. Spirometry Analysis (Sample Respondents 2-12) 241

*Bibliography* 252

*Index* 264

# List of Tables


4.1 Personal Profile of Nurses 89
4.2 Family Profile of Nurses 92
4.3 Medical History of Nurses (During Last One Year) 95
4.4 Details About Ailments of the Nurses 100
4.5 Caffeine Consumption 101
4.6 Nutritional Status of Nurses 103
4.7 Occupational Details of Nurses 105
4.8 Tips to Reduce Work Stress 109
4.9 Opinion of Nurses About Themselves 110
4.10 Type of Activities Performed by Nurses 112
4.11 Handling of Medical Equipment/Scientific Gadgets/Medical Accessories/Furniture 117
4.12 Comfort/Discomfort from the Use of Furniture 124
4.13 Experience in Handling of Medical Equipments/ Scientific Gadgets/Medical Accessories/Furniture 126
4.14 Occupational Hazards, Accidents, Risks, Injuries at Worplace (Since Last 1 Year) 133
4.15 Environmental Conditions During Field Experiments 135
4.16 Report of Nurses Regarding Environmental Parameters at Workplace 136
4.17 Sleep, Sleepiness and Related Factors 137
4.18 Factors Affecting Sleep Quality at Workplace 140
4.19 Factors Responsible for Troublesome Sleeping and Awakening 143
4.20 Social Consequences of Nursing Job 146
4.21 Job Satisfaction Among Nurses 148
4.22 Anthropometric Measurements of the Nurses (Sitting Position) 151
4.23 Body Mass Index of Nurses 155

4.24 Physiological Cost of Work of Nurses in Terms of Blood Pressure (mmHg) and Pulse Rate (per min) 156
4.25 Physiological Cost of Work of Nurses in Terms of Heart Rate (beats/min) 157
4.26 Physiological Cost of Work of Nurses in Terms of Energy Expenditure Rate (kJ/min) 159
4.27 Related Perceived Exertion of Nurses 160
4.28 REBA Analysis for Postural Assessment of Nurses 162
4.29 Test of Significance for REBA Analysis 168
4.30 Analysis of Variance for Blood Pressure, HR and EER 169
4.31 Chi-square for Sleep Quality and Performance Capacity 170
4.32 Chi-square Test for Job Satisfaction and Working Condition 171
4.33 Chi-square Test for Job Satisfaction and Communication Skills 171
4.34 Chi-square Test for Job Satisfaction and Coordination within Department 172
4.35 Chi-square Test for Job Satisfaction and Time Demand at Workplace 172
4.36 Chi-square Test for Job Satisfaction and Infrastructure Facility Available at Hospital 173
4.37 Chi-square Test for Overtime and Concentration 173
4.38 Chi-square Test for Overtime and Marital Strain 173

# List of Figures


| | | |
|---|---|---|
| 3.1 | Conceptual framework of the Study | 55 |
| 3.2 | Schematic Representation of Interaction of Variables | 56 |
| 3.3 | FVC graph | 60 |
| 3.4 | Schematic representation of sample selection | 81 |
| 4.1 | Physical Exercise Performed by Nurses | 101 |
| 4.2 | Rating of Appetite of Nurses | 103 |
| 4.3 | Rating of sleep quality of nurses | 140 |
| 4.4 | Physiological Cost of Work of Nurses in Terms of Blood Pressure (mmHg) | 157 |
| 4.5 | Physiological Cost of Work of Nurses in Terms of Heart Rate (beats/minute) | 158 |
| 4.6 | Physiological Cost of Work of Nurses in Terms of Energy Expenditure Rate (kJ/min) | 160 |
| 4.7 | Rated Perceived Exertion of Nurses | 161 |
| 4.8 | REBA Analysis for Postural Assessment of Nurses | 162 |
| 4.9 | Test Protocol for Respiration Rate | 165 |
| 4.10 | Spirometry Analysis (Sample Respondent 1) | 166 |
| 4.11 | Blood Lactate Concentration of Nurses | 167 |

# List of Plates


| | | |
|---|---|---|
| Plate 1 | Measurement of Body Height | 65 |
| Plate 2 | Measurement of Eye Height from Ground | 66 |
| Plate 3 | Measurement of Shoulder Height from Ground | 66 |
| Plate 4 | Measurement of Elbow Rest Height | 67 |
| Plate 5 | Measurement of Knee Height | 68 |
| Plate 6 | Measurement of Popliteal Height | 68 |
| Plate 7 | Measurement of Buttock Popliteal Length | 68 |
| Plate 8 | Measurement of Thigh Height | 69 |
| Plate 9 | Anthropometric Kit | 77 |
| Plate 10 | Spirometer | 78 |
| Plate 11 | Lactate Calibrator | 78 |
| Plate 12 | Activities Performed by the Nurses | 113 |
| Plate 13 | Activities Performed by the Nurses | 114 |
| Plate 14 | Activities Performed by the Nurses | 115 |
| Plate 15 | Handling of Scientific Equipments in Hospitals under Study | 122 |
| Plate 16 | Handling of Scientific Equipments in Model Hospital | 122 |
| Plate 17 | Awakward Posture Adopted by Nurses while Recording | 130 |
| Plate 18 | Ergonomically Suitable Posture while Recording | 130 |
| Plate 19 | Poor Working Situation | 131 |
| Plate 20 | Functional Working Situation | 131 |
| Plate 21 | Measuring Respiration with Spirometer | 164 |
| Plate 22 | Measurement of Blood Lactate | 164 |
| Plate 23 | Ergonomically Designed Furniture Available in the Market | 179 |
| Plate 24 | Shoulder Exercise | 185 |
| Plate 25 | Back Exercise | 185 |
| Plate 26 | Exercise for Arms | 185 |
| Plate 27 | Exercise for Arms | 185 |

| | | |
|---|---|---|
| Plate 28 | Nurses with Personal Protective Equipment | 188 |
| Plate 29 | Nurses with Personal Protective Equipment | 188 |
| Plate 30 | Comparison of Hospitals Under Study with Model Hospital in Terms of Furniture | 189 |
| Plate 31 | Comparison of Hospitals in Terms of Infrastructural Facilities | 192 |
| Plate 32 | Coordinated and Shared Responsibilities of Doctor and Nurse | 197 |
| Plate 33 | Involvement and Coordination of Male and Female Nurse in Patient Care During Night Shift | 198 |
| Plate 34 | Presence of Hi-Tech Facility Around | 198 |
| Plate 35 | Avoidance of Excessive Manually Handling Activities with Introduction of Hi-Tech Furniture | 199 |

# 1

# Introduction

Nursing, the profession of caring for the sick and the convalescent, the disabled and the helpless, is one of the noblest professions throughout the world. From the general ward to the operation theatre in the hospital, nursing is the most important component of patient care. The process of restoring patients to normal health depends as much, if not more, on nurses as on doctors or surgeons. In fact, the availability of effective nursing services is an indicator of the health of a country's medicare system. Nurses work in various spheres and settings. They may work in general hospitals run by the government or private sector, mental hospitals, rehabilitation nursing homes, homes for the aged or sanatoria. The work place dictates the type of environment in which a nurse has to adapt. The organizational and environmental conditions of work refer to the way in which the work is managed and structured.

The common aspect of all jobs in nursing is that there are always a lot of people; a nurse has to interact with and they are always expected to display a calm, perceptive approach during crises that are only to be expected in hospitals. Nursing covers a range of functions that vary with levels of qualification and the working environment. The main functional areas include nursing in general hospitals and health centres; and serving in rural or urban areas through Public Health Scheme.

Recently, the demand for 24 hour operations in various types of industries has also expanded worldwide. But 24 hour of operation in health industry is an old history of work pattern in the world since ages and it inevitably involves working in night shift. Various tasks related to health care of people in health industry are undertaken by worker particularly the nurses—day and night. An important aspect of the work environment of nurses is that they are required to work at any point in the 24 hour day.

Stress in the nursing profession is an ongoing worldwide problem. Of all health care professionals, nurses have been found to have especially high levels of stress. A study among a large sample of Swedish nurses revealed that more than 80 per cent of the nurses reported high or very high job strain (Petterson *et al.*, 1995). Job stress in the nursing profession has been associated with decreased job satisfaction, increased psychological and physical complaints and absenteeism. Work conditions that have been associated with stress outcomes are inappropriate levels of formalization of work procedures (too much or too little formalization of work procedures), lack of adequate communication within the organization, and organizational politics.

Shift workers working in different industries including health industry experience a circadian rhythm dysynchronization, which is a recurrent or persistent misalignment between a patient's sleep pattern and societal norms. The workers cannot sleep when sleep is needed and thus, will suffer from chronic sleep loss. These workers have greater sleep loss, unhealthy lifestyle behaviours (e.g. smoking, poor diet, alcohol abuse, and lack of exercise), increased stress levels, and a higher incidence of cardiovascular disease, hypertension, and gastrointestinal disorders (Shields, 2002).

In multi-shift work schedules, workers need to operate well when on duty, despite sleeping irregular hours. Daytime sleep is often of a shorter length and provides lower restorative values than a full night's sleep. During a night shift, alertness and performance often diminish as time progress. The term "shift work" describes regular employment outside the normal daytime hours. Night-shift work can cause not only occupational accidents due to severe sleepiness and a resulting reduction in alertness but also can introduce several health problems among these non-daytime shift workers. Similarly, in health industry, sleepless nights and irregular sleep of the health care workers especially of nurses have direct and sharp impact on the health and well-being of the patients.

Sleep is a complex neurological state, with its primary function of providing rest and restoring the body's energy levels. The importance of sleep could be seen from the fact that people spend about one-third of their lifespan in sleep. Reduction in the amount of sleep predisposes individuals to sleep deprivation, resulting in poor psychomotor performance. Nurses who work the night shift may be particularly subject to sleep deprivation because of irregularity of sleep hours and disruptions in the circadian cycle. Poor psychomotor performance has been associated with an increase in error, which can be translated into an unsafe work environment. The identification of sleep deprivation in nurses is essential for maintaining safe working conditions. The amount of sleep a person gets affects his or her physical health, emotional well-being, mental abilities, productivity and performance. Recent studies associate lack of sleep with serious health problems such as an increased risk of depression, obesity, cardiovascular disease and diabetes. Experts recommend that adults get between seven and eight hours of sleep each night to maintain good health and optimum performance. Persons who think they might be suffering from a sleep disorder are encouraged to consult with their primary care physician, who will refer them to a sleep specialist.

The impact of sleep is the result of the circadian interference with sleep during daylight hours and circadian suppression of pineal gland by light at night. Night work is associated with disturbed sleep and wakefulness, impaired alertness particularly in relation to the night shift. Circadian rhythm sleep disorders are characterized by complaints of insomnia and excessive daytime sleepiness that are primarily due to alterations in the internal circadian timing system or a misalignment between the timing of sleep and the 24 hour social and physical environment. Many sources also add the presence of associated daytime impairments, such as fatigue, irritability, decreased memory and concentration, and pervasive malaise affecting many aspects of daytime functioning. In a recent study, 32 per cent of night-shift workers reported symptoms of insomnia or excessive daytime sleepiness, whereas these symptoms were reported in only 18 per cent of day workers from the same sample population.

Several studies have reported that sleep problems are more common among health care personnel on rotating work shifts. There is substantial evidence that the prevalence of sleep disorders is an important occupational health problem, especially among health care professionals on night or on rotating work shifts. The quality of sleep has been found to be altered in hospital nurses working on rotating shift schedules, especially those working in morning and night shifts as well as in hospital nurses working in night shifts when compared with day shift nurses.

Alterations in the quality, quantity and pattern of sleep result in sleep disorders. Persistent and repeated interruption of sleep affects the health of an individual. Undiagnosed and untreated wake/sleep complaints cause not only misery to the sufferer, but it also has socio-economic consequences. Sleep disorders cover a wide spectrum of diseases. Though there are more than 100 identified sleep/wake disorders, most sleep complaints can be categorized into five, namely, hypersomnia, insomnia, circadian rhythm disorders, parasomnias, and sleep disorders associated with mental, neurological, and other medical disorders. Researches during the last 50 years, and the advances made in clinical sleep medicine, have lead to more effective treatments for the myriad human sleep disorders. It is not possible to assign a specific reason for many of the sleep disorders, but some aspects of sleep and wakefulness are genetically influenced. But, most commonly, sleepiness during waking hours, results from volitional or forced sleep deprivation during previous nights, due to social, economic and environmental reasons. So, public awareness about sleep disorders should be an essential part of any programme aimed at global management of sleep disorders.

The study of the role of demands or environmental stimuli in stress responses largely dictates investigations in occupational stress. Stress theory is based on the evaluation of how the body responds to demands of the external and internal environment, considering that stress is produced when demands exceed ones individual capacities to respond to stimuli. When the available response mechanisms are not effective, stress lingers. This may lead to negative health effects, such as high-blood pressure, depression and anxiety. With the development of these conceptual aspects—emphasizing the idea that any factor, physical or psychological, capable of affecting hormone levels could be considered a stressor—a large body of knowledge was developed highlighting the role of demands.

Recent studies have focused on the effects of prolonged anomalous exposure to artificial light, both in outdoor and indoor environments, on alterations in the principal neuroendocrine mediators and on potential pathological effects such as: increased risk of carcinogenesis, metabolic disorders (in particular obesity and diabetes), cardiovascular disease, acceleration of the ageing process and alterations in regulation of the immune system. Many other studies have examined the emotional value of light and its role in the treatment of mood disturbances.

Light is one of the most important factors in our interaction with the environment; it is indispensable to visual function and neuroendocrine regulation, and it is essential to our emotional perception and evaluation of the environment. Previous studies have demonstrated its effects on the psyche and also its therapeutic role and documented the existence of a retinal photoreceptor linked to the supra-chiasmatic nucleus. This receptor has been ascribed a role in the transmission of neuronal transmission arising from light stimuli to the pineal gland, seat of the biological clock which presides over the regulation of the circadian system *via* the retinal hypothalamic pathway.

Control of the biological clock and the release of several important hormones (which are cortisol, the stress hormone, and melatonin, the sleep hormone) are governed by the alternation of light and dark. Thus, exposure to light has important repercussions on human health and behaviour. A role in the regulation of the sleep/waking pattern, mood change, tension, depression, anger, body temperature and physical and cognitive performance has been attributed to daily and seasonal variations in light. Besides light, other environmental factors such as humidity, noise, temperature and air circulation seem to be correlated with psychological factors (irritation, tiredness, anxiety, confusion and agitation).

Previously, various countermeasures to prevent adverse effects due to night-shift work have been examined in various industries but not much research is conducted on health industries. Exposure to stimulant environment condition such as "light", "sound" and "temperature", intake of caffeine or pharmacological substances, and taking a nap has been investigated to enhance and sustain worker's alertness during night shift. Taking a nap particularly has known one of effective countermeasure to prevent increasing sleepiness and decreasing alertness among nurses which is exercised in the world.

The concept of control, in the psycho-social perspective, was first developed by psychologists and was deeply marked by the emphasis placed on the ability of influencing life events and self-esteem or depression effects. In this perspective, job control was rarely studied as a descriptive element of the work environment, i.e. as an important factor of the perception of autonomy the individual builds based on himself and his life. **Job satisfaction** is one of the central variables in work and organizational psychology and is seen as an important indicator of working life quality. **Job satisfaction** can be influenced by a variety of factors, including availability of functionally sound tools, equipments, supplements, furniture and furnishings at the workplace, quality of relationships with superiors and colleagues, the degree of fulfilment at work and prospects for promotion. Satisfied employees tend to be more productive and creative. Studies have shown a direct correlation between physician **satisfaction** and patient **satisfaction**.

**Rationale for the Study**

Long work hours and shift work adversely affect worker's health by increasing exposure to occupational hazards and reducing time for recovery. Research on shift workers, working in different production/service and other industries have been undertaken by different organizations; but not much attention has been paid to the industries where workers render their services for the health and care of people. Evidence shows increased working hours are associated with musculoskeletal injuries, needle sticks, and fatigue among nurses in developed as well as developing countries. Nursing job regularly include working long hours, shift work and mandatory or unplanned overtime. Before curing the patients, nurses themselves should be healthy and free from any risks at workplace to serve the patients as well as themselves with full dedication. The study of this kind especially on nurses has not been conducted till date in India. So, the present study will be of extreme importance for the welfare of society as a whole.

Since ages, the health industry is working in shift pattern, but focus was not given to this area. Multinational companies in India and their shift work has revealed that hospitals are also at risk particularly with regard to nurses who are the worst sufferers of the shift pattern and thus needs to be investigated in depth. Not much attention has been paid to conduct researches on sleep problems of the workers, working in 24 hours work industry. Thus, nurses also need care since they provide their excellent services to human beings day and night without caring for the own health. Therefore, the working environment of nurses needs serious attention. There is a dire need committed to provide safe working environment to this group of workers, i.e. nurses. Besides efforts need to be made to work out various approaches to protect them from any ill effect, thus making them fit to take care of patients.

## Objectives

1. To study the profile of nurses in the field of nursing, i.e. personal and family profile, medical history and selected anthropometric measurements.
2. To study the existing infrastructure facilities available in health care industry and handling of the same, i.e. environmental parameters, medical equipments, medical accessories/supplements/tools, furniture related to care of patients.
3. To study the occupational details (type of activities) and associated hazards/accidents/risks/injuries at the place of work.
4. To study the psychosocial and physiological cost of nursing work.
5. To suggest ergonomically suitable work schedule approaches or strategies for nursing work.

## Hypothesis

$H_1$: Action categories of REBA are independent of activities performed by nurses.

$H_2$: There is no significant difference in mean BP, mean HR, and Energy Expenditure Rate while performing various groups of activities by the nurses.

$H_3$: There is no significant association between sleep quality and performance of nurses.

$H_4$: There is no significant association between job satisfaction and working condition, communication skills, coordination within department, time demand, infrastructure facility available at health care industry.

$H_5$: Concentration ability and marital strain among nurses are independent of duration of overtime.

## Assumption

1. Sufficient sleep can improve the work performance.
2. Introduction of NAP strategies reduces the occupational risks in the health care centres.

**Limitations**

1. The study was conducted on 120 ward nurses only and thus the generalization would apply only to the similar work environment.
2. Since this was a research work of the student, a sample of only ward nurses of only selected hospitals was taken as sample.

# 2

# Review of Literature

To formulate the problem precisely and to pinpoint the importance of undertaking the same, it is essential to present brief review of the researches related directly and indirectly to the present study. Quite a number of studies have been conducted in abroad in order to explore the real status of nurses in the health care industries and occupational health hazards. In India, however, emphasis is not given to this inevitable community of nurses. In this chapter a brief resume of work done to the present study has been reviewed with respect to:

2.1 Studies related to anthropometric measurements
2.2 Physical features of the work environment
2.3 Occupational hazards/accidents/risks/injuries in nursing occupation
2.4 Sleep problems associated.with shift pattern in nursing job
2.5 Studies related to psychological problems related with nursing
2.6 Studies related to job satisfaction level of nurses
2.7 Physiological changes due to shift pattern in nursing
2.8 Studies related with Nap in nursing job

## 2.1 Studies Related to Anthropometric Measurements

The word "anthropometry" means measurement of the human body. It involves systematic measurement of the physical properties of human body, primarily dimensional descriptors of body size and shape. Anthropometry derived from the Greek words ***anthropos*** (man) and ***mentron*** (measure). The anthropometric data are used in ergonomics as reference data in planning ergonomic workplace layouts, to specify the physical dimensions of equipments, evaluating a wide range of products from clothing to spacecraft to "fit the task to the man" (Grandjean, 1980), thus enhancing operational ability, safety, convenience and comfort while performing tasks without augmenting work efficiency and reducing work cost.

Hira (1980) conducted a study on "An ergonomic appraisal of educational desk" and reported that the seat desk clearance of 16 cm was preferred by 95 per cent of the subjects, whereas most preferred desk height was 72-74 cm. The seat heights were found to be satisfactory whereas the seat depth were found to be very small by most of the subjects.

Evans *et al.* (1988) stated that anthropometric information for chair design is mainly concerned with providing data on stature of the people for whom the seats are designed.

Grandjean (1988) stated that the most favourable working height for handwork while standing is 50-100 mm below elbow level. The average elbow height is 980 mm for women. Author concludes that average-working heights of 880-930 mm for women will be convenient; besides these anthropometric considerations there must be allowance for the nature of the work.

Yaung *et al.* (1988) constructed a hydraulically adjustable chair with seven independent variables—seat height, seat angle, seat rocking, seat swivel, back rest distance, back rest height and back rest angle to evaluate comfort and biomechanical factors relevant to the design of a chair for industrial sewing operators. Overall body discomfort, electromyography (EMG) and height reduction (vertebral disc shrinkage) were used to evaluate these seven independent variables after making two females to work for 6 hours. The results indicated that to accommodate 90 per cent of the female population, seat height should be adjustable in the range of 10-15 cm (measured from the centre of the back rest to the centre of the seat pan), the back rest height should be fixed at 25 cm (measured from the centre of the back rest of the centre of the seat pan) and seat should be allowed to swivel freely.

The human geometry and the geometry of the product must be suitably fitted together (Kreifeldt, 1991) for safety as well as for functional reasons. Thus appropriate anthropometric applications are necessary for a "human compatible" designed product.

Anthropometric data could be used in ergonomics to ensure that physical mismatch between the dimensions of equipment, products and the corresponding use of dimensions of equipment, products and the corresponding use of dimensions are avoided (Pheasant, 1991).

Anthropometry is the approach, which deals with the measurements of the human external body dimensions in static and dynamic conditions (Chakrabarti, 1997). These include measurements of body parts, their strength, speed and their ranges of motion. External human body dimensional measurements are taken when a man is placed in a rigid and static position, whereas dynamic anthropometry is required more than static body measurements in the yield of design. The human body is not rigid but rather, always dynamic. Anthropometric data are fundamental to the design of safe and usable products (Norris and Wilson, 1997), and the benefits of using these data in designing process are widely recognized.

Thakur and Sharma (1998) ergonomically assessed various activities performed by women farmers. Anthropometric measurements of the women farmers in standing postures were taken to design and modify agricultural implements. Various products were designed taken into account the anthropometric measurements of hand and palm.

Anthropometry data sets are one way of bringing the physical dimensions of users into the designing process; however, there are limitations for design teams using these. Information sources are also fragmented making it difficult for the practicing designer to locate and compile relevant data (Porter *et al.*, 1999).

Adalarasu and Balasubramanian (2005) while evaluating chair for computer related works, reported that poorly designed office chairs in addition to intense computer work lead to musculoskeletal disorders known as computer related injuries (CRI).

Dewangan (2005) conducted a survey of thirty-three anthropometric dimensions from 280 male farmers belonging to 7 states of eastern region. Range, mean, standard deviation, coefficient of variation, 5th, 50th, and 95th percentile for each anthropometric dimension were calculated for entire region. The anthropometric dimensions of farm youths of the north eastern region were compared with those of the northern, eastern, southern and western region of India. It was found that the people of the north-eastern region had most of the body dimensions lower than those from other regions except southern and eastern regions of India. It was also stated that for efficient designing of tools and machines for higher productivity, the anthropometric data of the operators are very essential.

Workplace furniture design and user anthropometry have become an important consideration in designing ergonomically appropriate furniture (Van Wely, 1970; and Harris *et al.*, 2005).

Dhyani (2007) cited in her research study that, anthropometry is an integral part of human limitations and capabilities and the fact that the anthropometric dimensions vary significantly from individual to individual. It is essential to consider the range of variability in general body size, gender, racial/ethnic differences while designing the tools and equipment.

## 2.2 Physical Features of the Work Environment

Mckennel (1971) while studying noise sensitivity and performance differential reported that during noisy situation there is temporary drop in the number of correct additions per word period. Thus, more energy was used by the subjects during work, which was indicated by measures of oxygen consumption and muscle action potential. It was also observed that some people complained of more annoyance at high level of noise. He further reported that different people are affected differently by the same level of noise.

Fanger (1979) while studying local discomfort to the human body caused by non-uniform thermal environments stated that temperature between 19°C and 26°C are generally considered comfortable provided that the humidity is not too high. As humidity increases from 50 to 90 per cent at 26°C can increase the feeling of discomfort.

Mohanty (1980) conducted a study in which multiplication task was given to the students under periodic, non-periodic noise and quite conditions. Under periodic noise, 70.0 per cent of the students showed decline of output and 95.0 per cent complained of irritation and unpleasantness. Quiet conditions were found to be most suitable.

Rodgers (1980) also stated that raising the humidity from 50 to 90 per cent at 26°C can increase the feeling of discomfort. Further he revealed that humidity below 70 per cent is preferable in the summer months. The comfort zone of relative humidity lies from 20 to 85 per cent, with 35 to 65 per cent being the most common values.

Lindstrom and Vuori (1984) studied the relationship between environmental and individual factors with job satisfaction and psychological strain symptoms among a group of workers in an open plan office. Results revealed that disturbance in work performance due to noise were greater especially when the estimated noise level was higher. Symptoms of subjective strain were associated with poor ergonomics of the worksite and sudden loud noise in the work environment.

Klausewitz *et al.* (1986) categorized the effects according to different levels of noise and described that up to 23 dB noise, there is no disturbance whereas from 30-60 dB noise, most of the psychological effects at upper range occur, i.e. stress, and tension, further from 60 to 120 dB noise, psychological, physiological, ontological (ear diseases) effects occur and at above 120 dB noise, painful effects occur.

Sharma *et al.* (1988) reported that an individual spends more energy to perform a particular job in presence of extreme noise level than in normal conditions because more hazardous effects arise. Below 90 dB noise, there is no disturbance. At 90 to 100 dB noise, significant change in pulse rate and at 110 dB noise stimulation of reception in skin was observed. A noise level up to 140 dB can drive a man to instantly as it is extreme limit of human noise tolerance.

ISO 8995 (1989) revealed that a well lighted place means a better quality of work done in less time. With less strain on the eyes and expanding less mental and physical energy. In other words the quality of work done depends upon the amount of light entering in the place. Many working interiors are dim at illuminance that is lower than 200 lx. This is the reason that 200 lx is recommended as the minimum illuminance for workplace where work is executed for long periods.

## 2.3 Occupational Hazards/Accidents/Risks/Injuries in Nursing Occupation

Nag and Patel (1995) examined the risk potentials and accident patterns among the monthly rotating shift workers and permanent night workers in textile industries in India. At the beginning of the work shift, the production process raises possibilities for risks of accidents. This is particularly true in the case of morning shift. For example, after three hours of work there is demand of speedy work. This is considered a dangerous period and accident rate touches peak at the fourth hour of the shift. Beyond the fifth or sixth hour, however, human fatigue is probably responsible for further risk of accidents. Compared to the morning shift, however, the rate of accidents is relatively less on the afternoon shift, with no major difference between the first and second half of the shift. Despite that, the number of accidents on night shift is less than on other shifts, but there is a consistent rise in the percentage of accidents reaching a peak at fifth or sixth hour of work. In general, higher percentage of accidents in the later part of the night shift may be attributed to performance decrement, fatigue and lack of arousal associated with disturbed circadian rhythms. The results indicated that more accidents happened on first shift between three and four hours of work. Afternoon shift did not have many accidents. Third shift had the least of all. However, on third there was a peak in accidents at the 5th and 6th hour of work. It was reported that the main problems in accidents are concerned with the lack of organizational commitment and decision making in the issues related to occupational health and safety.

An examination of the worker's compensation claims made by nurses from the whole facility showed low back claims to be more common than neck and upper limb claims. It appears that nurses are more likely to make a worker's compensation claim for low back symptoms than neck and upper limb symptoms. In other words, worker's compensation claims do not accurately reflect the types of musculoskeletal symptoms actually experienced by nurses and affecting their ability to do their work. Five nurses from each unit were also observed during the entire morning and afternoon shifts to examine the work load and the effects of fatigue on the musculoskeletal system. Heart rate measurements and ratings of perceived exertion were taken. Activities performed and types of transfers carried out were also recorded. Nurses in one of the units had significantly more reported neck and shoulder symptoms than their counterparts. Observations of a sample of five nurses from each unit also showed higher ratings of perceived exertion in this unit. These differences were possibly confounded by the fact that nurses in the unit which experienced these problems were about 8 cm shorter and about 5 kg lighter than their counterparts. Differences in the work practices in the two units, especially methods of manual handling and use of ergonomic interventions were identified as important contributing factors (Lusted *et al.*, 1996).

Gitlin (1998) reported that the design of the structural environment should support, rather than restrict, a person's daily life. It also allows for the individual to meet physical, psychological and social needs, and promote a sense of well-being and safety.

The injury risk did not seem to be higher on the night shift in terms of frequency, but more severe accidents occured on the night than on day shifts. More injuries were observed at the end of the shift, at the 2nd part of the shift block, and in the summer. The accident rate was lower at weekend, especially on Sundays. It has been found that the night shift was not as dangerous as it might have been presumed, taking into account the lower level of human performance and accumulation of fatigue. The sharp rise of the accident rate in the second hour of the morning shift was observed, and it could be assumed that it reflected both the organizational factor; the presence of more workers and management personnel at this time of day, and the fatigue effect due to the early beginning of the shift at 6 a.m. It is assumed that delaying the shift's beginning to 7-7:30 a.m., could result in diminishing the worker morning fatigue and improving their well-being as well as alertness and vigilance (Oginska *et al.*, 1999).

Steele *et al.* (1999) surveyed emergency medicine physicians to compare the incidence of accidents or near misses in regular day shift *versus* evening or night shift workers, and found that 76 residents reported 96 accidents, and 553 reported 1146 near misses during the commute home. Nearly three quarters of the accidents and 80 per cent of the near misses occurred following a night shift. The number of incidents was significantly related to the number of night shifts worked per month.

Long work hours and shift work adversely impact workers' health by increasing exposure to occupational hazards and reducing time for recovery. Nursing job regularly include working long shifts, shift work, and mandatory or unplanned overtime. Evidence shows increased working hours associated with musculoskeletal injuries, needlesticks, fatigue among nurses in developed countries. There is a concern about nurses working long hours prioritizes patient safety over worker safety. Nurses working non-day shifts are at higher risk for occupational injury and illness. The more frequently a nurse works mandatory or unplanned overtime, the greater the odds of experiencing a work-related injury or illness, and missing work because of it (Castro *et al.*, 2007).

The static body position at the work station is clearly a risk factor for occurring osteomuscular pain. However, pain can also develop due to other factors such as working hours and sleep quality. The poor sleep quality and the habit of not taking naps can contribute to develop osteomuscular pain, as well as night shift working hours, which make also difficult to practice physical activities. The variables statistically associated to back osteomuscular pain were poor sleep; habit of not taking naps; increase of body weight during the last year; night shift (Lemos *et al.*, 2007).

Working at night is known as a risk factor for reduction in sleep duration, which has also been associated with body weight increase. Consequently, it might be suggested that the seniority in night work could also be associated with the increase in weight among night workers. There is an expected increase in body weight with age and years worked, both day and night work. Nevertheless, night work appears to result in a higher body mass index than day work (Marqueze *et al.*, 2007).

Shift work and non-standard working hours are associated with increased impairments of health and reduced social well-being. But not all regulations of working hours have an adverse health effect. More than half of the employees report no sleep disturbance, 36 per cent occasional and 9 per cent frequent sleeplessness regarding all three shift groups. There are only insignificant correlations between the shift groups and sleep patterns and the subjective sleep quality and quantity too. Shift work is not associated with more frequent sleep disturbances or a worse subjective sleep quality and quantity. The shift groups do not differ regarding the cardiovascular risk factors (blood pressure, lipo metabolism) and health behaviour (sport, smoking). Most of these risk factors rise with an increasing age and the effects are more strongly in men than in women. Shift work regulations which include no or only a small part of night-work do not have any probable negative health effects apparently. The known negative effects of the shift work are probably relevant at higher share of night-work only and along the disturbance accompanying the circadian rhythms (Ulbricht *et al.*, 2007).

## 2.4 Sleep Problems Associated with Shift Pattern in Nursing Job

Yamasaki (1998) reported that total sleep time was significantly greater in the non-African American day shift workers than in the other 3 groups. After controlling for work shift and race/ethnicity, longer sleep times predicted less dipping (absolute and relative) in blood pressure. Urinary norepinephrine and epinephrine were higher during work than non-work in both racial groups of day shift workers, but in evening + night shift workers the difference was small and in the opposite direction. These results indicate that being African American and working evening or night shifts are independent predictors of non-dipper status. Higher sleep blood pressure may contribute to the known adverse effects of shift work.

Moreover, effects of shift work on mood changes were studied on 1608 Japanese female nurses, working on rotating shift schedules, revealed that there were prominent changes of subjective fatigue, activity and confusion were observed especially when shift changes occurred. However, the mood changes were observed even after adjusting for the effect of sleep hours, indicating that irregular sleep pattern is not the only cause that affects mood (Hartel, 2000).

According to Ohida *et al.* (2000), sleep disorders caused by night-shift work in hospitals affect the job performance of many nurses. Therefore, relationship between sleep disorders and shift work among young female nurses in 11 hospitals in Japan was determined and statistically significant correlations were observed between working night shifts and the use of alcoholic beverages to help induce sleep, and between working night shifts and day time drowsiness. Statistically, significant differences were also observed between the two- and three-shift systems with regard to subjective sleep quality. Moreover, statistically significant correlations were observed between average hours of sleep and the following three items related to sleep: subjective sleep quality, difficulty in getting to sleep, and day time drowsiness. The results suggest that in the Japanese shift-work systems, sufficient hours of sleeping are needed for nurses who work night shifts to ensure good quality of sleep.

Mckenzie (2001) reported that a cross sectional study in Germany on sleeping disturbances and fatigue symptoms on sample size 3332 nurses on the effect of night shift found that night shift is associated to sleeping disturbances off duty but not to fatigue symptoms on duty. They conclude that fatigue is primarily related to quickly alteration work schedules but not to the fact of day shift or night shift. Also night shift is correlated to sleeping disturbance but it is unclear if night shift leads to fatigue symptoms.

Significant associations were observed between working on night shift and the use of alcoholic beverages to help induce sleep, and between working on night shift and daytime drowsiness. Significant differences were also observed between two- and three-shift systems with regard to subjective sleep quality. Moreover, average hours of sleep were significantly associated with three related sleep items: subjective sleep quality, difficulty in getting to sleep, and day-time drowsiness. Results suggest that in Japanese shift-work systems, sufficient sleep hours are needed for nurses who work on night shift to ensure good quality of sleep and consequently better services for patients (Ohida *et al.*, 2001).

A study conducted to examine shift related differences in chronic fatigue and the contribution of sleep quality anxiety and depression to chronic fatigue among a random sample (142) of female critical care nurses. Twenty-three per cent of this sample met the criteria for clinical depression, day and night nurses did not differ in their reports of chronic fatigue. Night nurses reported more depression and poorer sleep quality, depression and anxiety, depression and sleep quality were the most relevant to the explanation of chronic fatigue. This study suggests the need for studies of strategies to promote sleep and improve mood in critical care nurses (Perkins, 2001).

Almasi *et al.* (2006) reported that out of 128 nurses, more than 96 per cent were suffering from sleep disorders. Among them 0.8 per cent had only sleepiness during the day,

30.4 per cent had only nightly sleeplessness and 68 per cent had both nightly sleeplessness and sleepiness during the day. All nurses enrolled in the study 96.9 per cent of women and 96.7 per cent of men had sleep disorders. Rates of sleep disorders in married and single nurses were 99 and 90.32 per cent, respectively. Rate of sleep disorders among nurses who worked on rotating shifts was 97.54 per cent, while this rate in nurses who worked only on day shift was 83.33 per cent. Results of this study demonstrated high prevalence of sleep disorder among enrolled nurses—most probably because of shift working and extra working—that needs a serious attention. Rate of sleep disorders was higher in nurses who worked on shift, but the difference was not statistically significant.

Hobbs *et al.,* (2007) conducted a study on night shift and post shift sleepiness and reported that there is some indication that providing a 30 min nap reduces the negative effect of prolonged wakefulness and exercise may be beneficial as well. The multiple driving time periods appear to negatively impact driving incidences; the longer one had to maintain driving alertness, the more likely driving performance degraded. Driving performance varied considerably between individuals, both the mean level of performance and variability increase significantly when the sleep cycle is disrupted. Subjects were 4 times more likely to experience a driving error in periods 2 & 3. Period 2 was 20-35 min. after ending work; period 3, 40-55 min.

Night work is associated with disturbed sleep and wakefulness, particularly in relation to the night shift. Circadian rhythm sleep disorders are characterized by complaints of insomnia and excessive daytime sleepiness that are primarily due to alterations in the internal circadian timing system or a misalignment between the timing of sleep and the 24-h social and physical environment. In 86 shift-work nurses with insomnia disorders, administration of 5 mg of melatonin about 30 minutes before a night time sleep significantly decreased Sleep Onset Latency (SOL) and increased sleep quality as compared with placebo. Researcher further observed a significant improvement in falling asleep induced by 5 mg of melatonin (16 min) as compared to baseline, which supports the well known capacity of this hormone to change biological rhythms (Haghighi *et al.*, 2008).

Kalia (2008) reported that total sleep time was significantly greater in the non-African American day shift workers than in the other 3 groups. After controlling for work shift and race/ethnicity, we determined that longer sleep times predicted less dipping (absolute and relative) in blood pressure. Urinary norepinephrine and epinephrine were higher during work than non-work in both racial groups of day shift workers, but in evening+night shift workers the difference was small and in the opposite direction. These results indicate that being African American and working evening or night shifts are independent predictors of non-dipper status. Higher sleep blood pressure may contribute to the known adverse effects of shift work.

Nehme *et al.* (2008) reported that night work is associated with metabolic alterations. These include obesity, elevated serum lipids, hypertension among others. The study aimed to compare the effects of high-protein and high-carbohydrate night meal on sleepiness among night security guards, according to their body mass index. It was found that an interaction effect between time and body mass index for the week with high carbohydrate meal. The workers with body mass index above 30 $kg/m^2$ were sleepier than the others after eating the high-carbohydrate meal. There were no significant effects observed for the week with high-protein night meal. The results suggest that night meal content does have an effect on night worker sleepiness. However, this effect seems to be modulated by weight.

Sahu and Basu (2008) observed that evening type of personnel like slowly rotating or permanent night shift. The qualities of quantity of sleep are much better in evening chronotype compare to other two chronotypes when they engaged in night work in all three types of rotation. Total sleep hours are significantly less in morning type of personnel when they work in slowly rotating or permanent night shift. In physiological response curve it was observed that acrophase shift in evening chronotype of personnel are prominent. It helps them to adapt slow rotating night work. The alertness is low and exertion ratings are high in morning chronotype of people.

The impact of night and shift work on health is not positive referring to empirical studies of ergonomic research. Previous studies identified a link between night work and an increased incidence of sleep disturbances as well as increased risk parameters for cardiovascular diseases. This study had aims like do employees with high quantity of night work (G3), small quantity of night work (G2) or employees without night work (G1) differ in shift times, sleep aspects (sleep disturbances, sleep quality and quantity, splitted sleep) and health aspects (lipo metabolism, hypertension, sports and smoking). Employees with a high quantity of night work sleep less than employees with a lower quantity of night work. Employees with a high quantity of night work split their sleep much more often than employees with a lower quantity of night work. Night workers show higher systolic and diastolic blood pressure values. HDL-cholesterol concentration decreases with increasing quantity of night work. Other lipo metabolism parameters (total cholesterol, LDL cholesterol, triglycerides) do not differ between the different employee groups. Night and shift workers tend to show a more favourable health behaviour than day workers (sport activities, non-smoking). Night shift work is not associated with more frequent sleep disturbances or a worse subjective sleep quality or quantity (Ulbricht *et al.*, 2008).

## 2.5 Studies Related to Psychological Problems Related with Nursing

The need of professional, skilled nurses will increase as the population ages while the shortage of nurses is the reality already. Nurses are stressed further by inconvenient working hours like extensive working hours, weekend work, evening and night-time work, insufficient breaks during working shift, and even having to take on two jobs in order to make reasonable pay. Stress experienced in the field of nursing is on the increase even though work-related strain in other fields is declining. The growing conflict between the demand and the resources available creates an increasing amount of overload (Wickstrom, 2001).

The prevalence of psychological distress was 33.3 per cent, ranging from 20.0 per cent among lady nurses to 36.4 per cent, among nurse assistants. Strong dose-response gradients were observed between demand and psychological distress and the negative association between job control and psychological distress. Prevalence of psychological distress was higher (PR = 2.6; 95% CI: 1.81-3.75) among professionals in high-strain jobs (high demand, low control) when compared to professionals in low-strain jobs (low demand, high control), after adjustment by potential confounders in a logistic multiple regression model (Araújo *et al.*, 2003).

Studies have shown that certain unsatisfactory features of work such as poor opportunities to exert influence and insufficient social support networks increase the risk of careworkers' physical condition and functioning capability deteriorating (Brown *et al.*, 2006).

According to recent domestic estimates (Rauhala *et al.*, 2007), an increase of 30 per cent to the optimum level of strain in nursing work increases the number of sick leaves 1.5 times. At the yearly level, this means about 12 extra days for sick leaves.

The study of Abdalkader and Hayajneh (2008) describe the effect of night shift among nurses working in critical care units. The findings showed that female nurses had a significant difference on sufficient sleep, and interpersonal conflicts. In addition, the results indicated that nurses experience health problem and their work performance affected by the night shift. The study findings indicated that night shift affect critical care nurses well-being.

Erickson and Grove (2008) reported through their study that compared to their older counterparts, nurses under 30 years of age were more likely to experience feelings of agitation and less likely to engage in techniques to manage these feelings. Younger nurses also reported significantly higher rates of burnout and this was particularly true among those experiencing higher levels of agitation at work. We conclude by suggesting the need for increased awareness of the emotional demands facing today's nursing workforce as well as the need for more experienced nurses to serve as emotional mentors to those just entering the profession.

Morghen (2009) reported that comparing the number of hours worked per week by the doctors and nurses, it emerged that, although the former group worked longer hours, the latter tended to report higher levels of stress. The doctors who worked from 46 to 50 hours per week reported stress levels of 57 per cent and the nurses who worked from 37 to 45 hours per week reported stress levels of 46 per cent, a higher amount of stress per hour. The physicians declared a far higher capacity to influence their work flow (autonomy) than the nurses.

## 2.6 Studies Related to Job Satisfaction Level of Nurses

Job performance and job related stress of nurses was examined on 463 nurses working in rotating shift. The study revealed that the overall job performance was highest for nurses on day shift followed by the night, afternoon, and rotating shifts. Rotating shift nurses experienced the most job related stress, followed in turn by the afternoon day and night shift nurses (Coffey *et al.*, 1998).

Brooks and Swailes (2002) reported that permanent night shift nurses reported lower levels of commitment to nursing. As predicted, influence over shift patterns and realization of preferred shift pattern were positively associated with commitment to nursing, although the relationship was weak. Positive perceptions of career development opportunities were a stronger predictor of commitment to nursing.

In another study, Landrigan *et al.* (2004) demonstrated that intensive care unit interns working a traditional every third night extended 24-hours call schedule executed 5.6 times as many serious diagnostic errors than when they worked an intervention schedule that eliminated extended work shifts and reduced the number of hours worked per week.

About the prevalence of extended work periods and their effects on patient safety. Logbooks completed by 393 hospital staff nurses revealed that participants usually worked longer than scheduled and that approximately 40 per cent of the 5,317 work shifts they logged exceeded twelve hours. The risks of making an error were significantly increased when work shifts were longer than twelve hours, when nurses worked overtime, or when they worked more than forty hours per week (Rogers *et al.*, 2004).

Gelsema *et al.* (2005) examined the influence of organizational and environmental work conditions on the job characteristics of nurses and on their health and well-being. The direct influence of work conditions on outcomes was examined. Mediation of job characteristics in the relationships between work conditions and outcomes was tested by means of regression analysis. The results indicated that job characteristics, such as demands and control, mediated the relationship between work conditions, such as work agreements and rewards, and outcomes. By managing organizational and environmental conditions of work, job characteristics can be altered, and these in their turn influence nurses' job satisfaction and distress.

Kinzl *et al.* (2005) suggested that a high level of job satisfaction in anaesthetists correlates with interesting work demands and the opportunity to contribute skills and ideas. To improve job satisfaction, more attention should be paid to improve working conditions, including control over decision-making, and allowing anaesthetists to have more influence on their own work pace and work schedule.

Tanya *et al.* (2005) conducted a study to examine the influence of organizational and environmental work conditions on the job characteristics of nurses and on their health and well-being. The sample consisted of 807 registered nurses working in an academic hospital. The direct influence of work conditions on outcomes was examined. Mediation of job characteristics in the relationships between work conditions and outcomes was tested by means of regression analysis. The results indicated that job characteristics, such as demands and control, mediated the relationship between work conditions, such as work agreements and rewards, and outcomes. By managing organizational and environmental conditions of work, job characteristics can be altered, and these in their turn influence nurses' job satisfaction and distress.

Zverev (2005) reported that rotating shift work had significant effect on the amount of full meals. Comparison of the two groups of nurses indicated that volunteers in the study group had lower number of reported full meals per day, lower self-assessed appetite and eating pattern satisfaction during the night-shift phase of the rotating shift cycle than nurses on the day-shift schedule. All respondents in the study group and 40.9 per cent of nurses in the control group reported irregular eating pattern. Significant association was found between the self-reported health scored and appetite, amount of full meals and eating habit satisfaction in both groups of nurses. Nurses who reported irregular eating pattern had significantly lower subjective health score than nurses who consumed food regularly.

Abraham *et al.* (2006) identified several areas of tension in the nursing profession. The commitment to being competent providers of quality care was remarkably strong among the nurses, but they also perceived the barriers in the work environment to be multiple and complex. Concerns about the quality of leadership and management, insufficient staff, time demands and stressful work environment are experienced as obstacles in providing good nursing care. Four out of ten nurses (39.2%) would not choose nursing again as a career and more than half of the nurses (54.3%) have contemplated leaving the profession at some point in time. To effectively tackle the professional and workforce issues in nursing, investments should focus on redesigning a work environment that supports nurses in providing comprehensive professional care.

Nielsen *et al.* (2008) reported that intention to leave the workplace due to present working hours was highest among employees, who against their preference—had non-day working hours or weekend-work. It is thus important to take employees' preferences into account when planning and evaluating the work schedule. The aim of the study was to investigate whether a misfit between preferences and actual working hours for those working "odd hours" affected the intention to leave the workplace due to one's working hours. The fit between self-reported work-time preferences and actual work schedules was evaluated. Work schedule characteristics presented are non-day work and weekend work. "Fit" was defined as accordance between preferences and actual working hours.

According to Zieger (2009) in a large hospital, safety practices and results likely to be different than those of smaller facilities. The agency for healthcare research and quality suggests that small, rural hospitals score higher on quality than large urban facilities. Among the biggest gaps between the two categories of hospital was performance around handoffs and traditions, with rural hospitals performing 22 per cent better than urban facilities. This gap occurs, in part, because handoffs pose different types of problems for large and small facilities. With larger facilities, coordination and communication between different departments is particularly difficult.

## 2.7 Physiological Changes due to Shift Pattern in Nursing

Kobayashi *et al.* (1997) reported that three shift patterns, i.e. a day shift following a day shift, a night shift following a day shift, and a night shift following a half-day shift, were studied in terms of physical activity level, sympathetic and parasympathetic activity levels, cortisol, prolactin and changes in mood states. The change to the half-day shift increased the duration of sleep before night duty by about 86 min and brought wake-up times forward by about 1 h, resulting in increases in rest and time before work. In addition, the change was revealed to reduce the influence of reversed-phase circadian rhythms on autonomic nervous activity during the night shift. The score for sleepiness was significantly lower at 0500 hours following a half-day shift. There were some marginal but not significant differences in the scores reflecting the degree of vigour, tiredness and irritation during the night shift. Although the prolactin concentration was significantly decreased at the start of the night shift after the half-day shift, there was no difference in cortisol concentration between the usual night shift after a day shift and the night shift after the half-day shift. The half-day shift was not observed to cause any marked change in the fixed biorhythms of these nurses. The cortisol levels were low during the night shift, suggesting that the night shift itself is a high stress level, which is prejudicial to biodefense.

Lipkin *et al.* (1998) stated that shift workers are more likely to suffer cardiovascular and digestive disorders. Shift workers also experience headaches, muscle pain, respiratory infection and general malaise these in-turn result in higher rates of absenteeism employee turnover and higher costs associated with recruiting and training replacement employees.

Nonetheless, Steeland and Fine (1998) studied the effects of shift on worker who do not rotate, to determine whether current shift or recent change in shift was a risk factor for ischemic heart disease, they conduct a nested case control study of heart disease death at work within a cohort of 21,000 men. They found that there was little evidence of any difference in heart disease risk by current shift. There was some indication that recent change from afternoon or night shift to day shift had a protective effect initially which decrease over time on the other hand no corresponding negative was found for change from first to second third, but analysis were limited by small number of workers on night shift.

The problem with a night shift working is that, the human race is diurnal, who are functions during day time. Night workers report a number of health problems. Therefore, these negative effects have consequences not just for individual, but also for work place, as decreased alertness and reduced job performance that could endanger human lives and affect the quality of care at intensive care unit (Crofts, 1999).

Takahashi *et al.* (1999) studied the shift work-related problems between 16-hour night shift and 8-hour evening/night shifts among nurses in a university hospital with respect to subjective symptoms, physical activity, Heart Rate (HR), and sleep. The nurses of one group worked a 16-hour night shift under a rotating two-shift system, while those of the other group worked an 8-hour evening or night shift under a rotating three-shift system. The 16-hour night shift was staffed by three or four nurses who alternately took a 2-hour nap during the shift, and had at least one day off after each shift. Subjective symptoms and daily behaviour were measured every 30 min by the nurses before, during, after each shift as well as during days off using a time-budget method. Also, physical activity, Heart Rate (HR), and posture were recorded during shifts. The results showed similar or lower levels of sleepiness, difficulty in concentration, fatigue, physical activity, and HR during the 16-hour shift compared to the 8-hour shifts. No differences in subjective symptoms between the two shift schedules were observed before or after the shifts or during days off. The main sleep was longer after the shifts and during days off in the 16-hour shift group than in the 8-hour shift group. Our results suggest that the work-related problems in 16-hour night shift nurses may not be excessively greater than those in 8-hour evening/night shift nurses, as long as appropriate countermeasures are taken during and after the extended shift.

Costa (2001) indicates that women can be more vulnerable to shift-work in relation to both their more complex circadian and infradian (menstrual) hormonal rhythms and extra demands related to family life. This includes disorders such as menstrual pains abortion interference with fetal development, premature and low birth weight.

Chronobiological knowledge is increasing and the relationship between this knowledge and shiftwork is becoming clearer. This, in turn, is highlighting a need to facilitate a mix of permanent (day, evening and night) and rotational shift systems within individual wards or units. Is it perhaps time to allow greater flexibility in how individual nurses deal with the profession's need to care for patients throughout the 24 hours period? This review will focus on the 24 hours day-night or circadian rhythms and the consequences of the disruption of these rhythms as nurses undertake shiftwork and other activities which demand efficient functioning at times when an individual's circadian rhythms are expecting them to be at rest. As disruption of these rhythms is essentially unavoidable when 24 hours care is required, the choice becomes one of determining a preference for tolerable rhythm dysynchrony and shorter more frequently occurring episodes of night work, or some degree of rhythm synchrony and adaptation during slightly longer but less frequent episodes of rhythm disruption (Sandra, 2001).

Exposure to light at night suppresses the physiologic production of melatonin, a hormone that has antiproliferative effects on intestinal cancers. Although observational studies have associated night-shift work with an increased risk of breast cancer, the effect of night-shift work on the risk of other cancers is not known. We prospectively examined the relationship between working rotating night shifts and the risk of colorectal cancers among female participants in the nurses' health study. We documented 602 incident cases of colorectal cancer among 78m586 women who were followed up from 1988 through 1998. Compared with women who never worked rotating night shifts, women who worked 1–14 years or 15 years or more on rotating night shifts had multivariate relative risks of colorectal cancer. These data suggest that working a rotating night shift at least three nights per month for 15 or more years may increase the risk of colorectal cancer in women (Schernhammer *et al.*, 2003).

A study conducted by Noula *et al.* (2005) indicates that the health profile of nurses in Greece is relatively poor for this occupational group. In addition our study implies that some major health related behaviours are not considered directly by the group of nurses studied when self-rating their health. This may have a negative impact on their ability to promote health in their patient population. Further understanding of nurses' beliefs and behaviours is required in order to develop policies and strategies that will enhance their health promotion role. This information could be used in targeted health education and health promotion efforts in this group of health professionals.

Risk factors connected to life-style diseases increases the absenteeism of nurses in both day time work and in shift work. The joint occurrence of high cholesterol, overweight, high blood pressure and disturbed sugar levels lead to the risk of absenteeism 2.2 times higher than in cases where this combination of risk factors is non-existent (Kivimaki *et al.*, 2006).

Kudielka *et al.* (2007) reported that cortisol profiles including the cortisol rise in the first hour after awakening (CAR) were assessed during shift work and days off (eight saliva samples per shift). Participants were 102 healthy permanent day and night shift workers (comparison groups) and former permanent day and night shift workers after implementation of a new fast-forward rota including morning, evening, and night shifts. Results show that the CAR is detectable in day as well as night shifts. In permanent night workers cortisol profiles appear to be blunted during night work and days off. However, circadian cortisol profiles are not disturbed in former night workers who recently switched to the fast rotating shift schedule. In contrast, implementation of night work in former day workers seems to lead to initially blunted cortisol profiles that normalize after a short adjustment period. Results of a psychological assessment including exhaustion, chronic stress, effort–reward imbalance, and ratings of sleep quality and sleep length are also presented.

The study demonstrated that it was possible to increase the employees influence on their own working hours by implementing individualized computer-based planning of the work schedule. The intervention, in turn, did not affect biomarkers and self-reported risk factors for CVD. The aim of the study was to investigate the effect of work-time influence on biomarkers and self-reported risk factors for CVD among nursing personnel in the Danish eldercare sector. Though the intervention significantly increased the employees' self-reported work-time influence in the "high intensity" group compared with the reference group the intervention did not alter the participants' CVD-risk factor profile (Nielsen *et al.*, 2008).

Vannam and Kher (2008) studied the effects of night shift working on human circadian rhythm and found that the call centre ranked high for attrition due to health reasons, for sleeping disorders—83 per cent compared to industry average of 39.5 per cent, voice loss—8.5 per cent as against 3.9 per cent, other problems were ear problems (8.5 per cent), digestive disorders (14.9 per cent) and eyesight problems (10.6 pèr cent).

Epidemiological studies have found that long-term night-working women have a higher risk of breast cancer than women who do not work at night. According to the circadian rhythm disruption hypothesis the underlying mechanism involves suppression of melatonin production caused by exposure to light at night. Some evidence shows that melatonin has oncostatic and anti-oxidative properties, and also affects estrogen signalling and immune function. Artificial light at night might also disrupt circadian genes function, which can alter cell-cycle regulation. The results show differences between day and night melatonin syntheses in the expected direction in both group of nurses. Statistically significant differences between day and rotating night shift nurses were observed in evening samples, but not in morning samples (Beata *et al.*, 2009).

Korompeli *et al.* (2009) reported that mean reduction of cortisol level between the two measurements was statistically significantly greater for the 'rotating' than 'morning' shift group. There were no statistically significant differences between the two groups in overall mean change from the first to the second measurement of prolactin, triiodothyronine and thyroid-stimulating hormone. Levels of thyroxine increased statistically significantly in the 'rotating' group but not in the 'morning' group. The morningness scale score was greater for the 'rotating' group, while greater job satisfaction levels were found in the 'morning' group. Statistically significant correlations were found between thyroid-stimulating hormone, trüodothyronine, thyroxine and prolactin changes and specific scales of the SSI questionnaire. Ergonomic shift schedules sympathetic to the body clock and nurses' preferences should be adopted to mitigate the adverse effects on health.

## 2.8 Studies Related with Nap in Nursing Job

Takeyama *et al.* (2002) suggested that taking a night time nap was an effective way to reduce adverse effects due to first nocturnal work especially for morningness-type. According to the results taking a 2-hour nap later at night is expected to be more effective against the adverse effects. Task performances and subjective complaints of drowsiness and anxiety for morningness types were improved by taking a nap on the first night of night shifts.

Naps in the latter half of the night shift were superior to earlier naps in terms of sleep quality. However, performance declined after a 1-hour nap taken later in the night shift due to sleep inertia. This study suggests that appropriate timing of a short nap must be carefully considered, such as a 60-min nap during the night shift (Takeyama *et al.*, 2004).

Takeyama *et al.* (2005) reported that night time napping is an effective measure to prevent adverse effects due to night shift work. A characteristic of night time nap is that it can result in considerably deeper sleep. To promote night-time napping strategy in the workplace, consensus building while acting on conflicting interest is essential. Recently, participatory method for improvement of working condition has expanded worldwide. A characteristic of the activity is using action checklist and group work, and heightening motivation to improvement working condition between worker and manager. Through the activities, night-time napping strategy would be spread more in the workplaces and play a role as one of the effective tools for improving working conditions, work performance and safety in the future.

Night shifts interfere with circadian rhythms so that even adequate day-time sleep before a night shift may not be protective. As measured by the Psychomotor Vigilance Test, the nap group had fewer performance lapses. In the mood profile test, the nappers reported more vigour, less fatigue, and less sleepiness. However, measures of tension, depression, confusion, and anger, were the same for both groups. There were no aggregate difference in driving performance between the two groups. There were a substantial number of occurrences of dangerous driving in both groups. Across all participants, such events occurred during approximately 8 per cent of the drive, each event potentially lethal. However, a comparison of dangerous driving in the same individual between shifts showed that the driving of non-nappers worsened on night three, whereas that of napping subjects improved slightly. Analysis of driver alertness also showed trends suggesting the nap helped (Groch, 2006).

The results showed that a 120-min nap sustained early morning performance better than a 60-min nap. Taking a nap earlier or later did not affect the neurobehavioural performance tests, although participants slept more efficiently during naps later in the night shift. A negative effect of a nocturnal nap during the night shift on subsequent day-time and nocturnal sleep was not observed in the sleep architecture. It still remains unclear whether slow wave sleep plays an important role in sustaining early morning performance. In terms of work safety and sleep health, the results suggest that a longer and later nap is beneficial during night shifts (Kubo *et al.*, 2007).

Night time napping during a night shift is one of the effective strategies for sleepiness and fatigue among night shift workers. The findings suggested that the effect of sleep inertia on Visual Vigilance test performance was profound, but not on subjective sleepiness in late 60 condition. It is considered that the dissociation between performance and sleepiness might reflect an unstable state that participants cannot realize a decline in their performance by themselves (Kubo *et al.*, 2007).

Napping programmes at workplace are a reality in some industries, particularly in Japan. In Brazil, several hospitals allow nurses to sleep during the night shift, but this is really evaluated from the workers' health and well-being perspective. The concept of need for recovery from work can be useful for testing the role of napping/sleep during night shift on workers' health and well-being. The need for recovery is not a problem if workers have enough time to recover between periods of work. From this perspective, household duties would likely to interfere in the recovery process as they may influence the availability of time for recovering. Sleeping on the job during night-shifts for 2-3 hours is related to a better recovery from work among female nursing personnel provided that workers are not submitted to long domestic work hours (Costa *et al.*, 2008).

### Salient Findings from Review

The following conclusions can be drawn on the basis of review of literature—

1. Human body dimensional measurements are the ground on which the comfort and safety of the worker can be designed and efficiency can be improved in the form of product he/she is using.
2. Satisfactory environmental factors can enhance the quality of work and at the same time less time is consumed with comparatively less efforts.
3. Nursing has emerged as an area which has a lot of occupational hazards (physical as well as psychological), accidents, risks and injuries which seem to be developed during long working hours, shift patterns and overtime.
4. Disturbed circadian rhythm as a result of frequently changing shift pattern in nursing profession leads to changes in the physiological process.
5. Frequently rotating shift work and working in night leads to sleep disorders among nurses.
6. Psychological problems are prevalent among nurses ranging from stress to mood changes.
7. Job satisfaction leads to commitment in nursing profession, which is crucial to patient safety.
8. Napping strategies work as healing ailments for the wounds resulting from shift work which is a reality in the nursing field.

It is clear from the reviews that India is lagging behind in conducting studies which are related with ill effects of shift work especially in nursing field. This gap in the research provide a strong basis for taking such type of study which will be a boon to nursing community as for coming in limelight.

# 3

# Methodology

Research methodology is a systematic and scientific way to solve the research problem. It deals with the selection of sample, identification of variables, their measurement and the statistical tools used for analyzing the data. The methodology is given under following heads:

3.1 Research design
3.2 Conceptual framework
3.3 Selection of variables
3.4 Operational definitions
3.5 Selection, construction and description of tools
3.6 Sampling design
3.7 Method of data collection
3.8 Analysis of the data
  3.8.1 Categorization of variables
  3.8.2 Descriptive analysis
  3.8.3 Experimental analysis
  3.8.4 Statistical analysis

## 3.1 Research Design

A research design is the arrangement of processes for collection and analysis of data in accordance with the objectives of the research. In order to achieve the objectives of the study, descriptive-cum-experimental research design was selected. Descriptive research design was chosen to assess the personal and family profile of the ward nurses, medical history of ward nurses, infrastructure facility in health care industry, occupational details, occupational hazards in the nursing job and the psycho-social cost of nursing job. The main purpose of descriptive research design is the description of the state of affairs, as it exists at present.

On the other hand, experimental research design was used to find out anthropometrical measurements of ward nurses, postural stress while working in the hospital, environmental parameters and assessment of physiological cost of work of ward nurses.

## 3.2 Conceptual Framework

This represents the relationship of the variables with respect to the objectives of the study. It was proposed that if ergonomically suitable work schedule and work environment was introduced in the health care industries for the ward nurses, it reduced the occupational health hazards of the ward nurses. For this, it was important to identify the occupational hazards, accidents, risks, injuries of the work of ward nurses. To do this, we needed to record the anthropometric measurements of ward nurses, which ward nurses were handling besides studying the infrastructure facilities available in the health care industry. It was also proposed that to reduce any kind of hazard to these ward nurses, the physiological and psychological cost of work need to be studied along with types, duration and frequency of activities (conceptual framework in Figure 3.1).

## 3.3 Selection of Variables

A variable, as the name implies, is something which varies or variable is a concept which can take different value in a given range. The variables were selected according to the objectives of the study. The selected variables were categorized into independent and dependent variables. The schematic representation to show the hypothetical relationship between the variables considered for the study is given in Figure 3.2.

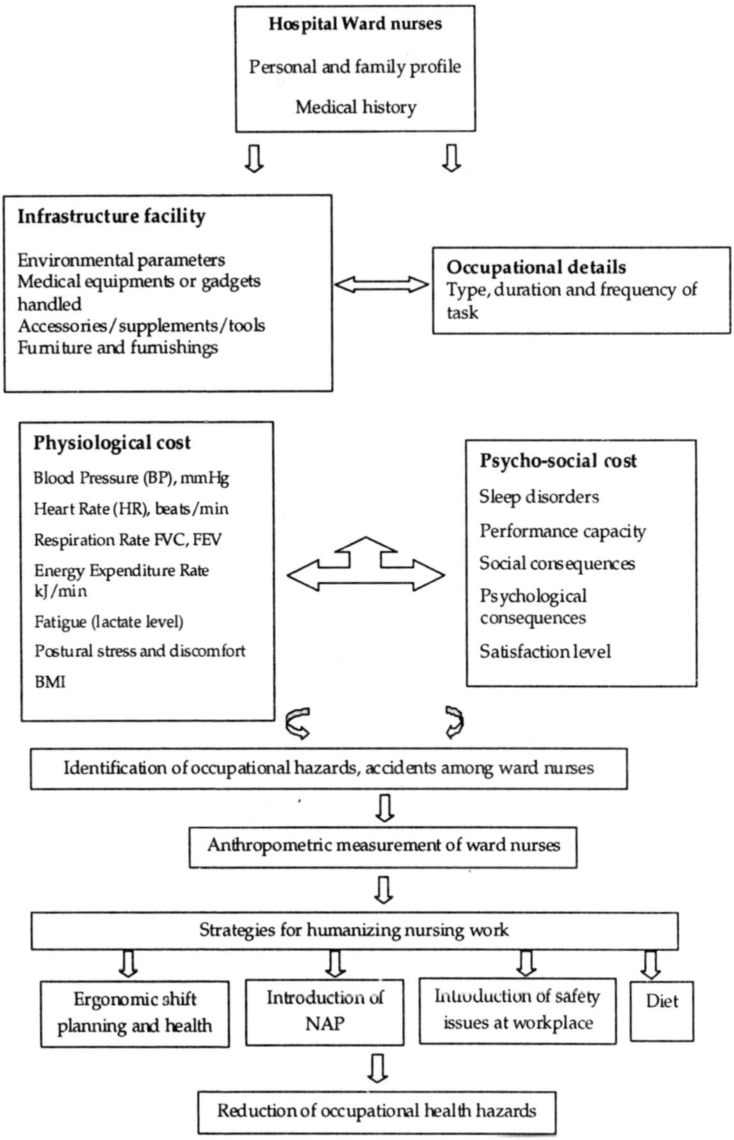


**Fig. 3.1:** Conceptual Framework of the Study

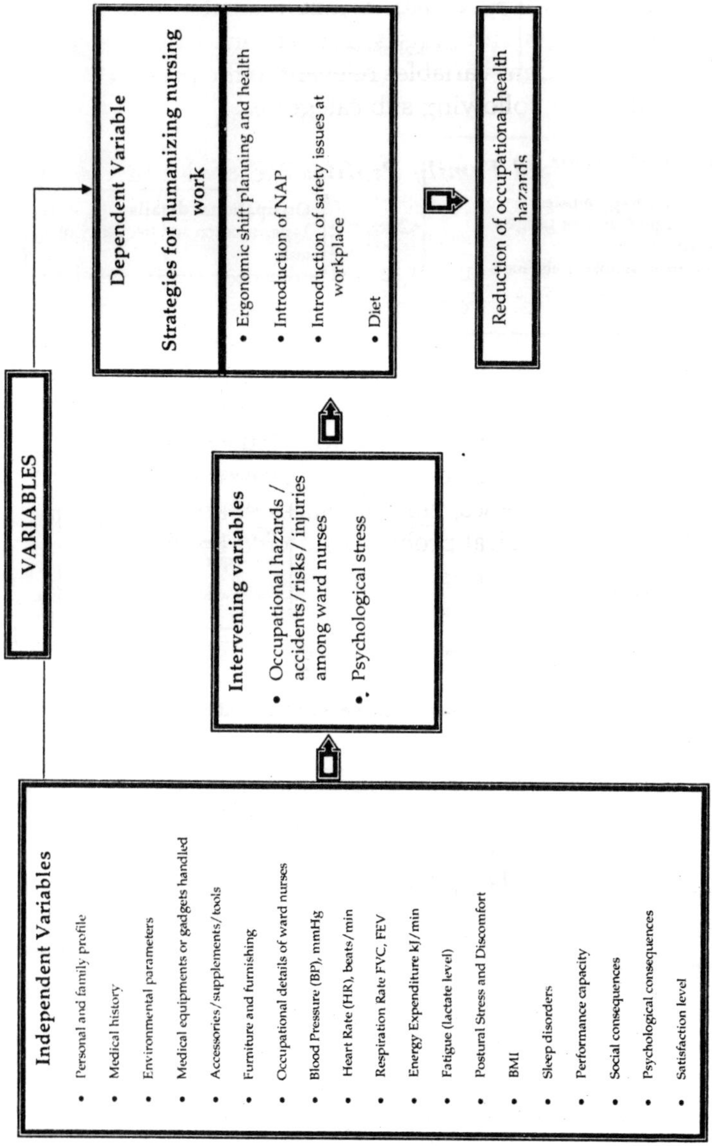


**Fig. 3.2:** Schematic Representation of Interaction of Variables

### 3.3.1 *Independent Variables*

An independent variable is antecedent to the dependent variable. It predicts and causes fluctuations in dependent variables. Independent variables relevant to the present study are grouped under following sub-categories:

1. ***Personal and Family Profile:*** Personal and family profile of nurses affect the level of involvement in nursing job and working pattern, therefore, this included the name, age, educational qualification, marital status, income of ward nurses, type of family, family composition, age of family members, relation with family members, educational level of members, occupation of family members and the family income.
2. ***Medical History:*** Medical history of the nurses provide health status thus dealt with different physiological (common illnesses, chronic illnesses, and symptoms) and psychological problems suffered by ward nurses during last one year.
3. ***Environmental Parameters:*** Environmental parameters directly affect the health and well-being of the nurses; therefore, various environmental parameters like illumination (light), temperature, humidity, noise, air circulation were included.
   (a) ***Illumination:*** Illumination affects the concentration of nurses in task and thus was included. It is the means of providing light measured in unit of Lux.
   (b) ***Ambient Temperature:*** Degree of hotness or coldness in the environment. Comfortable body temperature is 20°C and 23°C. It relates with human environment interaction.
   (c) ***Relative Humidity:*** Index of amount of water vapours in the air or it is the water vapour pressure at a given temperature. Humidity may affect to working of nurses.
   (d) ***Sound Level:*** Ability to hear clearly without stress and strain to ears. Sound is measured in decibel (dB). Excessive noise distracts the attention of nurses.

3. ***Medical Equipments or Gadgets Handled:*** They add the availability of medical equipments/scientific gadgets in the hospitals, the variety of equipments handled by the nurses, frequency and duration of handling of these equipments in a day by the ward nurses for assessing the comfortability of these equipments and the repetition in their handling along with frequent use of same muscles for longer duration which leads to musculo-skeletal disorders.
4. ***Medical Accessories/Supplements/Tools:*** They include the frequency and duration of using various medical accessories/supplements/tools in a day to assess the availability of different medical accessories/ supplements/tools in the hospitals, frequency and duration of handling of these accessories in a day by the ward nurses. Ward nurses are prone to use these repeatedly for a long period.
5. **Furniture:** They deal with the frequency and duration of using various furniture in a day to assess the postural discomfort associated with the use of different furniture.
6. **Occupational Details of Ward Nurses:** Occupational details of ward nurses include the duration of job, type of job, type of job shift, duration of shift, preference for shift, change in shift, overtime, duration of overtime, type of activities performed by the ward nurses and experience in handling of various medical equipments, accessories and furniture. These details were studied as they lead to disturbance in circadian rhythm and have direct impact on the sleep profile of the ward nurses.
7. **Blood Pressure (mmHg):** Due to extended working hour, prolonged overtime, ward nurses get stressed which may result in increase in blood pressure, so this parameter was measured to see the impact of various activities on the blood pressure.

Flow of blood between heart and the active musculature during dynamic muscular effort, blood is squeezed out of the muscle due to contraction but flows back easily during the subsequent relaxation.

(a) **Diastolic Pressure:** It is the lower level of blood pressure. The period of relaxation of the heart during which the heart chamber fills with blood.

(b) **Systolic Pressure:** It is the upper level of blood pressure. The period of contraction during which heart pumps blood into the arteries. The above pressures may change in different events.

**Mean Blood Pressure: Variations in different occupations are observed by different researches.** At normal resting heart rates mean blood pressure can be approximated using the more easily measured *systolic* and *diastolic pressures,* SP and DP:

Mean Blood Pressure (mmHg)
= DP+ 1/3 (SP-DP) ...(3.1)

Five values of measured blood pressure were averaged each time to make final assessment.

8. **Heart Rate (beats/min):** Research has shown that heart rate is increased as a result of shift pattern (Takahashi *et al.*, 1999), so this parameter was measured before, during and after performing various groups of activities. Five values of resting, working and recovery heart rate were measured (at the interval of 1 minute each) and were averaged to work out average heart rate.
9. **Respiration Rate:** The purpose behind taking this parameter was that after performing activities in different shifts and in different periods of the working day, a lot of exhaustion, ward nurses have to face, which may decrease their respiration capacity, so, respiration rate of ward nurses was taken after the completion of shift period.

   Respiration Rate is measured with the help of spirometer. It means the measuring of breadth specifically, a type of pulmonary (lung) function test that measures the amount in (volume) and/or speed (flow) of air that can be inhaled and exhaled. Lung function indices include as following:

(a) **Forced Vital Capacity (FVC):** It is the volume of air that can forcibly be blown out after full inspiration and measured in litres.

(b) **Forced Expiratory Volume (FEV):** It is the volume of air that can be forced out while taking a deep breadth. It is an important measure of pulmonary function. The forced expiratory volume in the first second is $FEV_1$.

(c) **$FEV_1$/FVC:** This is the ratio of $FEV_1$ to FVC. In healthy adults this should be approximately 75-80 per cent.

(d) **Peak Expiratory Flow (PEF):** It is the speed of the air moving out of subject's lungs at the beginning of the expiration and measured in litres per second (l/s).

10. **Energy Expenditure Rate (kj/min):** However, ward nurses perform moderate activities, but they do those in repetition and some activities for longer duration, which may result in fluctuation in energy demand, i.e. sometime higher or sometime requirement is low. Therefore, it becomes crucial to identify the actual Energy Expenditure Rate among ward nurses while performing activities.

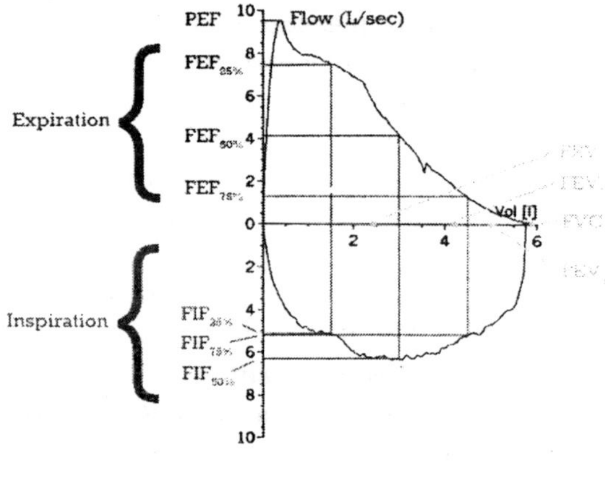

**Fig. 3.3:** FVC graph

11. **Energy Expenditure Rate (kJ/min):** However, ward nurses perform moderate activities, but they do those in repetition and some activities for longer duration, which may result in fluctuation in energy demand, i.e. sometime higher or sometime requirement is low. Therefore, it becomes crucial to identify the actual Energy Expenditure Rate among ward nurses while performing activities.

    The normal heart rate and increased heart rate during performance of tasks are measured and then energy expenditure is calculated with the help of following formula:

    Energy Expenditure Rate (kj/min)= 0.159 × Avg. working HR–8.72 ....(3.2)

12. **Fatigue (Lactate Level):** Studies have revealed that there are changes in subjective fatigue and confusion especially when shift changes occurred. Thus, fatigue is an important variable to be assessed in case of ward nurses, which affects the quality of work performed by the ward nurses.

    Fatigue is a measure of the amount of lactic acid in the blood. Lactate is a direct product of muscular work. During intense work, the muscle cells produce lactic acid, which rapidly diffuses into blood stream.

    Accumulation of lactic acid occurs, when there is a high demand for energy but the supply of $O_2$ to the cell is limited, as in intense working condition. The unit of measurement is mmol/l (mili-moles per litre of blood), (Anonymous, 1986). At rest the normal range for blood lactate is 0.5-2.2 mmol/l.

13. **Postural Stress and Discomfort:** The static body position and awkward postures adopted by the ward nurses for work performance result in occupational health hazards like lower back pain, osteomuscular pain etc. Ward nurses have to sit for longer periods for doing task like record keeping, which is injurious over a period of time. In the present study, data was

collected about the body postures, force used, type of movement. Deviation of the posture from the normal curvature of the body was assessed with REBA technique. **Rapid Entire Body Assessment (REBA)** is a whole body assessment tool which was initially designed to provide a pen and paper postural analysis tool to be used in the field by direct observations (Hignett and McAtamney, 2000). A final REBA score is generated giving an indication about the level of risk and urgency with which action should be taken on a five-point action level scale of $AL_0$ to $AL_4$, from 'no action required' through to 'action necessary now'.

(a) $AL_0$—Scoring 1(negligible risk level means no action is necessary)

(b) $AL_1$—Scoring 2 or 3 (low risk, further action may be needed)

(c) $AL_2$—Scoring 4 to 7 (medium risk level and change is required soon)

(d) $AL_3$—Scoring 8 to 10 (high risk and action necessary now)

(e) $AL_4$—Scoring 11+ (very high risk, action necessary now)

14. **Body Mass Index:** Sedentary professional life of ward nurses results in increase in weight over a period of time hindering the quality of work done and on the other hand obesity invites a lot of illness with it like hypertension, diabetes, risks for cardiovascular diseases. Thus, it becomes imperative to assess the BMI of ward nurses.

On the basis of weight and height of ward nurses, Body Mass Index was calculated for 120 ward nurses. It gives various grades of obesity and calculated by dividing the weight (kg) by height square (metre square). It gives four categories of obesity as following:

| Grade | BMI (Kg/mt$^2$) |
|---|---|
| I | >40 |
| II | 30-40 |
| III | 25-29.9 |
| Normal | <25 |

15. **Sleep Disorders:** Sleep related problems are common among shift workers particularly in case of night shift workers. The discrepancies in the circadian rhythm and inadequate amount of sleep due to shift work result in compensatory behaviour like sleepiness, drowsiness during working hour which might become a life threatening incidence on the part of patients and career of ward nurses is endangered also. Therefore, the above was included in the study.
16. **Performance Capacity:** Performance can vary in different types of shift pattern, and due to overtime and duration of overtime. So, it was assessed in the present study in terms of rating from poor, average, good, very good to excellent.
17. **Social Consequences:** There are circumstances when ward nurses have to deal with different types of patients or people which can result in mood swings. Social factor as variable includes physical insecurity at the hospitals, verbal abuses, marital strain and disbalance in the dual responsibilities performed by the ward nurses.
18. **Psychological Consequences:** It includes the situation of tension, vigour, stress, irritation, depression, anxiety, difficulty in concentration, fatigue, tiredness, confusion, anger, mood change, agitation during job affecting the performance, so are crucial to measure.
19. **Satisfaction Level:** Commitment in any profession needs job satisfaction so it is an urgent issue to emphasize the satisfaction level among ward nurses derived from the job.

### 3.3.2 *Intervening Variables*

Intervening variables may be defined as the phenomenon or characteristics hypothesized to be the outcome. These are measures to change imposed by the independent variables. Following intervening variables were identified in the study.

1. **Occupational Hazards, Accidents among Ward Nurses:** Nursing profession has a lot of hazards, injuries like needle sticks and accidents related with handling of equipments which was assessed in the present study.
2. **Psychological Stress**: It was considered as an important variable because stress affects the performance capacity of the ward nurses.

### 3.3.3 *Dependent Variables*

1. **Strategies for Humanizing Nursing Work**
   (a) **Ergonomic Shift Planning and Health:** It deals with planning the shift schedule as per the worker's health, functional capacity and well-being in order to make shift schedule less tiring and injurious.
   (b) **Introduction of NAP:** Nap is a short break of 30 or 60 minutes in between the shift in order to eliminate the ill effects of the prolonged working hours, thus was included.
   (c) **Introduction of Safety Issues at Workplace:** Safety on the part of ward nurses in the hospitals should be considered especially in night shift, thus this parameter need investigation.
   (d) **Diet:** A provision of proper diet for the ward nurses can be planned. This should be included as agenda in implementation programmes.
   (e) **Reduction of Occupational Health Hazards:** These above mentioned strategies if implemented at the hospital, will reduce the occupational health hazards among ward nurses, which need to be tested.

## 3.4 Operational Definitions

1. **Anthropometry:** Anthropometry refers to the measurement of the human individual for the purposes of understanding human physical variation. It is the systematic collection and correlation of measurements

of the human body. The following measurements were taken in sitting position:

(a) **Stature Height**: It is defined as the vertical distance from the floor to the top of the head (vertex).The person stands erect, looking ahead, the arms hanging loosely at the sides.

(b) **Body Height from Ground:** Body height from ground is the distance from ground to the top of the head. For measuring body height from ground, subject sits erect, feet resting on the ground with knees bent at right angles (Plate 1).

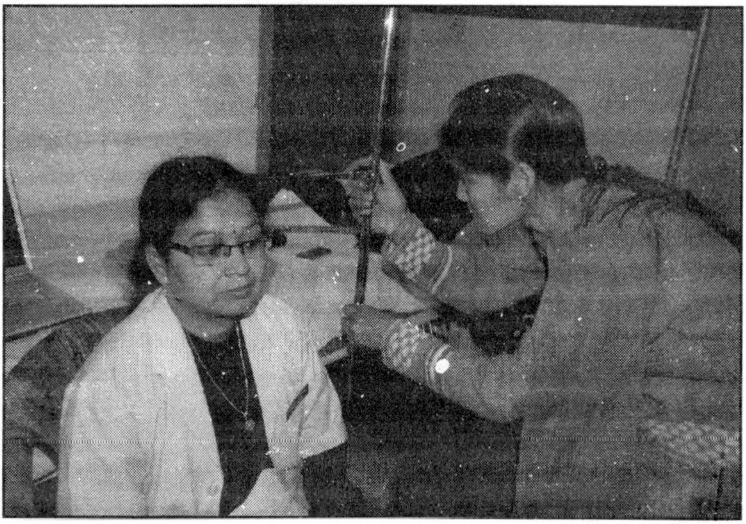

**Plate 1:** Measurement of Body Height

(c) **Body Height above Seat:** It is the vertical distance from sitting surface to the top of the head. Subject sits erect, his feet resting on the level ground with knees bent at right angles.

(d) **Eye Height from Ground:** It refers to the vertical distance from ground to the centre of right eye. Subject sits erect, feet resting on a surface with knees bent at right angles (Plate 2).

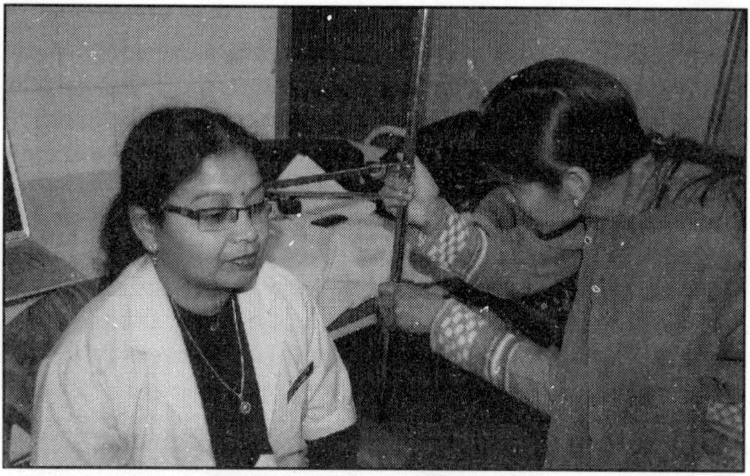

**Plate 2:** Measurement of Eye Height from Ground

(e) **Eye Height above Seat:** It is measured from sitting surface to the centre of right eye. Subject sits erect, his feet resting on a surface with knees bent at right angles.

(f) **Shoulder Height from Ground:** It refers to the vertical distance from ground to the mid-shoulder landmark in which subject sits erect, feet resting on a surface with knees bent at right angles (Plate 3).

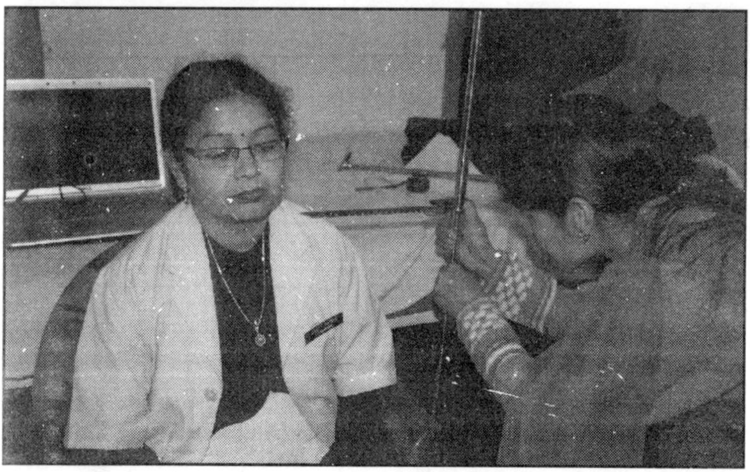

**Plate 3:** Measurement of Shoulder Height from Ground

(g) **Shoulder Height above Seat:** It is the vertical distance from sitting surface to the mid-shoulder landmark.

(h) **Elbow Rest Height from Ground:** It is defined as the height measured from ground to the bottom tip of the right elbow. To measure it, subjects sits erect, his right upper arm hanging at his side and his lower arm extended forward horizontally (Plate 4).

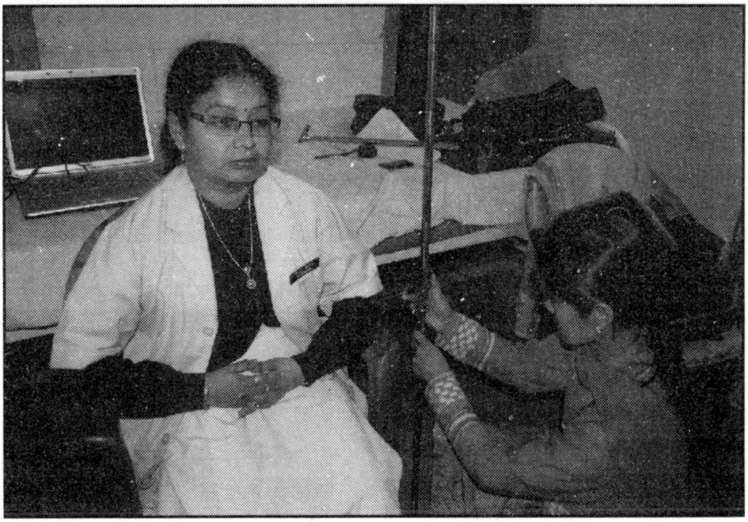

**Plate 4:** Measurement of Elbow Rest Height

(i) **Elbow Rest Height above Seat:** It refers to the vertical distance from sitting surface to the bottom tip of the right elbow for which subjects sits erect, his right upper arm hanging at his side and his lower arm extended forward horizontally.

(j) **Knee Height:** It is measured from foot rest surface to the top of the knee. Subjects sits erect, his feet resting on a level surface with knee bent at right angles (Plate 5).

(k) **Poplitcal Hcight:** Subjccts sits crect with his knee bent at right angles. Using anthropometer, measure vertical distance from foot rest surface to the underside of the right tendon of the biceps femoris muscle where it joins calf (Plate 6).

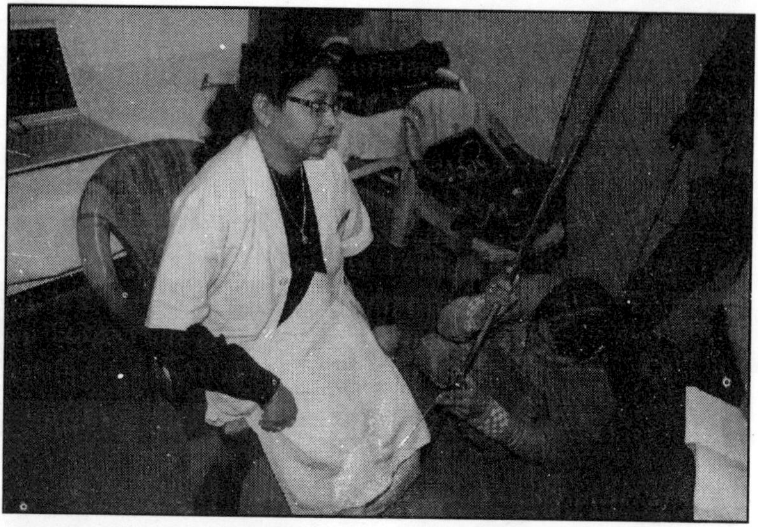

**Plate 5:** Measurement of Knee Height

**Plate 6:** Measurement of Popliteal Height

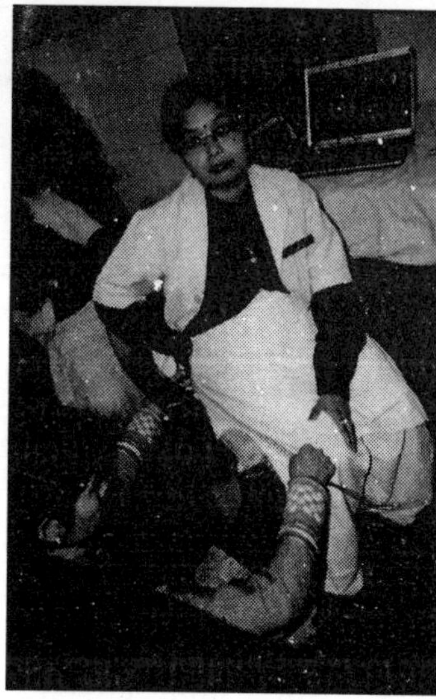

**Plate 7:** Measurement of Buttock Popliteal Length

(l) **Buttock Popliteal Length:** It is defined as the horizontal distance between area behind the knee to the highest point on the buttock. It was taken for the designing of seat depth. For this 5th percentile was taken so that the shortest person can also be accommodated easily (Plate 7).

(m) **Buttock Knee Length:** It refers to the horizontal distance from the rear most surface of the buttocks to top of the knee. For this measurement, subjects sits erect with his knee bent at right angles.

(n) **Thigh Height:** It is the height of mid-thigh from the sitting surface. Subject sits erect, his feet resting on a level surface with knees bent at right angles (Plate 8).

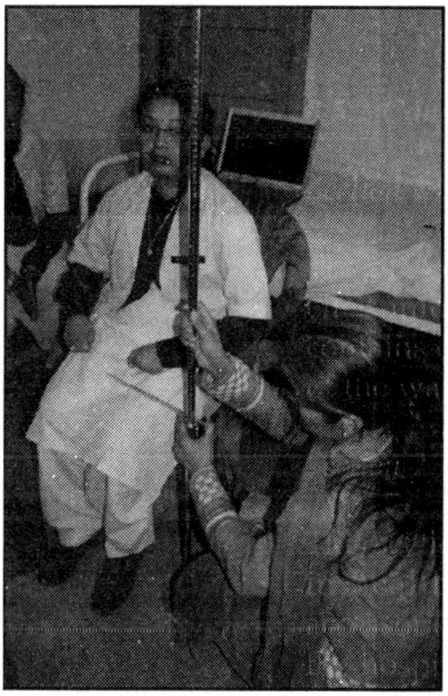

**Plate 8:** Measurement of Thigh Height

(o) **Hip Breadth:** It is used for designing seat width and for this 95th was used so that broadest person can be fitted properly.

(p) **Hand Length**: It is defined as the horizontal distance from wrist to tip of the middle finger. It is measured for the designing of hand rest of the chair.

(q) **Finger to Shoulder Length:** It is the horizontal distance from the tip of the middle finger to the mid-shoulder landmark.

(2) **Rated Perceived Exertion:** It is the method for subjective assessment of the exertion as a result of work performance. Though the heart rate is widely used to estimate occupational workload, it is often difficult to measure it in the tasks of short duration. The work scientists have recommended the use of another simple method to overcome this difficulty and provide equally reliable information for assessment of workload, i.e. subjective perception of exertion and that came out with a scale known as "Rating of Perceived Exertion (RPE)" based on extensive research (Gamberale, 1972; Astrila and Wendelin, 1974; Pendolf *et al.*, 1977; Borg, 1982 and Vargheses *et al.*, 1994). This scale has now been accepted as a practical method for rapid appraisal of all occupational work. It is the subjective evaluation of the exertion perceived by the subject on a scale rating 0 (no exertion) to 10 (maximum exertion).

(3) **Night Shift:** A night shift is either a group of workers who work during the night, or the period in which they work.

(4) **Insomnia:** Insomnia is commonly referred to as sleeplessness, or lack of sleep, insomnia can lead to severe fatigue, anxiety, depression and lack of concentration. Insomnia is serious, although unlike other diseases it does not kill. But only a sleep deprived person knows how lonely and how terrible this state can be. The International Classification of Sleep Disorders (ICSD) classifies SWSD as one of the dyssomnias, disorders with symptoms of either excessive sleepiness or insomnia.

(5) **Circadian Rhythms:** Many human physical functions follow a daily rhythm or a 24-hour cycle. These cycles are called circadian rhythms. These rhythmical processes are coordinated to allow for high activity during the day and low activity at night.

(6) **NAP:** Night time napping is an effective measure to prevent adverse effects due to night shift work. A characteristic of night time nap is that it can result in considerably deeper sleep. Taking night time naps suppressed increasing sleepiness, decreasing alertness during the period following awaking from a nap, and prevented disturbance of circadian rhythm.

(7) **Shift Roster**: It is a schedule showing how each staff member work their ordinary hours of work within a particular shift pattern.

(8) **Continuous Shift:** A 'continuous shift' is defined as working from beginning to end without being broken for reasons other than a meal break.

(9) **Fixed Shift Pattern**: A 'fixed shift pattern' is where the shift roster sets the same commencing and finishing hours for each shift to be worked on the same days each week throughout the shift roster.

(10) **Rotational Shift Pattern**: A 'rotational shift pattern' is where the shift roster sets different commencing and finishing times for the various shifts to be worked, and/ or different days each week, throughout a roster.

## 3.5 Selection, Construction and Description of Tools

### *3.5.1 Selection of the Tool*

Different tools were used as an instrument for collecting data for research work.

1. **Interview Schedule:** For collecting the relevant data as per the objectives of the study, a pre-coded structured interview schedule (Appendix 1) was constructed in consultation with advisory committee members to collect information on personal and family profile, medical history, medical equipments or gadgets handled, accessories/supplements/tools, furniture, occupational details of ward nurses, occupational hazards, accidents, risks, injuries.

2. **Checklist:** It was constructed to collect the information on psycho-social cost of work, i.e. sleep disorders, performance capacity, social consequences, and psychological consequences.
3. **Job Satisfaction Scale:** It was developed to study the satisfaction level, human performance of the ward nurses.
4. **Data Table and Worksheet:** For anthropometric measurements, environmental parameters, physiological responses and postural analysis, data table and worksheet were developed.
5. **Software:** Software as BPL ARPEMIS was used for pulmonary lung function.

### *3.5.2 Construction and Description of Tools*

*Section 1*

The pre-coded interview schedule was constructed in order to elicit information about the background of ward nurses. It contains data on personal and family profile, medical history of the ward nurses.

*Section 2*

This section dealt with the availability of infrastructure facility in health care industry, medical equipments handled, accessories, supplements and tools and furniture available in the hospitals.

*Section 3*

It comprised occupational details, types of activities performed by ward nurses, their experience in handling of various gadgets.

*Section 4*

This section included checklist for identification of occupational hazards/accidents/risks or injuries faced by ward nurses in the hospitals.

*Section 5*

This section comprised checklist related with sleep, sleepiness and related disorders among ward nurses, nutrition and health, social consequences and job satisfaction scale.

*Section 6*

This section includes experimental tables and software used to record information of selected physical parameters, physiological cost of work in terms of blood pressure, heart rate and respiration rate, environmental parameters (ambient room temperature, relative humidity, light level and sound level) in recorded period.

*Section 7*

This section adopts REBA Employee Assessment Worksheet developed by Hignett and McAtamney (2000) for postural analysis of ward nurses.

The above instrument prepared initially was distributed to a panel of 5 judges for establishing its content validity. They were requested to judge the clarity and relevance of the instrument. The judges were experts from various colleges and departments i.e. College of Agriculture (Department of Agriculture Communication), College of Basic Sciences and Humanities (Department of Maths, Statistics and Computer), College of Sciences (Department of Physiology), College of Technology (Department of Computer Engineering) and College of Home Science (Department of Family Resource Management) of Govind Ballabh Pant University of Agriculture and Technology. Some questions were modified and added as suggested by the judges.

### 3.5.2.1 *Development of Job Satisfaction Scale*

A three-point rating satisfaction scale was developed to measure the extent of satisfaction derived by the ward nurses from their job.

*(i) Item Collection*

A variety of items contributing towards the satisfaction derived from job by the ward nurses were collected from the literature and concerned experts in the field. Items relevant to study, on occupational details of ward nurses were collected.

Following criteria were considered while selecting items for the scale:

- The statement should be as simple as possible.
- They should be clear, brief and straightforward.
- Double negatives should not be present in any statement.
- They should have a certain difficult value and that should promote thinking of the ward nurses.

These items were then thoroughly screened and cited in order to make them more simple, clear and meaningful to elicit maximum information.

*(ii) Establishment of Content Validity of Tool*

Validity is the most critical criterion and indicates the degree to which an instrument measures what it is support to measure. In other words, validity is the extent to which differences found with a measuring instrument reflect true differences among those being tested.

Content validity is the extent to which a measuring instrument provides adequate coverage of the topic under study. It was determined by using a panel of persons, which judges how well the measuring instrument meets the standards. For content validity of the satisfaction scale, ten experts were selected from the College of Agriculture and

College of Home Science, Govind Ballabh Pant University of Agriculture and Technology, Pantnagar. These experts were requested to judge the content validity of the scale. For this a score sheet was prepared for the judges and the screening of this was done on the basis of following criteria:

(a) Those statements, selected by 70 per cent or more judges on relevance were retained in the scale.
(b) Those statements, which were not clear by 70 per cent or more judges, were reformed to make them more clear and meaningful.

*(iii) Pre-Testing and Establishment of Reliability*

A pilot study was conducted to establish the feasibility of the instrument on a sample of 33 female ward nurses. The responses of ward nurses on each statement of scale was quantified by assigning score, where score 1 was assigned to response "Disagree", score 2 was assigned to response "Agree", and score of 3 was assigned to response "Strongly agree".

Minor changes were made in the instrument on the basis of pilot study which was then utilized for the final data collection.

*(iv) Establishment of Reliability of Scale*

Reliability is the level of internal consistency or stability of the measuring devices. The reliability, therefore, refers to the test consistency. The reliability of the scale was tested with the application of split-half technique. The zero order correlation between even and odd numbered items was worked out as a measure of reliability. The coefficient of reliability was computed with the help of Spearmen Brown Prophecy Formula as given below:

$$r = \frac{(\Sigma xy)}{\sqrt{(\Sigma x)^2.(\Sigma y)^2}} \qquad ...(3.3)$$

Following equation was used to understand reliability coefficient of the scales:

$$r_{11} = \frac{2r_{½}I/II}{I + r_{½}I/II}$$

Where,

$r_{11}$ = reliability coefficient of whole test

$r_{½}$ I/II = reliability coefficient of half test

The correlation coefficient and reliability coefficient computed values were 0.65 and 0.78, respectively, thereby revealing commendable reliability of the scale.

### 3.5.3 *Pre-Testing of Interview Schedule*

The interview schedule so prepared was pretested on 10 non-sample ward nurses to check the feasibility of schedule and to ensure that no difficulty is experienced in getting right type of responses. On the basis of pretested results necessary modifications in the interview schedule were made in consultation with advisory committee and it was finalized for data collection.

### 3.5.4 *Instruments Used*

Various instruments were used for taking the measurements and recording responses. Their accuracy was checked from time to time. The description of instruments is given as follows:

1. **Measuring Tape:** A narrow measuring tape marked in feet, inches and centimetres was used for taking the various dimensions of the table and chair used by ward nurses in hospitals and few measurements of ward nurses also.
2. **Anthropometric Kit:** It contains the rod which is used to measure the various human dimensions (Plate 9).
3. **Weighing Machine:** A portable weighing machine was used to record the weight of the ward nurses. It was calibrated in kilograms.

**Plate 9:** Anthropometric Kit

4. **Heart Rate Monitor:** It was used to measure the heart rate of selected ward nurses which consists of three parts, namely the polar coded transmitter, the elastic strap and the wrist receiver. Polar coded transmitter was attached to the elastic strap and the length of the strap was adjusted to fit snugly and comfortable. The grooved electrode area was tied around the chest, where the water was applied to make it wet for close touch with body and the buckle was locked. Polar logo was kept in central upright position. The receiver was put on the wrist of the subject as an ordinary watch. Select button was pressed, heart rate measurement started, and heart rate reading appeared in the bottom line in a few seconds. Then the stop watch was pressed by pressing set/start/stop. Stop watch started running. Automatic recording of the heart rate information started.
5. **Blood Pressure Monitor:** It gives the blood pressure, pulse pressure of the subjects.

6. **Lux Meter:** Light intensity in the working and resting area of the ward nurses is recorded with this instrument.
7. **Sound Level Meter:** It measures the level of sound in working and resting area of the ward nurses.
8. **Thermohygrometer:** It is used to record the temperature and humidity in the working and resting area of the ward nurses.
9. **Spirometer:** It is used to measure lung capacity (respiration capacity) in terms of FVC, FEV, PEF and the ratio of $FEV_1/FVC$ (Plate 10).

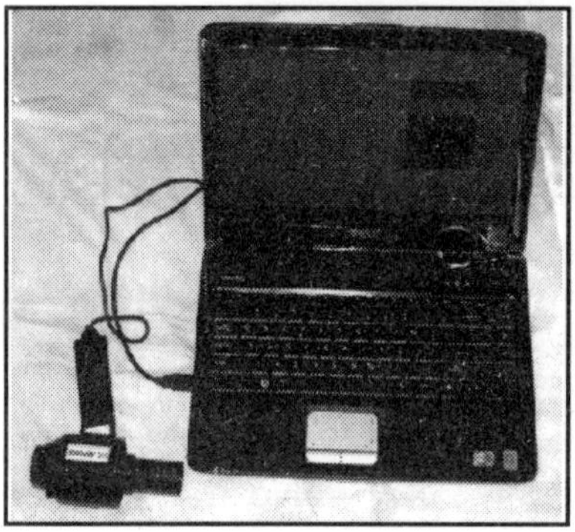

**Plate 10:** Spirometer

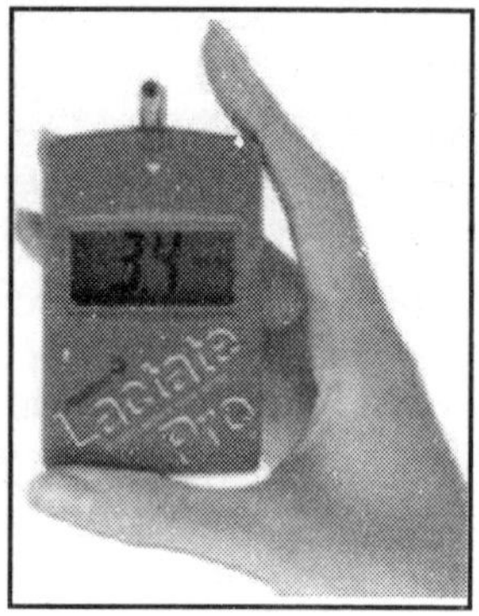


**Plate 11:** Lactate Calibrator

10. **Lactate Instrument:** This instrument is used to measure the fatigue level of ward nurses (Plate 11).

### 3.6 Sampling Design

Purposive-cum-random sampling technique was used to select the study area and samples. After data collection and interpreting the results, infrastructure facility, working condition and status of ward nurses in hospitals was validated in the light of standard hospital of capital, i.e. Sir Ganga Ram Hospital. For this purpose, the codes of the hospitals were taken into consideration.

### 3.6.1 Selection of Locale

For the present study, Uttarakhand state was selected purposively as the investigator belonged to it. Districts like Udham Singh Nagar and Nainital were selected purposively from the state as these were near to the place of residence of the investigator. From district Udham Singh Nagar, Sardar Ballabhbhai Patel Community Health Centre, Kichha and University Hospital, G.B. Pant University of Agriculture and Technology, Pantnagar, J.L.N. District Hospital, Rudrapur as Government hospitals and Kishore Hospital and Endoscopy Centre, Kichha, Deep Hospital, Jivandeep Hospital and Futela Hospital, Rudrapur as private hospitals were selected purposively. In Nainital district, block Haldwani was selected from which Female Hospital and Base Hospital as Government hospitals and Forest Hospital, Krishna Nursing Home as private hospitals were selected purposively as location of these hospitals was near to place of residence.

### 3.6.2 Sample Size

For selection of ward nurses from these above mentioned hospitals, simple random sampling technique without replacement (SRSTWOR) was used as number of ward nurses varied from hospital to hospital and selection of equal number of ward nurses was not possible. The selection procedure of ward nurses is shown in Figure 3.4. It was further observed that number of ward nurses was small in case of private hospitals as compared to number of ward nurses in Government hospitals, so a ratio of 70 ward nurses from Government and 50 from private hospitals was maintained. Thus, making a total of 120 ward nurses. Out of these 120 ward nurses, 10 per cent ward nurses (12 ward nurses) were randomly selected (irrespective of the fact that whether they belonged to Government hospital or private hospital) for collection of experimental data. The 120 ward nurses were interviewed for collecting information on various objectives. The selection of locale and ward nurses is shown in Figure 3.4.

### 3.7 Method of Data Collection

The data for the present investigation was collected in two different phases in the following order:

*Phase 1*

The descriptive data from 120 ward nurses was collected by using the pre-coded interview-cum-record schedule through personal contact from the key informants. Following protocol was used for this phase.

- Personal and family profile, medical history, selected anthropometric measurements, infrastructure facility available at health care industry, i.e. environmental parameters, medical equipments or gadgets handled, accessories/supplements/tools and furniture used by them, occupational details of ward nurses, occupational hazards, accidents, risks, injuries, psycho-social cost of work.
- REBA analysis of ward nurses for postural stress.

*Phase 2*

Experimental data was collected from 12 ward nurses with the help of scientific instruments personally. Environmental parameters in 5 government and 6 private hospitals (patient ward and duty room) were also recorded. Following test parameters were measured from experiments:

- Physiological cost of work in terms of Blood Pressure, Heart Rate, Energy Expenditure Rate of ward nurses.
- Rated Perceived Exertion of ward nurses
- Spirometry analysis of ward nurses.
- Blood lactate analysis of ward nurses

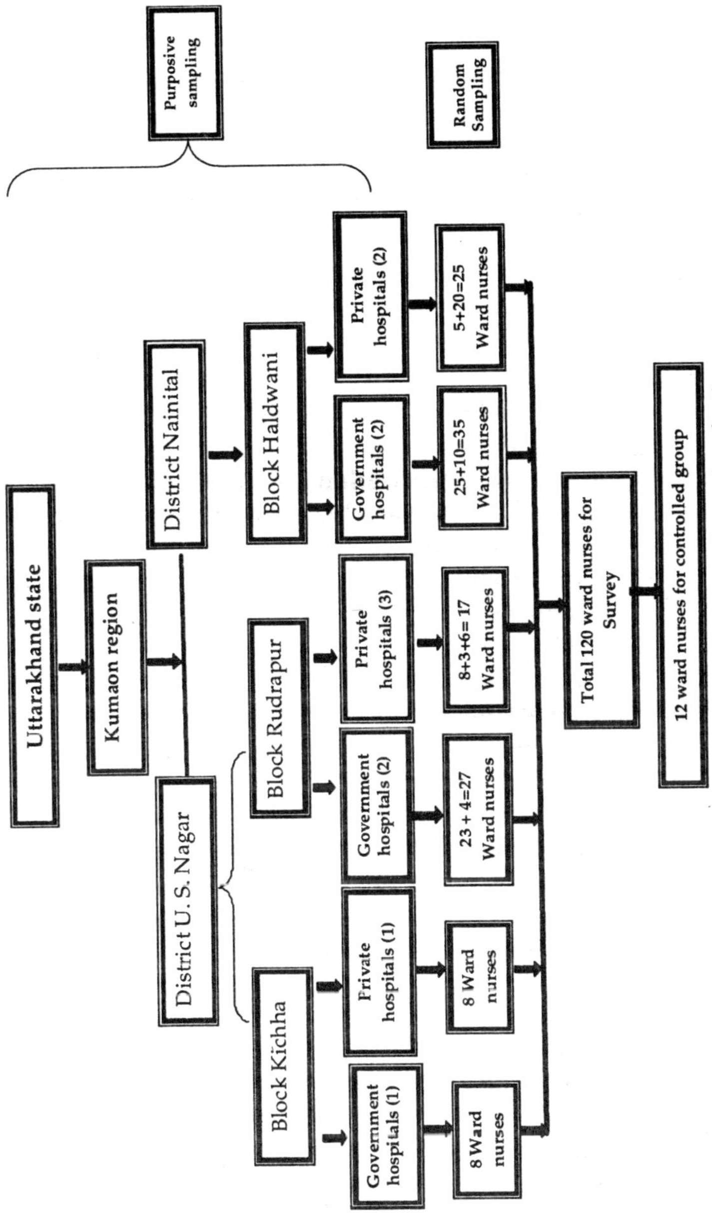


**Fig. 3.4:** Schematic representation of sample selection

## 3.8 Analysis of the Data

### *3.8.1 Categorization of the Variables*

Categorization is the first step in any analysis. Categories are formed according to research problem and purpose. For the present study, variables were categorized as given below:

(i) **Age:** Age was measured in terms of numbers of full years the ward nurses completed at the time of interview. It was categorized as follows:
1. 20 – 30 years
2. 30– 40 years
3. 40 – 50 years

(ii) **Educational Qualification:** Operationally, education referred as the formal education attained by the ward nurses. It was categorized as:
1. High School
2. Intermediate
3. Graduation
4. Nursing diploma

(iii) **Marital Status:** It is categorized as:
1. Married
2. Single, never married
3. Single, divorced
4. Single, widowed

(iv) **Personal Income (Rs. per month):** It refers to the monthly income in terms of money accrued from their occupation, categorized as:
1. <10,000
2. 10,000 – 20,000
3. 20,000 – 30,000

(v) **Family Income (Rs./month)**
1. 20,000 – 40,000
2. 40,000 – 60,000
3. 60,000 and above

(vi) **Extent of Satisfaction Derived**

The responses of ward nurses on each statement of satisfaction scale were quantifies by assigning scores:

| Statements | Responses | Score |
|---|---|---|
| | Dissatisfied | 1 |
| | Satisfied | 2 |
| | Strongly Satisfied | 3 |

(vii) **Activity Profile:** It involves different types of activities which are performed by ward nurses in the hospitals and these activities were assessed with experimental group of ward nurses. The activities were categorized on the basis of time involved in performing them. The categories are given as follows:

1. Group I Activities—They include giving medicine, dripping, giving injection and weight check-up.
2. Group II Activity—This group involves injury and wound care (dressing), measuring heart rate, record keeping and filing.
3. Group III Activity—It consists of mobility of patients, first aid and emergency and measuring blood pressure.

### *3.8.2 Descriptive Analysis*

The information collected were coded into the coding sheets and was then transferred into tabular form. The data were coded according to code numbers assigned and were analyzed using descriptive statistics. The findings were presented in frequencies, percentages, means, standard deviations and percentiles and weighted mean score. They were computed for analyzing the personal and family profile, medical history, occupational details, hazard analysis, postural analysis etc.

**Frequency:** It is sum of responses (in numbers).

**Percentage:** For making sample comparison the percentage values were calculated by dividing the frequency of a particular cell by total number of samples, multiplying by 100.

$$P = n/N \times 100 \qquad ...(3.5)$$

**Mean :** Mean is the most common measure of central tendency and it can be defined as the value which we get by dividing the total of the values of various given items in a series by the total number of items.

$$\text{Mean} \sum X_i / n = \frac{X_1 + X_2 + .... + X_n}{n} \qquad ...(3.6)$$

where,

$\Sigma$ = Symbol for summation

$X_i$ = Value of the ith item $X_1, X_2, X_3....$

n = Total number of items

**Standard Deviation and Error:** Standard deviation is the most extensively used measure of dispersion of a series and is commonly denoted by the symbol σ (pronounced as sigma). It is defined as the square root of the average of square of deviation.

$$\sigma = \sqrt{\left\{\Sigma\left(X_i - \overline{X}\right)^2\right\}/n-1} \qquad ...(3.7)$$

$$\text{Standard Error (SEm)} = \sigma/\sqrt{n} \qquad ...(3.8)$$

**Percentile:** To calculate percentile values of anthropometric measurements, the formula used was

$$\text{5th P} = M - 1.645 \times S.D. \qquad ...(3.9)$$
$$\text{95th P} = M + 1.645 \times S.D.$$

Where,

P = Percentile

M = Mean

S.D. = Standard Deviation

**Pheasant (1996) Mean Score**: Scoring techniques were used for calculating mean scores for self-opinion of ward nurses, social consequences and satisfaction level.

Opinion of ward nurses about themselves was assessed in the continuum from "much less than usual (1), same as usual (2), more than usual (3). Medical equipments/furniture were assessed as comfortable (3), somewhat comfortable (2) and uncomfortable (1). Social consequences were also assessed with a continuum from never (1), occasionally (2), sometimes (3), fairly often (4) to very often (5). Satisfaction level three point continuum scale was used to assess the job satisfaction of ward nurses and scores were assigned according to the satisfaction derived by them that is Dissatisfied (1), Satisfied (2), Strongly Satisfied (3).

Total scores pertaining to each factor were computed by summation of points given to it by the ward nurses. The mean score of each factor was then calculated by using the following formula:

$$\text{Weighted mean score} = \frac{\text{Total scores earned by each factor}}{\text{Total number of the ward nurses}} \quad ...(3.10)$$

$$= \sum \frac{f_i X_i}{N}$$

Where,
$f_i$ = frequency
$X_i$ = Scores given by the ith respondent to a factor
N = Total number of ward nurses

### 3.8.3 *Experimental Analysis*

For analysis of experimental data, percentage and mean values were calculated.

### 3.8.4 *Statistical Analysis*

For hypothesis testing chi-square and ANOVA were applied.

# 4

# Results and Discussion

The findings of the investigation as a result of statistical analysis of the descriptive and experimental data have been presented in this chapter. The entire descriptive analysis was done on the basis of selected government and private hospitals of districts Udham Singh Nagar and Nainital of the Uttarakhand State. The findings of the study were produced through composite summary tables and pictorial graphs and they are in concurrence with the said objectives. They are described under different sub-heads as follows:

4.1 Personal profile of nurses
4.2 Family profile of nurses
4.3 Medical history of nurses
4.4 Details about ailments of nurses
4.5 Caffeine consumption
4.6 Physical exercise performed by nurses
4.7 Nutritional status of nurses
4.8 Occupational details of nurses
4.9 Tips to reduce work stress
4.10 Opinion of nurses about themselves
4.11 Type of activities performed by nurses
4.12 Handling of medical equipment/scientific gadgets/ medical accessories/furniture
4.13 Comfort/discomfort from the use of furniture
4.14 Experience in handling of medical equipments/ scientific gadgets/medical accessories/furniture
4.15 Occupational hazards, accidents, risks, injuries at work place

4.16 Environmental parameters at work place
    4.16.1 Environmental conditions during field experiments
    4.16.2 Report of nurses regarding environmental parameters at work place
4.17 Psycho-social parameters
    4.17.1 Sleep, sleepiness and related factors
    4.17.2 Rating of sleep quality of nurses
    4.17.3 Factors affecting sleep quality at work place
    4.17.4 Factors responsible for troublesome sleeping and awakening
    4.17.5 Social consequences of nursing job
    4.17.6 Job satisfaction among nurses
4.18 Physiological parameters
    4.18.1 Anthropometric measurements of nurses
    4.18.2 Body Mass Index of nurses
    4.18.3 Physiological cost of work of nurses (BP, HR, EER)
    4.18.4 Rated perceived exertion of nurses
    4.18.5 Rapid Entire Body Assessment (REBA) analysis for postural discomfort of nurses
    4.18.6 Spirometry analysis of nurses
    4.18.7 Blood lactate analysis of nurses involved in various group of activities
4.19 Testing of hypothesis
4.20 Ergonomically suitable work schedule approaches and strategies for nursing work

**4.1 Personal Profile of Nurses**

Table 4.1 shows the personal profile of nurses of Government and private hospitals, which is described as follows:

***4.1.1 Age***

The age of nurses varied from 20 to 50 years. In totality, majority of the nurses (43.33 per cent) fell in the age category of 30-40 years followed by 29.17 per cent in the age group of

40-50 years. On the whole, the mean age of nurses was 39.96 ± 0.77 whereas, in particular the mean age of Government and nurses from private hospitals was 35.76 ± 1.02 and 33.84 ± 1.16 years respectively.

Data here revealed that private hospitals usually employed to young girls as nurse who were not much trained and qualified, which was not the case with Government hospitals.

**Table 4.1:** Personal Profile of Nurses

| *S. No.* | *Personal characteristics* | *Government hospital (n= 70)* | *Private hospital (n= 50)* | *Total (N=120)* |
|---|---|---|---|---|
| 1. | **Age (years)** | | | |
| | (a) 20-30 | 17 (24.29) | 16 (32) | 33 (27.50) |
| | (b) 30-40 | 33 (47.14) | 19 (38) | 52 (43.33) |
| | (c) 40-50 | 20 (28.57) | 15 (30) | 35 (29.17) |
| | **Mean±SEm** | 35.76±1.02 | 33.84±1.16 | 39.96±0.77 |
| 2. | **Educational qualification** | | | |
| | (a) High School | 2 (2.86) | 8 (16) | 10 (8.33) |
| | (b) Intermediate | 21 (30) | 24 (48) | 45 (37.50) |
| | (c) Graduate | 47 (67.14) | 18 (36) | 65 (54.17) |
| | (d) Nursing Diploma | 64 (91.43) | 9 (18) | 73 (60.83) |
| 3. | **Marital status** | | | |
| | (a) Married | 64 (91.43) | 42 (84) | 106 (88.33) |
| | (b) Unmarried | 4 (5.71) | 8 (16) | 12 (10)) |
| | (c) Single, widowed | 2 (2.86) | — | 2 (1.67) |
| 4. | **Income (Rs./month)** | | | |
| | (a) < 10,000 | — | 31 (62) | 31 (25.83) |
| | (b) 10,000-20,000 | 32 (45.71) | 19 (38) | 51 (42.50) |
| | (c) 20,000-30,000 | 38 (54.29) | — | 38 (31.67) |
| | **Mean±SEm** | 17,960 ± 559.79 | 7,471 ± 541.32 | 13,674 ± 621.31 |

*Note* : Figures in parentheses indicate the percentage values.

### *4.1.2 Educational Qualification*

With regard to educational status, differences were seen between nurses of Government hospitals and nurses from private hospitals. Educational level varied from high school to graduation with additional nursing diploma courses. It was observed that majority of the nurses (54.17 per cent) were graduate followed by 37.50 per cent who were educated up to intermediate. As observation was initiated in both Government and private hospitals, it was found that in case of nurses from Government hospitals, maximum of 67.14 per cent nurses were graduate and very few (2.86 per cent) were educated up to high school level. Regarding nurses from private hospitals, highest education was intermediate in 48 per cent of cases, whereas, a few of 16 per cent were educated up to high school. In total, a big proportion of nurses (60.83 per cent) were having nursing diploma out of which 91.43 per cent nurses were coming from Government hospitals.

It indicated that in Government hospitals, degree or diploma course related with nursing was necessary for the process of recruitment, whereas in case of private hospitals, good qualification was not the matter of concern but these hospitals used to recruit nurses on the basis of duration of experience in hospitals.

### *4.1.3 Marital Status*

Marital status is an important factor to be considered in case of studying nursing job which may directly affect their job because they are performing shift job particularly in night. It increases their workload physically as well as psychologically. The data regarding marital status, shows that 88.33 per cent nurses were married and very few (1.67 per cent) were widowed. Only 10 per cent of nurses were unmarried. With regard to Government hospitals majority (91.43 per cent) of nurses was married followed by unmarried (5.17 per cent) and 2.86 per cent were widowed. In case of private hospitals also, majority (84 per cent) were married and about 16 per cent nurses were unmarried.

### *4.1.4 Income (Rs. Per month)*

Income is a very important variable which directly affects the job satisfaction of nurses. It is clear from Table 4.1 that mean income of nurses was Rs. 13,674 ± 621.31 per month, Rs. 17,960 ± 559.79 per month in case of government and for private hospitals, it was Rs. 7,471 ± 541.32 per month. Further, it was observed from the table that maximum of nurses, i.e. 42.5 per cent were earning between Rs. 10,000 and Rs. 20,000 per month followed by 31.67 per cent nurses who had income in the range of Rs. 20,000-30,000 per month and a comparatively less proportion (25.83 per cent) had income below Rs. 10,000 per month. In case of nurses from government hospitals majority, i.e. 54.29 per cent had income between Rs. 20,000 and Rs. 30,000 per month and for private, majority (62 per cent) was falling in income category below Rs.10,000 per month.

It showed that there was a wide gap between the income of 2 groups of nurses, one who was coming from government hospital and the other who belonged to private hospitals. It can be concluded that private hospitals were paying less to their employees who were less qualified also.

## 4.2 Family Profile of Nurses

It was necessary to go into detail of family profile of nurses because it affects the daily routine of nurses and increases the workload of nurses both at hospital and at home.

### *4.2.1 Family Type*

Major proportion of nurses (65.83 per cent) belonged to nuclear family followed by joint family system (34.17 per cent). It is obvious from the data that nuclear family system was prevalent among nurses as they were not able to perform the responsibilities of joint family system.

### *4.2.2 Family Composition*

A large proportion of nurses (73.33 per cent) were having family composition of 1-4 members. It was followed by 4-8-member family composition (26.67 per cent). As the family size increases, workload is also increased and thus small family size was more prevalent.

### *4.2.3 Age (years) of Family Members*

It was observed that age of family members of most of the nurses (70 per cent) fell into the category of more than 30 years followed by 17.50 per cent who were below 15 years of age.

### *4.2.4 Educational Level of Members*

Regarding education of family members, family members of maximum of the nurses (38.33 per cent) were educated up to high school followed by 25.83 per cent who were graduate and above. However, very few (only 5 per cent) were illiterate. These illiterate members were old people in the family.

### *4.2.5 Occupation of Family Members*

Majority (70.83 per cent) of the family members of the nurses were in service and 29.17 per cent were in business.

### *4.2.6 Family Income (Rs. per month)*

On the whole, mean income of family of nurses was Rs. 30,822±842.34 per month with Rs. 33,651±1128.34 per month for Government hospital nurses and Rs. 26,860±1037.56 per month for nurses from private hospitals. It was further observed from Table 4.2 that 86.67 per cent nurses had family income in the range of Rs. 20,000-40,000 per month followed by 10.83 per cent whose family income was Rs. 40,000-60,000 per month. Particularly with regard to nurses from Government hospitals, maximum of nurses, i.e. 78.57 per cent had family income in the range of Rs. 20,000-40,000 per month followed by Rs. 40,000-60,000 per month (17.14 per cent). In case of nurses from private hospitals, it was observed that 98 per cent nurses were having family income between Rs. 20,000-40,000 per month.

**Table 4.2:** Family Profile of Nurses

| S. No. | Characteristics | Government hospital (n= 70) | Private hospital (n= 50) | Total (N=120) |
|---|---|---|---|---|
| 1. | **Family Type** | | | |
| | (a) Nuclear | 50 (71.43) | 29 (58) | 79 (65.83) |
| | (b) Joint | 20 (28.57) | 21 (42) | 41 (34.17) |
| 2. | **Family Composition** | | | |
| | (a) Small (1-4 members) | 50 (71.43) | 38 (76) | 88 (73.33) |
| | (b) Medium (4-8 members) | 20 (28.57) | 12 (24) | 32 (26.67) |
| 3. | **Age (years) of Family Members** | | | |
| | (a) < 15 | 14 (20) | 7 (14) | 21 (17.50) |
| | (b) 15-30 | 12 (17.14) | 3 (6) | 15 (12.50) |
| | (c) > 30 | 44 (62.86) | 40 (80) | 84 (70) |
| | **Mean± SEm** | 28.78±1.57 | 31.93±1.99 | 30.23±1.24 |
| 4. | **Educational Level of Members** | | | |
| | (a) Illiterate | 4 (5.71) | 2 (4) | 6 (5) |
| | (b) Primary School | 7 (10) | 3 (6) | 10 (8.33) |
| | (c) High School | 16 (22.86) | 30 (60) | 46 (38.33) |
| | (d) Intermediate | 19 (27.14) | 8 (16) | 27 (22.50) |
| | (e) Graduate and above | 24 (34.29) | 7 (14) | 31 (25.83) |
| 5. | **Occupation of Family Members** | | | |
| | (a) Service | 57 (81.43) | 28 (56) | 85 (70.83) |
| | (b) Business | 13 (18.57) | 22 (44) | 35 (29.17) |
| 6. | **Family Income (Rs./month)** | | | |
| | (a) 20,000-40,000 | 55 (78.57) | 49 (98) | 104 (86.67) |
| | (b) 40,000-60,000 | 12 (17.14) | 1 (2) | 13 (10.83) |
| | (c) 60,000 and above | 3 (4.29) | — | 3 (2.5) |
| | **Mean± SEm** | 33,651± 1,128.34 | 26,860± 1,037.56 | 30,822± 842.34 |

*Note*: Figures in parentheses indicate the percentage values.

Increased family income in case of nurses from government hospitals as compared to nurses from private hospitals reflected higher contribution in raising the income of the family.

## 4.3 Medical History of Nurses (during last one year)

Table 4.3 shows the medical history of nurses since last one year. It was crucial to diagnose the occurrence of illness/sickness among nurses as it has an impact on health status of themselves as well as their patients. It also affects the sickness absenteeism.

### *4.3.1 Physiological Problems*

#### *4.3.1.1 Common Illness*

On the whole, it was observed that maximum of 40 per cent nurses were suffering from headache followed by bodyache (34.17 per cent), whereas minimum of 17.50 per cent nurses were suffering from back pain. In case of nurses from Government hospitals, again temporary headache due to job was reported by 27.14 per cent nurses, and for private, it was temporary back-pain (42 per cent) as a result of job performance. Thus, most common illness among nurses was observed to be headache. Headache, muscular pain and general malaise from shift work were also stated by Lipkin *et al.* (1998).

#### *4.3.1.2 Chronic Illness*

Regarding occurrence of chronic illness among nurses, it was revealed from Table 4.3 that most prevalent chronic illness was anaemia among 19.17 per cent nurses and least common was thyroid problem (2.50 per cent). Based on the observation of chronic illness among Government hospitals, most frequent chronic illness was Blood Pressure (17.14 per cent) which was continuous due to other sources rather than job and the least common was continuous problem of gastrointestinal disorders (2.86 per cent) due to job related factors. Similar type of study was conducted by Lipkin *et al.* (1998), who reported that shift workers were more prone to digestive disorders due to irregular eating habits and change to shift pattern had a direct effect on the metabolic system of the shift workers.

Observation of private hospitals reveals that again temporary anaemia due to other sources (apart from job) was prevalent among 12 per cent nurses. A few proportion of nurses (4 per cent) reported problem of thyroid. In line with these findings, health profile of workers assessed by Steeland and

Fine (1998) revealed that there was little evidence of any difference in heart disease risk by shift.

#### *4.3.1.3 Symptoms*

As far as symptoms of illness were concerned, it was revealed that most common symptom among maximum of 44.17 per cent nurses was tiredness and very few (3.33 per cent) nurses felt excessive perspiration. As category-wise data was analyzed, it was observed that 37.14 per cent nurses from Government hospitals reported symptom of temporary tiredness from job, whereas, very few (2.86 per cent) felt temporary muscle tightness due to other sources. Regarding nurses from private hospitals, it was revealed from the data that most common symptom was tiredness (22 per cent) and the least common was excessive perspiration (4 per cent). Further, it was clear from Table 4.3 that both were temporary in nature and were occurring due to job.

### *4.3.2 Psychological Problem*

Nursing job allows a lot of psychological problems like depression, arrogance, anger, emotional problem etc. Among all the psychological problems, fatigue in patient care was felt by about 41.67 per cent nurses and the least problem was reported to be frequent absenteeism (4.17 per cent). As data were analyzed for particular category, it was inferred from Table 4.3 that among nurses from Government hospitals again temporary fatigue in patient care due to job was reported by 38.57 per cent nurses and only 7.14 per cent nurses each had problem of memory loss and poor communication due to job. In case of nurses from private hospitals, it was found that maximum of 18 per cent nurses were having feeling of increased negativity and irritation from job which was temporary in nature and the least common temporary psychological problem was poor communication (2 per cent) due to their long hour of job. These types of negative effects were also found by Crofts (1999) in his study and reported

**Table 4.3:** Medical History of Nurses (During Last One Year)

| S. No | Illness | Occurrence | Government (n=70) | | | | Private (n=50) | | | |
|---|---|---|---|---|---|---|---|---|---|---|
| | | | Temporary | | Continuous | | Temporary | | Continuous | |
| | | | From job | Other sources | From job | Other sources | From job | Other sources | From job | Other sources |
| | **A. Physiological Problems** | | | | | | | | | |
| | ***1. Common Illness*** | | | | | | | | | |
| (a) | Cough, cold, fever | 38 (31.67) | — | 12 (17.14) | — | — | 14 (28) | 12 (24) | — | — |
| (b) | Headache | 48 (40) | 19 (27.14) | 4 (5.71) | — | — | 17 (34) | 8 (16) | — | — |
| (c) | Bodyache | 41 (34.17) | 14 (20) | 7 (10) | — | — | 20 (40) | — | — | — |
| (d) | Back-pain | 21 (17.50) | — | — | — | — | 21 (42) | — | — | — |
| (e) | Skin-rashes, Allergy | 26 (21.67) | 12 (17.14) | 6 (8.57) | — | — | 4 (8) | 4 (8) | — | — |
| | ***2. Chronic illness*** | | | | | | | | | |
| (a) | Diabetes Mellitus | 15 (12.5) | — | — | — | 11 (15.71) | — | — | — | 4 (8) |
| (b) | Respiratory diseases | 16 (13.33) | 6 (8.57) | 3 (4.29) | — | — | — | 2 (4) | 3 (6) | 2 (4) |
| (c) | BP problem | 20 (16.67) | — | — | — | 12 (17.14) | 4 (8) | — | — | 4 (8) |

(*contd.*)

**Table 4.3** *(contd.)*

| S. No | Illness | Occurrence | Government (n=70) | | | | Private (n=50) | | | |
|---|---|---|---|---|---|---|---|---|---|---|
| | | | Temporary | | Continuous | | Temporary | | Continuous | |
| | | | From job | Other sources | From job | Other sources | From job | Other sources | From job | Other sources |
| (d) | Anaemia | 23 (19.17) | 3 (4.29) | 11 (15.71) | — | — | 3 (6) | 6 (12) | — | — |
| (e) | Gastrointestinal disorder | 20 (16.67) | — | 5 (7.14) | 2 (2.86) | 7 (10) | — | 6 (12) | — | — |
| (f) | Thyroid | 3 (2.50) | — | — | — | — | — | — | — | 3 (6) |
| | **3. Symptoms** | | | | | | | | | |
| (a) | Muscle tightness | 14 (11.67) | 7 (10) | 2 (2.86) | — | 2 (2.86) | 3 (6) | — | — | — |
| (b) | Excessive perspiration | 4 (3.33) | — | — | — | — | 2 (4) | 2 (4) | — | — |
| (c) | Tiredness | 53 (44.17) | 26 (37.14) | 14 (20) | — | — | 11 (22) | 2 (4) | — | — |
| | **B. Psychological Problems** | | | | | | | | | |
| (a) | Increased negativity, irritation | 29 (24.17) | 10 (14.29) | 7 (100) | — | — | 9 (18) | 3 (6) | — | — |
| (b) | Greater physical demand | 33 (27.50) | 16 (22.86) | 8 (11.43) | — | — | 9 (18) | — | — | — |
| (c) | More relationship problem | 36 (30) | 25 (35.71) | 3 (4.29) | — | — | 8 (16) | — | — | — |

*(contd.)*

**Table 4.3** *(contd.)*

| S. No | Illness | Occurrence | Government (n=70) | | | | Private (n=50) | | | |
|---|---|---|---|---|---|---|---|---|---|---|
| | | | Temporary | | Continuous | | Temporary | | Continuous | |
| | | | From job | Other sources | From job | Other sources | From job | Other sources | From job | Other sources |
| (d) | Depression | 17 (14.17) | 6 (8.57) | 6 (8.57) | — | — | 2 (4) | 3 (6) | — | — |
| (e) | Frequent bad mood | 36 (30) | 11 (15.71) | 14 (20) | — | — | 6 (12) | 5 (10) | — | — |
| (f) | Unable to concentrate | 25 (20.83) | 11 (15.71) | 7 (10) | — | — | 2 (4) | 5 (10) | — | — |
| (g) | Lack of energy | 29 (24.17) | 14 (20) | 8 (11.43) | — | — | 3 (6) | 4 (8) | — | — |
| (h) | Memory loss | 18 (15) | 5 (7.14) | 7 (10) | — | — | 5 (10) | 1 (2) | — | — |
| (i) | Poor communication | 16 (13.33) | 5 (7.14) | 7 (10) | — | — | 1 (2) | 3 (6) | — | — |
| (j) | Arrogant | 23 (19.17) | 9 (12.86) | 8 (11.43) | — | — | 5 (10) | 1 (2) | — | — |
| (k) | Postural fatigue | 45 (37.50) | 26 (37.14) | 10 (14.29) | — | — | 7 (14) | 2 (4) | — | — |
| (l) | Fatigue in patient care | 50 (41.67) | 27 (38.57) | 11 (15.71) | — | — | 9 (18) | 3 (6) | — | — |
| (m) | Sleep deprivation | 22 (18.33) | 17 (24.29) | — | — | — | 5 (10) | — | — | — |

*(contd.)*

**Table 4.3** (*contd.*)

| S. No | Illness | Occurrence | Government (n=70) | | | | Private (n=50) | | | |
|---|---|---|---|---|---|---|---|---|---|---|
| | | | Temporary | | Continuous | | Temporary | | Continuous | |
| | | | From job | Other sources | From job | Other sources | From job | Other sources | From job | Other sources |
| (n) | Performance anxiety | 24 (20) | 9 (12.86) | 4 (5.71) | — | 2 (2.86) | 6 (12) | 3 (6) | — | — |
| (o) | Fear of crowd | 20 (16.67) | 6 (8.57) | 5 (7.14) | — | — | 5 (10) | 4 (8) | — | — |
| (p) | Emotional outbursts | 23 (19.17) | 7 (10) | 8 (11.43) | — | — | 4 (8) | 4 (8) | — | — |
| (q) | Anger outbursts | 23 (19.17) | 6 (8.57) | 8 (11.43) | — | — | 4 (8) | 5 (10) | — | — |
| (r) | Work related stress | 35 (29.17) | 7 (10) | 11 (15.71) | 8 (11.43) | — | 5 (10) | 4 (8) | — | — |
| (s) | Low self-confidence | 22 (18.33) | 8 (11.43) | 6 (8.57) | — | — | 6 (12) | 2 (4) | — | — |
| (t) | Frequent absenteeism | 5 (4.17) | — | — | — | — | 3 (6) | 2 (4) | — | — |
| (u) | Low motivation | 32 (26.67) | 15 (21.43) | 10 (14.29) | — | — | 4 (8) | 3 (6) | — | — |

*Note* : Figures in parentheses indicate the percentage values.

that they have consequences not just for individual, but also for workplace as decreased alertness and reduced job performance could endanger human lives and affect the quality of care of the patients.

It can be concluded that due to less number of nurses in private hospitals as compared to Government hospitals, workload is more and at the same time they are not trained, so it results in negativity and irritation.

## 4.4 Details About Ailments of Nurses

Ailments of nurses were also recorded in order to know their health status during last one year. It is very obvious from Table 4.4 that 33.33 nurses were receiving medication for illness and out of which 47.14 per cent from Government hospitals and 14 per cent nurses from private hospitals. The types of illness as reported by nurses were blood pressure (16.67 per cent), diabetes (12.50 per cent), thyroid (2.5 per cent), and gallstone (1.67 per cent). When analyzing the data in particular category, it was found that in Government hospitals, few nurses were suffering from illness like blood pressure (22.86 per cent) followed by diabetes (21.43 per cent) and thyroid (2.86 per cent), whereas in case of private hospitals, nurses had problem of blood pressure (8 per cent) and gallstone (4 per cent). As reported by Kivimaki *et al.* (2006), the joint occurrence of high cholesterol, overweight, high blood pressure and disturbed sugar levels lead to 2.2 times high absenteeism than the case when these problems do not occur.

### *Hospitalization*

Nurses were asked about they ever have been hospitalized for any reason and it was found out that a little proportion, i.e. 11.67 per cent nurses were hospitalized out of which 8.57 per cent from Government hospitals and 16 per cent from private hospitals. Only 1.67 per cent nurses on the whole undergone surgery for gall bladder.

### Protection from Dangerous Substances

Regarding protection from exposure to dangerous substances, data from Table 4.4 reveal that only 7.5 per cent nurses on the whole were well protected from dangerous substances out of that 12 per cent from Government hospitals and 4.29 per cent nurses were in case of private hospitals.

**Table 4.4:** Details about Ailments of the Nurses

| S. No | Details | | Government (n=70) | Private (n=50) | Total (N=120) |
|---|---|---|---|---|---|
| 1. | **Medication for illness** | | 33 (47.14) | 7 (14) | 40 (33.33) |
| 2. | **Illness** | Diabetes | 15 (21.43) | — | 15 (12.50) |
| | | Blood pressure | 16 (22.86) | 4 (8) | 20 (16.67) |
| | | Thyroid | 2 (2.86) | 1 (2) | 3 (2.50) |
| | | Gall stone | — | 2 (4) | 2 (1.67) |
| 3. | **Hospitalization** | | 6 (8.57) | 8 (16) | 14 (11.67) |
| 4. | **Surgery** | | 2 (2.86) | — | 2 (1.67) |
| 5. | **Type of surgery** | Gall stone | 2 (2.86) | — | 2 (1.67) |
| 6. | **Protection from dangerous substances** | | 6 (12) | 3 (4.29) | 9 (7.50) |
| 7. | **Sick leave in past 6 month** | 2-3 days | 1 (1.43) | 2 (4) | 5 (4.17) |
| | | 1 week | 2 (2.86) | — | 3 (2.5) |

Figures in parentheses indicate the percentage values

The detail about nurses in Table 4.4 related with sick leaves taken by them during past 6 months revealed that 4.17 per cent nurses on the whole had taken 2-3 days sick leave followed by 2.5 per cent nurses with 1 week leave. In particular only 2.86 per cent nurses from Government hospitals and 4 per cent from private hospitals took sick leaves for week and days respectively. It was revealed that nurses were not allowed to take leaves and their health status also affects the health of their patients. So, nurses were found to take very few sick leaves.

## 4.5 Caffeine Consumption

As nurses have to work continuously for 6-12 hours in the shifts they have to depend upon beverages like tea and coffee. This is required to keep themselves fresh and awaken and to perform better while taking care of patients with refreshing mood. It is observed from Table 4.5 that on the whole, tea was consumed 1-2 times per shift by 40 per cent nurses, 58.57 per cent nurses from Government hospitals and 3-4 times by 46 per cent nurses from private hospitals. In case of coffee consumption, it was consumed single time by 10 per cent of nurses.

**Table 4.5:** Caffeine Consumption

| *S. No.* | *Beverage* | *Frequency* | *Government (n=70)* | *Private (n=50)* | *Total (N=120)* |
|---|---|---|---|---|---|
| **1.** | **Tea** | 1-2 times | 41 (58.57) | 7 (14) | 48 (40) |
| | | 3-4 times | 5 (7.14) | 23 (46) | 28 (23.33) |
| **2.** | **Coffee** | 1 time | 9 (12.86) | 3 (6) | 12 (10) |

*Note*: Figures in parentheses indicate the percentage values.

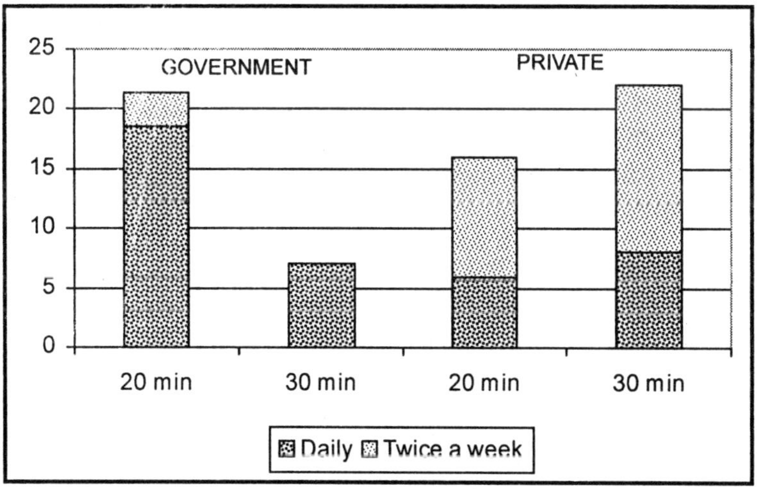


**Fig. 4.1:** Physical Exercise Performed by Nurses

## 4.6 Physical Exercise Performed by Nurses

The details regarding physical exercise done by nurses are given in Figure 4.1, which is important factor for the physical fitness. It was observed that maximum (18.33 per cent) nurses on the whole, were performing daily exercise and 5.83 per cent nurses performed exercise twice a week. Particularly with regard to nurses from Government hospitals 18.57 per cent performing exercise on daily basis and approximately 8 per cent from private hospitals performed exercise daily. However, 2.86 per cent from Government hospitals and 10 per cent nurses from private hospitals performed exercise twice a week.

From the results, it is revealed that nurses do not get time for exercise, which is a matter of concern because exercise is necessary to keep oneself physically fit especially in case of nurses, whose most of the time is spent in static or sitting position along with awkward posture.

## 4.7 Nutritional Status of Nurses

The statements related with nutritional status of nurses are enclosed in Table 4.6. It is evident from the data that majority of the nurses (72.5 per cent) were taking full meal daily followed by 58.33 per cent who were able to take meals at the same time on each shift. Poor appetite was reported by 31.67 per cent nurses and a small proportion (10.83) of nurses on the whole received nutritional counselling for health maintenance. The data regarding nutritional status in a particular category, it was observed that a good proportion of nurses (70 per cent) was able to take full meals daily, but comparatively less percentage of nurses (5.71 per cent) received nutritional counselling for health maintenance. Near about same situation was observed in private hospitals.

The reason behind irregular eating pattern and poor appetite may be owned to shift job, and overtime to provide 24 hour facility.

**Table 4.6:** Nutritional Status of Nurses

| S. No. | Details | Government (n=70) | Private (n=50) | Total (N=120) |
|---|---|---|---|---|
| 1. | Take full meals daily | 49 (70) | 38 (76) | 87 (72.50) |
| 2. | Take meals at the same time on each shift | 36 (51.43) | 34 (68) | 70 (58.33) |
| 3. | Poor appetite | 20 (28.57) | 18 (36) | 38 (31.67) |
| 4. | Receive nutritional counselling for health maintenance | 4 (5.71) | 9 (18) | 13 (10.83) |

*Note*: Figures in parentheses indicate the percentage values.

Figure 4.2 shows the rating of appetite of nurses as reported by the nurses. It is evident from the figure that a good proportion of nurses (52.86 and 46 per cent from Government and private hospitals) had fairly good appetite, which shows nutritional status among nurses is good.

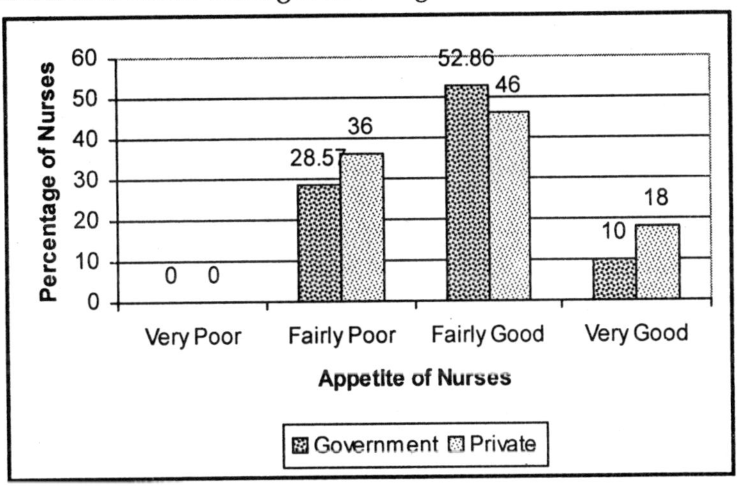


**Fig. 4.2:** Rating of Appetite of Nurses

## 4.8 Occupational Details of Nurses

Occupational details (Table 4.7) included job duration, type of job, type of job shift, duration of shift, preference for shift etc.

### *4.8.1 Job Duration*

On the whole, data pertaining to job duration reveals that majority of nurses (52.5 per cent) worked as nurses for less than 5 years and only 11.67 per cent nurses were working for 10-15 years. When category-wise data was analyzed, it was found that maximum nurses from Government hospitals (38.57 per cent) were having job experience of more than 15 years, whereas in case of nurses from private hospitals (90 per cent) had job experience for less than 5 years. As an interesting case, very few (4 per cent) nurses worked in this job for 10-15 years which shows lesser stability of nurses in the private sector as compared to Government hospitals. The reason behind this may be less payment for the work done and less facilities provided by the private hospitals.

### *4.8.2 Job Type*

All the nurses were full time permanent employee, i.e. both in case of Government as well as private hospitals.

### *4.8.3 Type of Job Shift*

Job shift were categorized as rotating 6 hours, rotating 8 hours, rotating 12 hours, permanent day, permanent evening and permanent night shift. The data in Table 4.7 reveals that among whole, maximum of the nurses (50.83 per cent) were working on rotation of 8 hours job followed by rotating 6 hours (28.33 per cent). Very few nurses (3.33 per cent) were having rotating 12 hours job shift. As category-wise data was analyzed, it was observed that in case of nurses from Government hospitals, 58.57 per cent had rotating 8 hours job shift and a small proportion (5.71 per cent) was working in rotating 12 hours job pattern. Regarding nurses from private hospitals, it can be concluded that maximum of 40 per cent nurses worked in rotating 8 hours job shift and a few of 10 per cent nurses worked for permanent night shift job.

Because of a good number of staff in the Government hospitals, nurses were having night shifts in alternate 15 days or 1 month, whereas with regard to private hospitals, nurses had to go for night shift very frequently. The differences in various types of shifts were revealed by Takahashi *et al.* (1999) who reported similar or lower level of sleepiness, difficulty in concentration, fatigue, physical activity, and heart rate during the 16 hour shift as compared to 8 hour shift.

### *4.8.4 Duration of Shift*

Duration of shift refers to the period for which a particular shift prevails. It is clear from Table 4.7 that maximum of the nurses (35 per cent) had 15 days duration of shift and minimum of 18.33 per cent nurses reported shift duration of 7 days. Regarding data in a particular category, it was observed that in Government hospitals, maximum nurses (38.57 per cent) had a shift for 10 days followed by 30 days shift (32.86 per cent), whereas in case of nurses from private hospitals, maximum of 44 per cent nurses were having shift duration for 15 days.

### *4.8.5 Preference for Shift*

Preference of nurses was asked for 6 hours, 8 hours job shift and revealed that maximum of the 44.17 per cent preferred to

**Table 4.7:** Occupational Details of Nurses

| *S. No* | *Occupational details* | | *Government (n=70)* | *Private (n=50)* | *Total (N=120)* |
|---|---|---|---|---|---|
| 1. | **Job duration (yrs)** | (a) < 5 | 18 (25.71) | 45 (90) | 63 (52.50) |
| | | (b) 5-10 | 13 (18.57) | 3 (6) | 16 (13.33) |
| | | (c) 10-15 | 12 (17.14) | 2 (4) | 14 (11.67) |
| | | (d) >15 | 27 (38.57) | — | 27 (22.50) |
| 2. | **Job Type** | Full time permanent | 70 (100) | 50 (100) | 120 (100) |
| 3. | **Type of Job Shift** | (a) Rotating 6 hr | 25 (35.71) | 9 (18) | 34 (28.33) |
| | | (b) Rotating 8 hr | 41 (58.57) | 20 (40) | 61 (50.83) |
| | | (c) Rotating 12 hr | 4 (5.71) | — | 4 (3.33) |
| | | (d) Permanent day | — | 7 (14) | 7 (5.83) |
| | | (e) Permanent evening | — | 9 (18) | 9 (7.5) |

*(Contd.)*

| *S. No* | *Occupational details* | | *Government (n=70)* | *Private (n=50)* | *Total (N=120)* |
|---|---|---|---|---|---|
| | | (f) Permanent night | — | 5 (10) | 5 (4.17) |
| 4. | **Duration of Shift** | (a) 7 days | — | 22 (44) | 22 (18.33) |
| | | (b) 10 days | 27 (38.57) | — | 27 (22.50) |
| | | (c) 15 days | 20 (28.57) | 22 (44) | 42 (35) |
| | | (d) 30 days | 23 (32.86) | 6 (12) | 29 (24.17) |
| 5. | **Preference for Shift** | | | | |
| | **I. 6-hour Shift** | (a) Morning to day | 24 (34.29) | 29 (58) | 53 (44.17) |
| | | (b) Day to night | 22 (31.43) | 8 (16) | 30 (25) |
| | **II. 8-hour Shift** | (a) Morning to day | 18 (25.71) | 13 (26) | 31 (25.83) |
| | | (b) Day to night | 6 (8.57) | — | 6 (5) |
| 6. | **Change in Shifts** | | 67 (95.71) | 11 (22) | 78 (65) |
| 7. | **Frequency of Changing the Shifts** | > 2 times | 19 (27.14) | — | 19 (15.83) |
| | | No set pattern | 58 (82.86) | 11 (22) | 69 (57.50) |
| 8. | **Reasons for Changing Shifts** | Ill health | 6 (8.57) | 2 (4) | 8 (6.67) |
| | | On call from hospital | 61 (87.14) | 9 (18) | 70 (58.33) |
| 9. | **Over-time** | | 6 (8.57) | 42 (84) | 48 (40) |
| 10. | **Duration of Overtime** | 4-6 hrs/week | 6 (8.57) | 14 (28) | 20 (16.67) |
| | | 6-8 hrs/week | — | 28 (56) | 28 (23.33) |
| 11. | **Dual Role of Nurses** | | 24 (34.29) | 40 (80) | 64 (53.33) |

*Note*: Figures in parentheses indicate the percentage values.

work for 6 hours morning to day shift, and 25.83 per cent preferred to work for 8 hours morning to day shift. Particularly with regard to nurses from Government hospitals, it was observed that maximum nurses, i.e. 34.29 per cent preferred morning to day shift in 8 hours job and 31.43 per cent nurses were favouring 6 hours day to night shift. In case of nurses from private hospitals, it is revealed that a large proportion (58 per cent) nurses preferred 6 hours morning to day shift followed by 26 per cent who preferred 8 hours morning to day shift.

It was revealed that nurses preferred day shift as compared to night shift because of comfortable working in the day time. Night shift is not good from the health point of view. As reported by Schernhammer *et al.* (2003) who indicated women working 1-15 years or more on rotating night shift had multivariate risks of developing colorectal cancer.

### *4.8.6 Change in Shifts*

Sometime shift was changed by nurses but only in case of emergency. Table 4.7 further reveals that in summative response 65 per cent nurses changed their shift (95.71 per cent nurses from Government hospitals and 22 per cent from private hospitals).

### *4.8.7 Frequency of Changing the Shifts*

As far as frequency of changing the shift is concerned, it was pointed out in Table 4.7 that majority of nurses (57.50 per cent) had no set pattern and this was true among 82.86 per cent nurses from Government hospitals and rest of 22 per cent from private hospitals.

### *4.8.9 Reasons for Changing Shifts*

Reasons for changing the shift were ill health or on call from hospitals. On the whole, majority of nurses (58.33 per cent) gave reason for changing the shift as when call is received from the hospital. Similar trend was observed in 87.14 per cent from Government and 18 per cent from private hospitals.

### *4.8.10 Overtime*

Overtime is also requirement when there is a shortage of staff in the hospitals. Overtime work was reported by 40 per cent nurses on the whole out of which 84 per cent nurses were from private hospitals, but it was very low, i.e. 8.57 per cent for nurses from Government hospitals. Study conducted by Sandra (2001) revealed that disruption of circadian rhythm is essentially unavoidable when 24 hou- care is required, so overtime becomes urgent.

### *4.8.11 Duration of Overtime*

Duration of overtime was 6-8 hours per week as reported by 23.33 per cent in totality followed by 16.6 per cent who worked overtime for 4-6 hours per week. In case of nurses from Government hospitals, only 8.57 per cent of nurses worked overtime for 4-6 hour/week, whereas 56 per cent nurses from private hospitals worked for 6-8 hours per week for overtime work and 28 per cent nurses worked overtime for 4-6 hours in a week. Thus, duration of overtime was more in private hospitals which has ill effect on the health of the nurses.

### *4.8.12 Dual Role of Nurses*

Nursing job requires working in odd hours and for long hours, in night shifts also and therefore, a lot of struggle that nurses have to face for performing household and other activities. It is obvious from Table 4.7 that on the whole 53.33 per cent nurses reported that they had dual responsibilities. Out of which 34.29 per cent nurses from Government hospitals and 80 per cent nurses from private hospitals faced struggle due to dual job. The reason behind struggle among nurses of private hospitals was overtime and duration of overtime. The results can be supported with the study of Costa (2001) who indicated that women (nurses) are more vulnerable to shift work in relation to both their more complex hormonal rhythm and extra demand related to family life, so, overexertion results in ill health.

## 4.9 Tips to Reduce Work Stress

It is crucial to know that how nurses reduces their work stress. On the whole, 73.33 per cent nurses spent their leisure time with tea and coffee and minimum of 1.67 per cent nurses were going for cinema in order to get rid of stress for some time. The data pertaining to tips to reduce work stress by nurses working in Government hospitals reveals that majority (78.57 per cent) of nurses preferred to spend time by taking tea or coffee and very few (2.86 per cent) were able to go for outing or cinema. However, in case of nurses from private hospitals, nurses (66 per cent) preferred to consume beverages like tea or coffee and watching T.V. (26 per cent). Only 4 per cent nurses spent time with cooking.

**Table 4.8:** Tips to Reduce Work Stress

| *Time for yourself besides work* | *Government (n=70)* | *Private (n=50)* | *Total (N=120)* |
|---|---|---|---|
| (a) Listen to your favourite music to relax | 23 (32.86) | 5 (10) | 28 (23.33) |
| (b) Just lying on the bed | 27 (38.57) | 3 (6) | 30 (25) |
| (c) Taking tea or coffee | 55 (78.57) | 33 (66) | 88 (73.33) |
| (d) Go for outings or cinema | 2 (2.86) | — | 2 (1.67) |
| (e) Spend time with your family | 46 (65.71) | 10 (20) | 56 (46.67) |
| (f) Cooking | 3 (4.29) | 2 (4) | 5 (4.17) |
| (g) Reading favourite magazines | 12 (17.14) | — | 12 (10) |
| (h) Yoga | 3 (4.29) | — | 3 (2.5) |
| (i) Watching Television | 28 (40) | 13 (26) | 41 (34.17) |

*Note*: Figures in parentheses indicate the percentage values.

## 4.10 Opinion of Nurses about Themselves

Self-opinion of nurses was recorded in order to get an idea about their personality and it is presented in Table 4.9. On the whole, it is obvious that maximum nurses from Government hospitals (30 per cent) searched for social support to reduce their stress closely followed by 28.57 per cent who were able to enjoy normal day-to-day activities. Only 14.29 per cent nurses agreed that they felt inability to relax. The reason of loosing self-confidence might be long hour of work performance and lack of rest between shifts. In case of nurses from the private hospitals, 30 per cent nurses searched for social support to reduce their stress. A least proportion of nurses (12 per cent) got edgy and bad tempered. Similar type of study conducted by Brown *et al.* (2006) showed that certain unsatisfactory features of work like insufficient social support system increase the risk of deterioration in physical condition of nurses.

**Table 4.9:** Opinion of Nurses about Themselves

| S.No. | Opinion of nurses | MLU | SAU | MTU | MS | Total (N=70) | MLU | SAU | MTU | MS | Total (N=50) |
|---|---|---|---|---|---|---|---|---|---|---|---|
| 1. | Able to enjoy normal day-to-day activities | 7 (10) | 9 (12.86) | 4 (5.71) | **0.53** | 20 (28.57) | 9 (18) | 3 (6) | 1 (2) | **0.36** | 13 (26) |
| 2. | Loose self-confidence | 4 (5.71) | 8 (11.43) | 2 (2.86) | **0.37** | 14 (20) | 6 (12) | 2 (4) | — — | **0.20** | 8 (16) |
| 3. | Getting edgy and bad tempered | 9 (12.86) | 2 (2.86) | — | **0.18** | 11 (15.71) | 6 (12) | — — | — — | **0.12** | 6 (12) |
| 4. | Frightened with crowded places | 8 (11.43) | 3 (4.29) | — | **0.20** | 11 (15.71) | 3 (6) | 2 (4) | 4 (8) | **0.38** | 9 (18) |
| 5. | Feel inability to relax | 2 (2.86) | 2 (2.86) | 6 (8.57) | **0.34** | 10 (14.29) | 2 (4) | 8 (16) | 2 (4) | **0.48** | 12 (24) |
| 6. | Loose your balance | 9 (12.86) | 2 (2.86) | 8 (11.43) | **0.53** | 11 (15.71) | 3 (6) | 1 (2) | 6 (12) | **0.46** | 10 (20) |
| 7. | Search for social support to reduce your stress | 9 (12.86) | 4 (5.71) | 8 (11.43) | **0.59** | 21 (30) | 3 (6) | 5 (10) | 7 (14) | **0.68** | 15 15 (30) |

**MLU**—Much Less Than Usual (1), **SAU**—Same As Usual (2), **MTU**—More Than Usual (3), **MS**—Mean Score
*Note*: Figures in parentheses indicate the percentage values.

## 4.11 Type of Activities Performed by Nurses

Activities like helping in medical tests, giving medicine to patients, injury care (dressing), measuring blood pressure, and heart rate were performed by all nurses of Government hospitals for less than 20 times and for less than 40 minutes. Data pertaining to activities performed by nurses from private hospitals is outlined and it is clearly evident from Table 4.10 that all of the nurses performed activities like help in medical tests by 86 per cent, giving medicine by 72 per cent, injury care (dressing) by 86 per cent of nurses, measuring blood pressure and heart rate by 72 per cent, for less than 20 time and for 40-80 minutes in a day. All of the nurses from Government hospitals were found to assist in surgery for less than 20 time and for more than 80 minutes, whereas in private hospitals 84 per cent performed it for 20-40 time and for more than 40-80 minutes by all.

Glucose dripping was performed for less than 20 times by majority (78.57 per cent) of nurses from Government hospitals for less than 40 minutes in duration (57.14 per cent) followed by 27.14 per cent nurses who performed it for 40-80 minutes in a day. With regard to nurses from private hospitals, all of them performed dripping for 20-40 times and for less than 40 minutes in a day.

Record keeping, giving injection, drug administration and storage were performed by 95.71 per cent nurses for less than 20 times and for less than 40 minutes in a day in Government hospitals. Few nurses 12 per cent were checking weight of patients on a regular basis for more than 40 times for 40-80 minutes (Table 4.10 and Plates 12-14).

## 4.12 Handling of Medical Equipment/Scientific Gadgets/ Medical Accessories/Furniture

A variety of medical equipments/scientific gadgets, furniture and accessories which are used by nurses is given in Table 4.11. Data reveals the frequency and duration of using each and every medical equipments, accessories and furniture in a day both in Government and private hospitals.

**Table 4.10:** Type of Activities Performed by Nurses

| S. No. | Activities | Government (n=70) | | | | | | Private (n=50) | | | | | |
|---|---|---|---|---|---|---|---|---|---|---|---|---|---|
| | | Frequency in times | | | Duration in Min. | | | Frequency in times | | | Duration in Min. | | |
| | | < 20 | 20-40 | > 40 | < 40 | 40-80 | >80 | < 20 | 20-40 | > 40 | < 40 | 40-80 | >80 |
| 1. | Help in Medical Tests | 70(100) | — | — | 70(100) | — | — | 50(100) | — | — | 7(14) | 43(86) | — |
| 2. | Giving medicine | 70(100) | — | — | 70(100) | — | — | 50(100) | — | — | 7(14) | 36(72) | 7(14) |
| 3. | Injury care(dressing) | 70(100) | — | — | 70(100) | — | — | 50(100) | — | — | — | 43(86) | 7(14) |
| 4. | Measuring B.P. | 70(100) | — | — | 70(100) | — | — | 50(100) | — | — | 7(14) | 36(72) | 7(14) |
| 5. | Measuring Heart rate | 70(100) | — | — | 70(100) | — | — | 50(100) | — | — | 7(14) | 36(72) | 7(14) |
| 6. | Assisting in surgery | 70(100) | — | — | — | — | 70(100) | 8(16) | 42(84) | — | — | 50(100) | — |
| 7. | Dripping | 55(78.57) | — | 4(5.71) | 40(57.14) | 19(27.14) | — | — | 50(100) | — | 50(100) | — | — |
| 8. | Supervision on health and infection control | 7(10) | — | — | 7(10) | — | — | 50(100 ) | — | — | 50(100) | — | — |
| 9. | First aid and emergency | 59(84.29) | — | — | 59(84.29) | — | — | 48(96) | — | — | 39(78) | 9(18) | — |
| 10. | Record keeping | 67(95.71) | — | — | 65(92.86) | 2(2.86) | — | 32(64) | 18(36) | — | 50(100) | — | — |
| 11. | Giving injection | 67(95.71) | — | — | 70(100) | — | — | 50(100) | — | — | 50(100) | — | — |
| 12. | Drug administration, storage | 67(95.71) | — | — | 66(94.29) | 1(1.43) | — | 36(72) | — | 14(28) | 50(100) | — | — |
| 13. | Bathing and toileting | — | — | — | — | — | — | 46(92) | — | 4(8) | 50(100) | — | — |
| 14. | Mobility of patients | 49(70) | — | — | 48(68.57) | 1(1.43) | — | 39(78) | — | 11(22) | 50(100) | — | — |
| 15. | Regular weight check—up | 62(88.57) | — | — | 62(88.57) | — | — | 44(88) | — | 6(12) | 44(88) | 6(12) | — |

*Note*: Figures in parentheses indicate the percentage value .

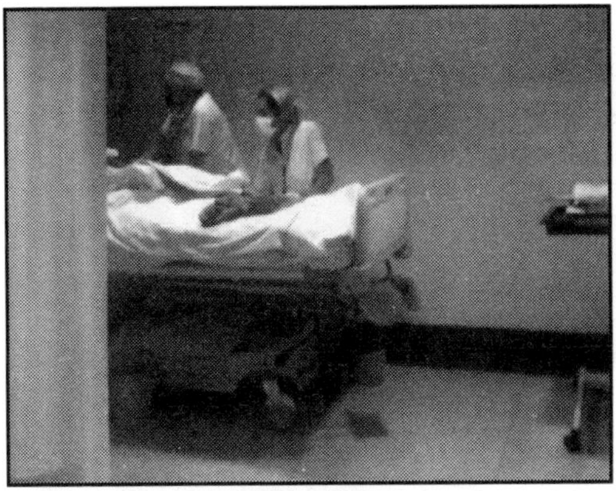

**Medical Test**

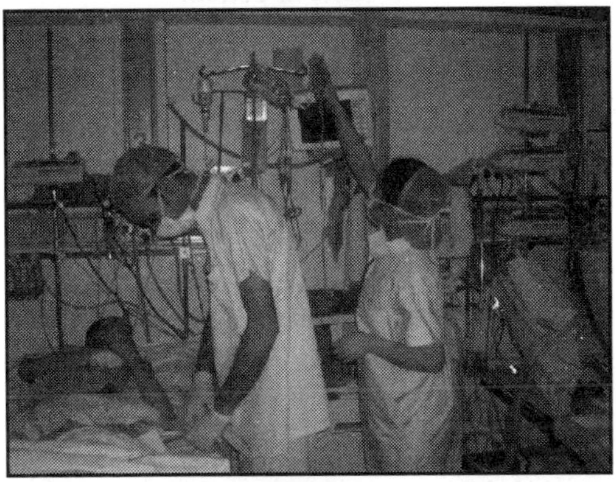

**Dripping**

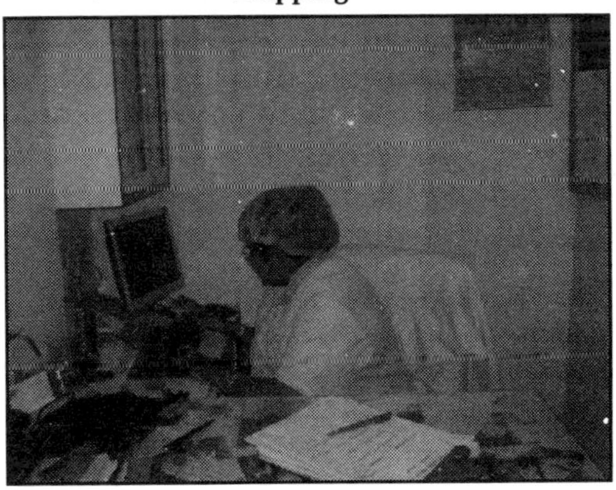

**Record Keeping**

**Plate 12: Activities Performed by the Nurses**

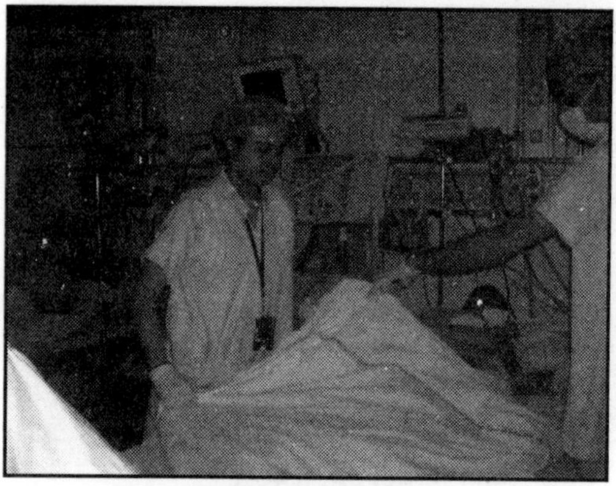

**Mobility of Patient**

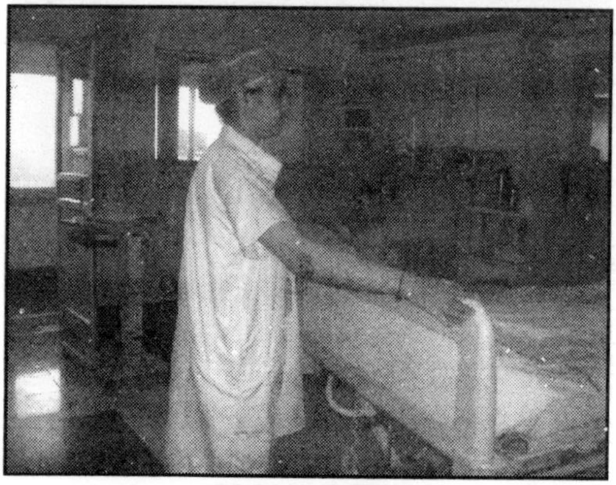

**Making the Bed**

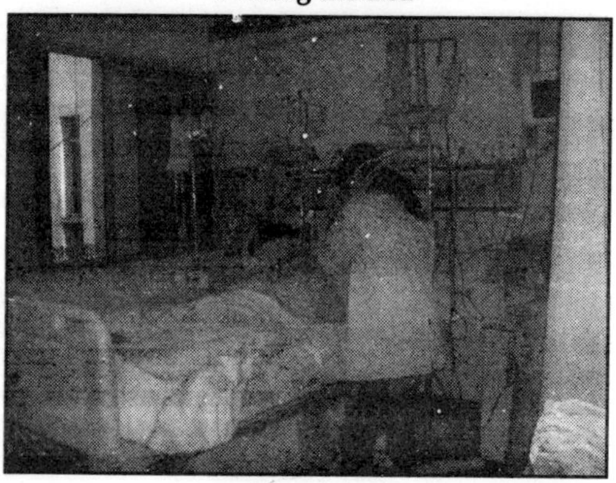

**Physiotherapy**
**Plate 13: Activities Performed by the Nurses**

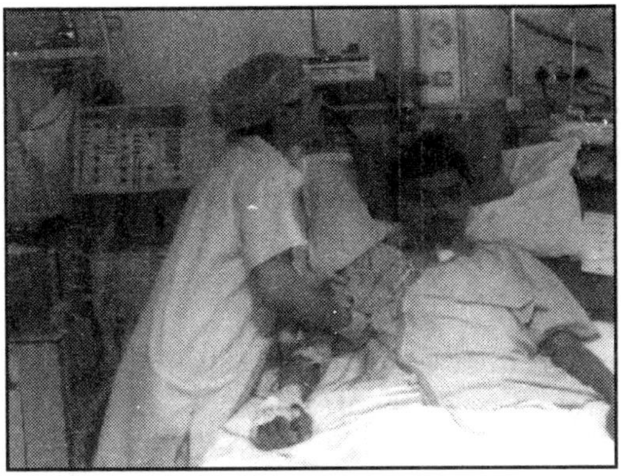

**Measuring Body Temperature**

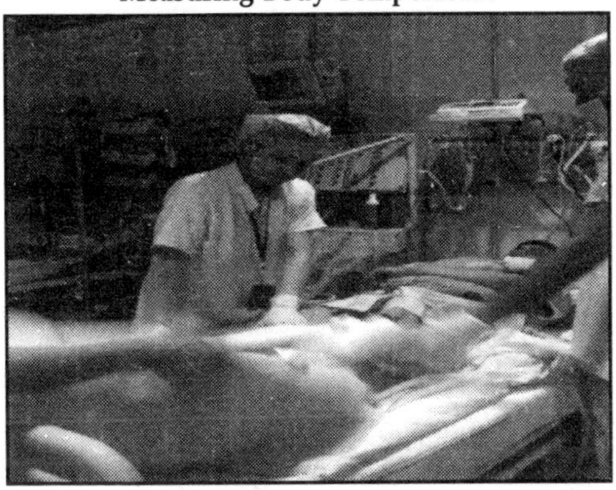

**Changing Bedsheet**

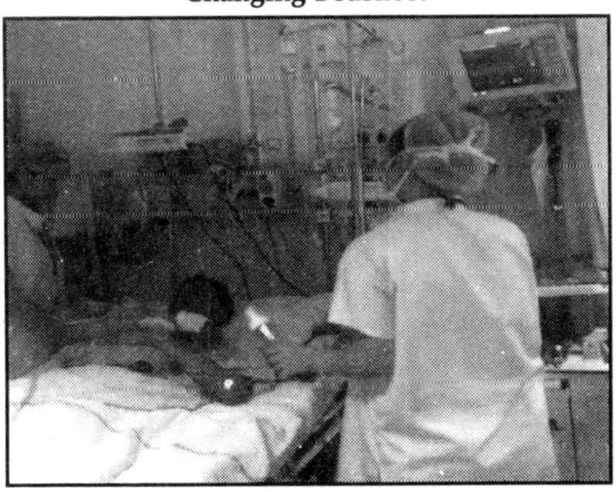

**Giving Medicine**

**Plate 14: Activities Performed by the Nurses**

### *4.12.1 Medical Equipments*

Most frequently used medical equipments were Heart rate monitor, weighing machine, ECG ultrasound machine, X-ray machine, first aid kit, instrument sterilizer, paediatric equipment, dental instruments, autoclaves, obstetric labour tables telescope, ophthalmic instruments, orthopedic instruments, endoscopic instruments, ICU Bed for less than 20 time and less than 40 minutes in duration in a day among the nurses from Government hospitals.

Again in case of nurses among private hospitals, BP apparatus, Heart rate monitor, weighing machine, ECG, ultrasound machine, X-ray machine, thermometers, oxygen therapy instrument, first aid kit, incubator, instrument sterilizer, paediatric equipment, dental instruments, autoclaves, obstetric labour tables telescope, ophthalmic instruments, orthopedic instruments, endoscopic instruments, ICU bed were frequently used for less than 20 times and for less than 40 minutes (Table 4.11 and Plates 15-16).

### *4.12.2 Medical Accessories*

Most frequently used medical accessories were medical disposable and dressing bandages by all the nurses from Government hospitals for less than 20 times and less than 40 minutes. They were followed by patient gowns chemicals, by glasswares nurses for less than 40 minutes as well as 40-80 minutes. Regarding nurses from private hospitals, it was observed that most frequently used accessories were medicine trolley, dressing trolleys, food service cart, dressing bowl, commode chair. All the nurses used these accessories for less than 20 times and for less than 40 minutes. Generally, Government hospitals have all the health departments so, medical equipments, accessories were available in variety whereas, the private hospitals were specialized in one particular branch of the medical science so, number of medical equipments and accessories were less.

**Table 4.11:** Handling of Medical Equipment/Scientific Gadgets/Medical Accessories/Furniture

| S. No. | Equipment Medical equipment | Government (n=70) | | | | | | Private (n=50) | | | | | |
|---|---|---|---|---|---|---|---|---|---|---|---|---|---|
| | | Frequency in times per day | | | Duration in Min. per day | | | Frequency in times per day | | | Duration in Min. per day | | |
| | | < 20 | 20-40 | > 40 | < 40 | 40-80 | >80 | < 20 | 20-40 | > 40 | < 40 | 40-80 | >80 |
| 1. | BP apparatus | 5 (7.14) | 40 (57.14) | — | 50 (71.43) | — | — | 40 (80) | 10 (20) | — | 36 (72) | 14 (28) | — |
| 2. | Heart rate monitor | 43 (61.43) | 3 (4.29) | — | 46 (65.71) | — | — | 46 (92) | 4 (8) | — | 28 (56) | 22 (44) | — |
| 3. | Weighing machine | 53 (75.71) | 4 (5.71) | — | 53 (75.71) | 4 (5.71) | — | 46 (92) | 4 (8) | — | 31 (62) | 19 (38) | — |
| 4. | ECG | 39 (55.71) | — | — | 31 (44.29) | 8 (11.43) | — | 46 (92) | 4 (8) | — | 36 (72) | 14 (28) | — |
| 5. | Ultrasound machine | 57 (81.43) | — | — | 57 (81.43) | — | — | 41 (82) | 9 (18) | — | 48 (96) | 2 (4) | — |
| 6. | X-ray machine | 64 (91.43) | — | — | 64 (91.43) | — | — | 40 (80) | 10 (20) | — | 36 (72) | 14 (28) | — |
| 7. | Thermometers | 34 (48.57) | 36 (51.43) | — | 70 (100) | — | — | 41 (82) | 9 (18) | — | 34 (68) | 16 (32) | — |
| 8. | Oxygen therapy instrument | 67 (95.71) | — | — | 1 (1.43) | 22 (31.43) | 44 (62.86) | 41 (82) | 9 (18) | — | 44 (88) | 6 (12) | — |
| 9. | First aid kit | 44 (62.86) | 26 (37.14) | — | 66 (94.29) | 3 (4.29) | — | 40 (80) | 10 (20) | — | 41 (82) | 9 (18) | — |

(contd.)

**Table 4.11** (*contd.*)

| *S. No.* | *Equipment Medical equipment* | *Government (n=70)* | | | | | | *Private (n=50)* | | | | | |
|---|---|---|---|---|---|---|---|---|---|---|---|---|---|
| | | *Frequency in times per day* | | | *Duration in Min. per day* | | | *Frequency in times per day* | | | *Duration in Min. per day* | | |
| | | *< 20* | *20-40* | *> 40* | *< 40* | *40-80* | *>80* | *< 20* | *20-40* | *> 40* | *< 40* | *40-80* | *>80* |
| 10. | Incubator | 62 (88.57) | — | — | — | 23 (32.86) | 39 (55.71) | 39 (78) | 11 (22) | — | 49 (98) | 1 (2) | — |
| 11. | Instrument sterilizer | 69 (98.57) | 1 (1.43) | — | 45 (64.29) | 10 (14.29) | 15 (21.43) | 41 (82) | 9 (18) | — | 50 (100) | — | — |
| 12. | Paediatric equipment (71.43) | 50 (11.43) | 8 | — (81.43) | 57 (1.43) | 1 | — (80) | 40 (20) | 10 | — (96) | 48 (4) | 2 | — |
| 13. | Dental instruments | 43 (61.43) | 13 (18.57) | — | 56 (80) | — | — | 32 (64) | 11 (22) | — | 39 (78) | 3 (6) | — |
| 14. | Autoclaves | 60 (85.71) | 7 (10) | — | 62 (88.57) | 5 (10) | — | 39 (78) | 11 (22) | — | 50 (100) | — | — |
| 15. | Obstetric labour tables telescope | 58 (82.86) | — | — | 55 (78.57) | 3 (4.29) | — | 43 (86) | 7 (14) | — | 46 (92) | 4 (8) | — |
| 16. | Gynaecological instruments | 18 (25.71) | 22 (31.43) | — | 32 (45.71) | 8 (11.43) | — | 50 (100) | — | — | 23 (46) | 27 (54) | — |
| 17. | Ophthalmic instruments | 39 (55.71) | 19 (27.14) | — | 34 (48.57) | 22 (31.43) | 2 (2.86) | 50 (100) | — | — | 50 (100) | — | — |
| 18. | Orthopedic instruments | 32 (45.71) | 25 (35.71) | — | 57 (81.43) | — | — | 50 (100) | — | — | 50 (100) | — | — |
| 19. | Endoscopic instruments | 26 (37.14) | 26 (37.14) | — | 52 (74.29) | — | — | 44 (88) | 6 (12) | — | 50 (100) | — | — |

(*contd.*)

**Table 4.11** (*contd.*)

| S. No. | Equipment / Medical equipment | Government (n=70) | | | | | | Private (n=50) | | | | | |
|---|---|---|---|---|---|---|---|---|---|---|---|---|---|
| | | Frequency in times per day | | | Duration in Min. per day | | | Frequency in times per day | | | Duration in Min. per day | | |
| | | < 20 | 20-40 | > 40 | < 40 | 40-80 | >80 | < 20 | 20-40 | > 40 | < 40 | 40-80 | >80 |
| 20. | ICU Bed | 24 (34.29) | — | — | 22 (31.43) | 2 (2.86) | — | 42 (84) | 8 (16) | — | 50 (100) | — | — |
| | **Medical accessories** | | | | | | | | | | | | |
| 21. | Medicine trolley | 16 (22.86) | 31 (44.29) | — | 47 (67.14) | — | — | 50 (100) | — | — | 50 (100) | — | — |
| 22. | Dressing Trolley | 17 (24.29) | 30 (42.86) | — | 47 (67.14) | — | — | 50 (100) | — | — | 50 (100) | — | — |
| 23. | Food service cart | 20 (28.57) | 29 (41.43) | — | 49 (70) | — | — | 50 (100) | — | — | 50 (100) | — | — |
| 24. | Dressing bowl | 21 (30) | 36 (51.43) | — | 57 (81.43) | — | — | 50 (100) | — | — | 50 (100) | — | — |
| 25. | Instrument trolley | 19 (27.14) | 31 (44.29) | — | 46 (65.71) | 4 (5.71) | — | 39 (78) | 11 (22) | — | 39 (78) | 11 (22) | — |
| 26. | Surgical table | 39 (55.71) | — | — | 35 (50) | 4 (5.71) | — | 44 (88) | 6 (12) | — | 40 (80) | 10 (20) | — |
| 27. | Wash Basin Stand | 65 (92.86) | — | — | 65 (92.86) | — | — | 36 (72) | 14 (28) | — | 50 (100) | — | — |
| 28. | Commode Chair | 57 (81.43) | — | — | 57 (81.43) | — | — | 50 (100) | — | — | 50 (100) | — | — |

(*contd.*)

**Table 4.11** *(contd.)*

| S. No. | Equipment Medical equipment | Government (n=70) | | | | | | Private (n=50) | | | | | |
|---|---|---|---|---|---|---|---|---|---|---|---|---|---|
| | | Frequency in times per day | | | Duration in Min. per day | | | Frequency in times per day | | | Duration in Min. per day | | |
| | | < 20 | 20-40 | > 40 | < 40 | 40-80 | >80 | < 20 | 20-40 | > 40 | < 40 | 40-80 | >80 |
| 29. | Wardrobes | 67 (95.71) | — | — | 22 (31.43) | 40 (57.14) | 5 (7.14) | 36 (72) | 14 (28) | — | 50 (100) | — | — |
| 30. | Hearing telephone | 45 (64.29) | — | 3 (4.29) | 48 (68.57) | — | — | 45 (90) | 5 (10) | — | 50 (100) | — | — |
| 31. | Sanitory gloves | 39 (55.71) | — | 31 (44.28) | 35 (50) | 4 (5.71) | 31 (44.28) | 44 (88) | 6 (12) | — | 40 (80) | 10 (20) | — |
| 32. | Glucose drips | 57 (81.43) | — | — | 57 (81.43) | — | — | 50 (100) | — | — | 50 (100) | — | — |
| 33. | Medical disposable | 70 (100) | — | — | 70 (100) | — | — | 29 (58) | 21 (42) | — | 50 (100) | — | — |
| 34. | Dressing bandages | 70 (100) | — | — | 70 (100) | — | — | 45 (90) | 5 (10) | — | 50 (100) | — | — |
| 35. | Patient's gowns | 67 (95.71) | — | — | 27 (38.57) | 40 (57.14) | — | 36 (72) | 14 (28) | — | 50 (100) | — | — |
| 36. | Knifes, blades | 39 (55.71) | — | 31 (44.28) | 35 (50) | 4 (5.71) | 31 (44.28) | 44 (88) | 6 (12) | — | 40 (80) | 10 (20) | — |
| 37. | Surgical sponges, forceps | 34 (91.43) | 36 (51.43) | — | 70 (100) | — | — | 36 (72) | 14 (28) | — | 50 (100) | — | — |
| 38. | Chemicals, glasswares | 67 (95.71) | — | — | 27 (38.57) | 40 (57.14) | — | 36 (72) | 14 (28) | — | 50 (100) | — | — |

*(contd.)*

**Table 4.11** (*contd.*)

| S. No. | Equipment / Medical equipment | Government (n=70) | | | | | | Private (n=50) | | | | | |
|---|---|---|---|---|---|---|---|---|---|---|---|---|---|
| | | Frequency in times per day | | | Duration in Min. per day | | | Frequency in times per day | | | Duration in Min. per day | | |
| | | < 20 | 20-40 | > 40 | < 40 | 40-80 | >80 | < 20 | 20-40 | > 40 | < 40 | 40-80 | >80 |
| | **Furniture** | | | | | | | | | | | | |
| 39. | Hospital beds | 24 (34.29) | 42 (60) | 2 (2.86) | 68 (97.14) | — | — | 38 (76) | 12 (24) | — | 50 (100) | — | — |
| 40. | Hospital chairs | 14 (20) | 44 (62.86) | 2 (2.86) | 60 (85.71) | — | — | 32 (64) | 6 (12) | 12 (24) | 50 (100) | — | — |
| 41. | Stretchers | 64 (91.43) | — | — | 64 (91.43) | — | — | 6 (12) | — | — | 50 (100) | — | — |
| 42. | Wheelchair | 20 (28.57) | 48 (68.57) | — | 68 (97.14) | — | — | 50 (100) | — | — | 50 (100) | — | — |
| 43. | Stool | 20 (28.57) | 48 (68.57) | — | 68 (97.14) | — | — | 50 (100) | — | — | 50 (100) | — | — |
| 44. | Stands and racks | 23 (32.86) | 45 (64.29) | — | 68 (97.14) | — | — | 36 (72) | 7 (14) | 7 (14) | 50 (100) | — | — |
| 45. | Bediside table | 24 (34.29) | 45 (64.29) | — | 69 (98.57) | — | — | 43 (86) | 7 (14) | — | 50 (100) | — | — |
| 46. | Baby cradle | 66 (94.29) | — | — | 61 (87.14) | 6 (8.57) | — | 50 (100) | — | — | 50 (100) | — | — |

*Note*: Figures in parentheses indicate the percentage values.

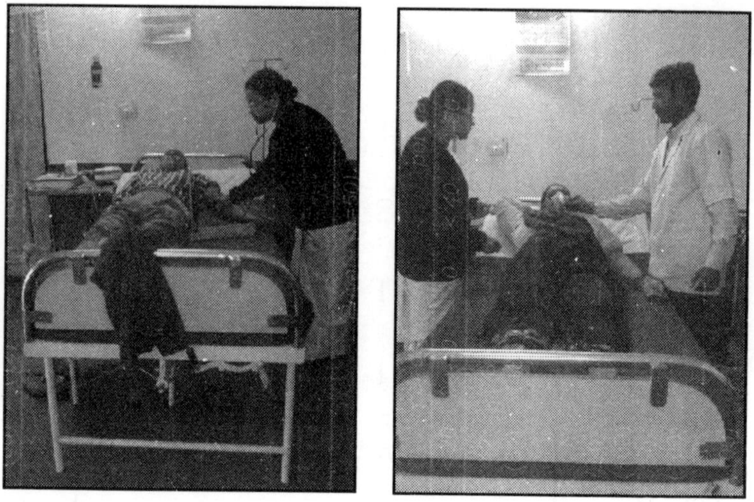

**Plate 15:** Handling of Scientific Equipments in Hospitals under Study

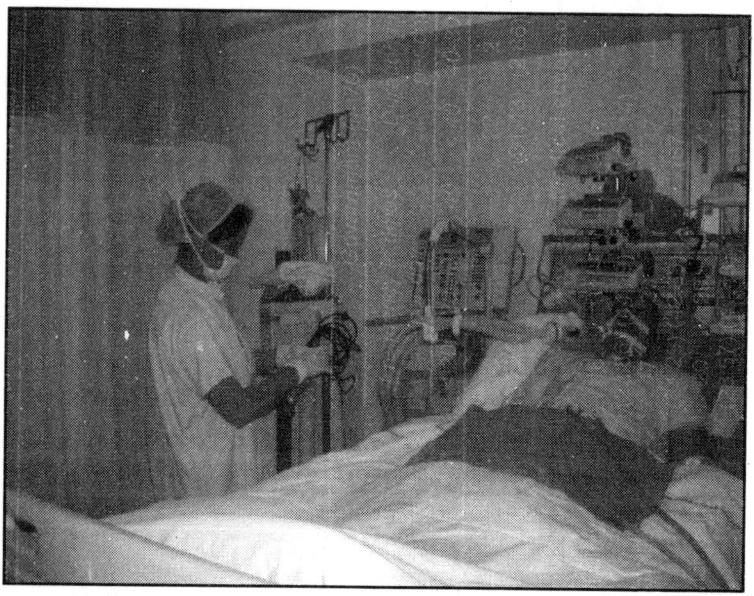

**Plate 16:** Handling of Scientific Equipments in Model Hospital

### *4.12.3 Furniture*

There were no special relaxing chairs for nurses in any hospitals. The chair provided to nurses was used by them for more than 40 times (38.57 per cent) and for less than 40 minutes by all of them. Other furniture which were used by Government hospitals were baby cradle (94.29 per cent for less than 20 times and 87.14 per cent used for less than 40 minutes), stretchers (91.43 per cent for less than 20 times and for less than 40 minutes), single foot step and double foot step (80 per cent for less than 20 times and 81.43 per cent used these articles for less than 40 minutes). In case of nurses from private hospitals, all of them used furniture like wheel chair, stool and baby cradle for less than 20 times and for less than 40 minutes.

## 4.13 Comfort/Discomfort from the Use of Furniture

Furniture details like high/low furniture and associated comfort or discomfort are crucial for better work performance.

### *4.13.1 Dimensional Features of Furniture*

On the whole, 11.67 per cent nurses reported that their furniture is too high to sit and a small proportion (4.17 per cent) felt that their furniture is too low. When category-wise data was analyzed, it was found that 12.86 per cent nurses from Government and 10 per cent nurses from private hospitals found the furniture to be high. Again the same proportion of nurses (10 per cent) only from private mentioned their furniture as too low.

Same results were shown by Adalarasu and Balasubramanian (2005) who reported that poorly designed office chair in addition to intense work leads to musculoskeletal disorders. So, human geometry and the dimensions of the product must be suitably fitted together as revealed by Kreifeldt (1991).

**Table 4.12:** Comfort/Discomfort from the Use of Furniture

| S. No | Details | Government (n=70) | Private (n=50) | Total (N=120) |
|---|---|---|---|---|
| 1. | Dimensional details of furniture | | | |
| | (a) Too high | 9 (12.86) | 5 (10) | 14 (11.67) |
| | (b) Too low | — | 5 (10) | 5 (4.17) |
| 2. | Structural details of furniture | | | |
| | (a) Hard texture | 9 (12.86) | 17 (34) | 26 (21.67) |
| | (b) Sharp edges | 5 (7.14) | 2 (4) | 7 (5.83) |
| | (c) Cushioned | 10 (14.29) | 3 (6) | 13 (10.83) |
| 3. | Material used in furniture | | | |
| | (a) Wooden | 60 (85.71) | 49 (98) | 109 (90.83) |
| | (b) Metallic | 6 (8.57) | 19 (38) | 25 (20.83) |
| | (c) Plastic | 13 (18.57) | 42 (84) | 55 (45.83) |
| | (d) Painted | 25 (35.71) | 14 (28) | 39 (32.5) |
| 4. | Other information | | | |
| | (a) Heavy furniture rather than lightweight | 32 (45.71) | 15 (30) | 47 (39.17) |
| | (b) Sturdy chair/table | 32 (45.71) | 21 (42) | 53 (44.17) |
| | (c) Plastic or rubber gliding tips on the ends of the legs | — | 22 (44) | 22 (18.33) |
| | (d) Properly fixed wheels | 14 (20) | 43 (86) | 57 (47.5) |

*Note*: Figures in parentheses indicate the percentage values.

### *4.13.2 Structural Features of Furniture*

Structural features like hard texture was felt by 21.67 per cent nurses followed by cushioned furniture (10.83 per cent) and sharp edges (5.83 per cent). When data was analyzed for individual category of nurses from Government hospitals, it was found that maximum of 14.29 per cent reported their furniture is cushioned followed by hard texture (12.86 per cent). In case of nurses from private hospitals, hard textured furniture was reported by 34 per cent followed by 6 per cent nurses who had cushioned furniture.

### *4.13.3 Material Used in Furniture*

The data pertaining to material used in furniture of different hospitals on the whole, reveal that majority (90.83 per cent) of nurses had wooden furniture, followed by plastic furniture

(45.83 per cent) and painted (32.5 per cent). In case of nurses from Government hospitals maximum (85.71 per cent) had wooden furniture followed by 35.71 per cent nurses whose furniture was painted. Regarding nurses from private hospitals majority (98 per cent) of them possessed wooden furniture closely followed by plastic furniture (84 per cent).

### *4.13.4 Other Information*

On the whole, maximum (47.5 per cent) nurses reported that their furniture had properly fixed wheels. Chair or table was reported to be sturdy when pressure is put on them by 44.17 per cent nurses followed by 39.17 per cent nurses who felt their furniture is heavy. Particularly in relation to nurses from Government hospitals a commendable proportion (45.17 per cent each) reported their furniture is heavy and it is sturdy when pressure is put on it. In case of nurses from private hospitals, majority (86 per cent) reported that wheels are properly fixed on their furniture and it was followed by presence of plastic or rubber gliding tips on the ends of the legs by 44 per cent nurses.

## 4.14 Experience in Handling of Medical Equipments/ Scientific Gadgets/Medical Accessories/Furniture

Nurses were asked about experience in handling of various gadgets while performing different tasks and it is given in Table 4.13.

### *4.14.1 Medical Equipments*

It is evident from Table 4.13 that highest mean score value was given to Blood Pressure apparatus and Oxygen Therapy instrument (2.44 each) by 47.14 per cent and 62.86 per cent nurses respectively from Government hospitals felt them comfortable. Least mean score value (1.71) was calculated in the case of X-ray machine by 50 per cent nurses who reported it is uncomfortable. It can be further envisaged from Table 4.13 that in case of nurses from private hospitals, highest mean score

**Table 4.13:** Experience in Handling of Medical Equipments/Scientific Gadgets/Medical Accessories/Furniture

| *S. No.* | *Medical equipments* | *Government (n=70)* | | | | *Private (n=50)* | | | |
|---|---|---|---|---|---|---|---|---|---|
| | | *C* | *SC* | *UC* | *MS* | *C* | *SC* | *UC* | *MS* |
| 1. | BP apparatus | 33 (47.14) | 35 (50) | 2 (2.86) | 2.44 | 47 (94) | 3 (6) | — | 2.94 |
| 2. | Heart rate monitor | 24 (34.29) | 25 (35.71) | 21 (30) | 2.04 | 33 (66) | 17 (34) | — | 2.66 |
| 3. | Weighing machine | 20 (28.57) | 20 (28.57) | 30 (42.86) | 1.86 | 33 (66) | 17 (34) | — | 2.66 |
| 4. | ECG | 16 (22.86) | 20 (28.57) | 34 (48.57) | 1.74 | 33 (66) | 17 (34) | — | 2.66 |
| 5. | Ultrasound machine | 16 (22.86) | 20 (28.57) | 34 (48.57) | 1.74 | 24 (48) | 26 (52) | — | 2.48 |
| 6. | X-ray machine | 15 (21.43) | 20 (28.57) | 35 (70) | 1.71 | 30 (60) | 15 (30) | 5 (10) | 2.50 |
| 7. | Oxygen therapy instruments | 44 (62.86) | 13 (18.57) | 13 (18.57) | 2.44 | 24 (48) | 26 (52) | — | 2.48 |
| 8. | Incubator | 33 (47.14) | 27 (38.57) | 10 (14.29) | 2.33 | 8 (16) | 42 (84) | — | 2.16 |
| 9. | Instrument sterilizer | 29 (41.43) | 27 (38.57) | 14 (20) | 2.21 | 18 (36) | 32 (64) | — | 2.36 |
| 10. | Autoclave | 33 (47.14) | 27 (38.57) | 10 (14.29) | 2.33 | 30 (60) | 15 (30) | 5 (10) | 2.50 |
| 11. | Obstetric tables telescope | 33 (47.14) | 24 (34.29) | 13 (18.57) | 2.29 | 16 (32) | 21 (42) | 13 (26) | 2.06 |
| 14. | Gynaecological instruments | 33 (47.14) | 34 (48.57) | 3 (4.29) | 2.43 | 15 (30) | 30 (60) | 5 (10) | 2.20 |
| 15.. | Ophthalmic instruments | 27 (38.57) | 27 (38.57) | 16 (22.86) | 2.16 | 15 (30) | 30 (60) | 5 (10) | 2.20 |
| 16. | Orthopedic instruments | 24 (34.29) | 33 (47.14) | 13 (18.57) | 2.16 | 15 (30) | 30 (60) | 5 (10) | 2.20 |

(*Contd.*)

**Table 4.13** (*Contd.*)

| *S. No* | *Medical equipments* | *Government (n=70)* | | | | *Private (n=50)* | | | |
|---|---|---|---|---|---|---|---|---|---|
| | | *C* | *SC* | *UC* | *MS* | *C* | *SC* | *UC* | *MS* |
| 17. | Endoscopic instruments | 23 (32.86) | 20 (28.57) | 27 (38.57) | 1.94 | 15 (30) | 30 (60) | 5 (10) | 2.20 |
| 18. | ICU Bed | 18 (25.71) | 25 (35.71) | 27 (38.57) | 1.87 | 19 (27.14) | 25 (50) | 6 (12) | 2.26 |
| | **Medical accessories** | | | | | | | | |
| 19. | Surgical table | 27 (38.57) | 30 (42.86) | 13 (18.57) | 2.20 | 34 (68) | 16 (32) | — | 2.68 |
| 20. | Washbasin stand | 28 (40) | 36 (51.43) | 6 (8.57) | 2.31 | 4 (8) | 13 (26) | 33 (66) | 1.42 |
| 21. | Armoires/Wardrobes | 40 (57.14) | 30 (42.86) | — | 2.57 | 33 (66) | 17 (34) | — | 2.66 |
| 22. | Sanitory gloves | 14 (20) | 18 (25.71) | 32 (45.71) | 1.57 | 33 (66) | 17 (34) | - | 2.66 |
| | **Furniture** | | | | | | | | |
| 23. | Hospital beds | 30 (42 86) | 31 (44.29) | 9 (12.86) | 2.30 | 16 (32) | 34 (68) | — | 2.32 |
| 24. | Hospital chair | 15 (7 14) | 18 (40) | 37 (52.86) | 1.69 | 16 (32) | 34 (68) | — | 2.32 |
| 25. | Baby cradle | 28 (40) | 40 (57.14) | 2 (2.86) | 2.37 | 17 (34) | 33 (66) | — | 2.34 |
| 26. | Wheelchair | 17 (24.29) | 40 (57.14) | 13 (18.57) | 2.06 | 25 (50) | 25 (50) | — | 2.50 |
| 27. | Stool | 28 (40) | 38 (54.29) | 4 (5.71) | 2.34 | 33 (66) | 17 (34) | — | 2.66 |
| 28. | Stands and racks | 22 (31.43) | 40 (57.14) | 8 (11.43) | 2.20 | 34 (68) | 16 (32) | — | 2.68 |
| 29. | Hospital stretcher | 40 (57.14) | 30 (42.86) | — | 2.57 | 34 (68) | 16 (32) | — | 2.68 |

*Note*: Figures in parentheses indicate the percentage values.
C—Comfortable (3), SC—Somewhat comfortable (2), UC—Uncomfortable (1), MS—Mean Score

value (2.94) was calculated for equipments like Blood pressure apparatus which was found to be comfortable by 94 per cent nurses. Obstetric labour tables telescope was found as uncomfortable by 26 per cent nurses with mean score as 2.06.

### 4.14.2 Medical Accessories

Among medical accessories, highest mean score (2.57) was obtained by armoire/wardrobe found as comfortable by 57.14 per cent nurses from Government hospitals. Least mean score (1.57) was calculated for sanitary gloves as found to be uncomfortable by maximum of 45.71 per cent nurses. The data in relation to nurses from private hospitals, it was revealed that highest mean score (2.68) was given to surgical table for which 68 per cent nurses reported that it is comfortable, whereas washbasin stand got the least mean score of 1.42 and found to be uncomfortable by 33 per cent of nurses.

### 4.14.3 Furniture

Under the category of furniture and furnishings, hospital stretcher got highest mean score of 2.57 as reported to be comfortable by 57.14 per cent nurses, whereas least mean score (1.69) was given to hospital chair and reported as uncomfortable by 52.86 per cent nurses. In case of private hospitals, stand and racks along with hospital stretcher got highest mean score value (2.68 each) and were found to be comfortable by 68 per cent nurses, whereas least mean score (2.32 each) was given to hospital bed and chair and observed to be somewhat comfortable by maximum (68 per cent) of the nurses.

## 4.15 Occupational Hazards, Accidents, Risks or Injuries at Workplace

Hazards, accidents, risks or injuries are the common incidence at the hospital and the research reports have revealed that rate of accidents is relatively more in the morning shift as compared to afternoon shift.

### *4.15.1 Mechanical Hazards*

The results regarding mechanical hazards as experienced by nurses (on an average) revealed that majority (94.17 per cent each) of the nurses were encountering problem with repetitive motion and awkward posture during work schedule followed by 71.67 per cent and 67.5 per cent nurses who reported injuries with sharp edges and accidents with manual handling respectively. As far as data with regard to nurses from Government hospitals was concerned, it was found that all the nurses were encountered with reported repetitive motion and awkward posture followed by manual handling (84.29 per cent) whereas, very few (5.7 per cent) had injuries with lifting the material. In case of private hospitals further repetitive motion and awkward posture were experienced by majority (86 per cent) of nurses. A small proportion (16 per cent) of nurses reported accidents with lifting equipments manually. The findings can be supported by the study of Castro *et al.* (2007) who reported increased working hours are associated with musculoskeletal injuries, needlesticks, fatigue among nurses in developing countries.

The reason behind this may be that nurses most of the time work continuously in sitting position and sometimes continuously in standing position in awkward posture which is injurious in long run leading to musculoskeletal disorders.

### *4.15.2 Biological Hazards*

Hazards may occur through contact with biological waste during pathological waste etc. which may be infectious to the nurses who have to perform these tests. In the summative responses, biological hazards like skin infection were reported by about 34.17 per cent followed by rashes/allergy (13.33 per cent). When data was analyzed with regard to nurses from Government hospitals particularly, it was observed that rashes/allergy and skin infection were common biological hazards among nurses (17.14 per cent each). In case of nurses from private hospitals about 58 per cent reported skin infections and only 8 per cent were suffering from skin rashes/allergy.

**Plate 17:** Awkward Posture adopted by Nurses while Recording

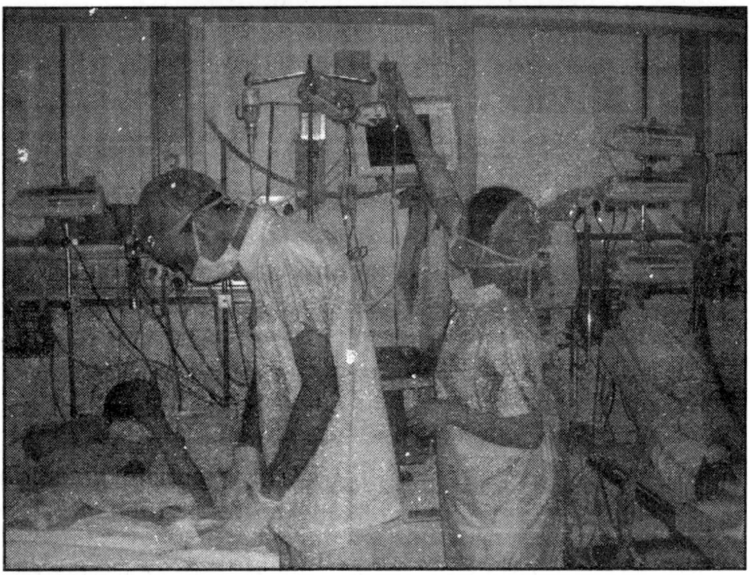

**Plate 18:** Ergonomically Suitable Posture while Recording

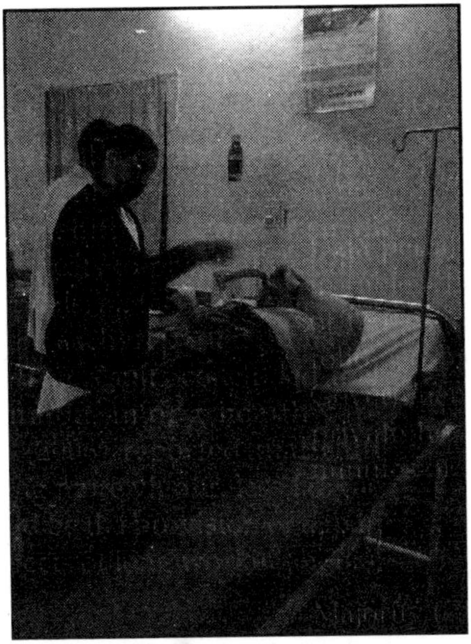

**Plate 19:** Poor Working Situation

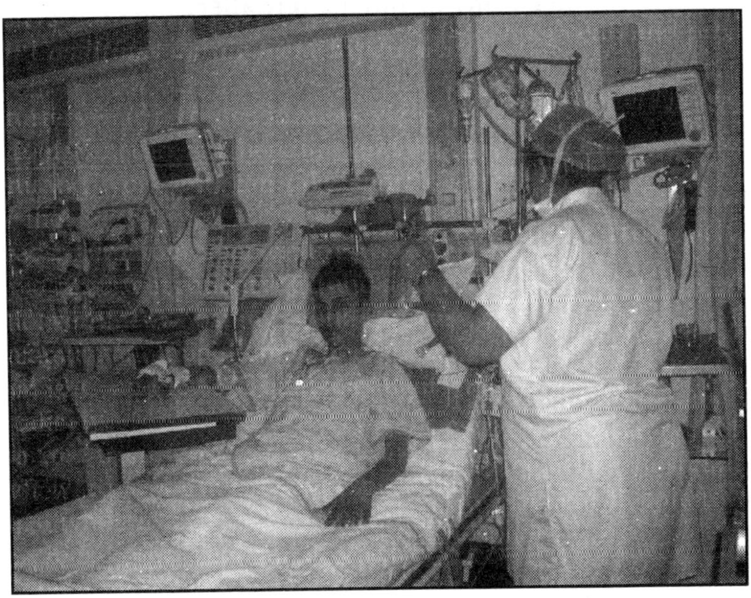

**Plate 20:** Functional Working Situation

As compared to nurses from private hospitals, nurses of Government hospitals are more prone to biological hazards which showed that private hospitals do not maintain the health and hygiene practices.

### *4.15.3 Chemical Hazards*

Chemical hazards may happen while using different chemicals (acids or alkalies), cleaning compounds, exhaustion of waste anesthetic gases through X–ray machines, ultrasound machines etc. It can be envisaged from Table 4.14 that most of the nurses (40.83 per cent each) got injured with solvents and dust followed by 33.33 per cent who were having infections with cleaning compounds. It was further found that in relation to nurses from Government hospitals, 38.57 per cent nurses had injury through contact with solvents and cleaning compounds whereas only 7.14 per cent reported problems with waste anesthetic gases. In case of nurses from private hospitals, majority (64 per cent) of nurses felt allergy with waste anesthetic gases and a few of 12 per cent complained of skin burns from acid.

### *4.15.4 Physical Hazards*

Physical hazards are a combination of hazards from noise, radiation, heat and cold. It is evident from Table 4.14 that majority of nurses, i.e. 60 per cent felt noise hazards, radiation, heat and cold (30.83 per cent each). Data pertaining to nurses from Government hospitals revealed that maximum (42.86 per cent) of nurses reported hazards with noise and very few were in problem with radiation hazards (4.29 per cent). In case of nurses from private hospitals, 84 per cent had hazards of noise followed by radiation, i.e. 68 per cent. The more number of hazards like noise is not a serious problem especially in private hospitals and even in Government hospitals and it could be assumed that it reflected both the organizational factor, the presence of more people like relatives of the patients and management personnel.

### 4.15.5 Psycho-Social Hazards

Psycho-social parameters include the hazards which increase the psycho-social cost of work of an individual and thus termed as psycho-social hazards.

**Table 4.14:** Occupational Hazards, Accidents, Risks, Injuries at Workplace (Since Last 1 Year)

| S. No. | Type of Hazards | Sources of Hazard | Frequency of Incidence | | |
|---|---|---|---|---|---|
| | | | Government (n=70) | Private (n=50) | Total (N=120) |
| 1. | **Mechanical/ Ergonomics/ Repetitive Strain Injuries (RSI)** | (a) Lifting | 4 (5.71) | 8 (16) | 12 (10) |
| | | (b) Sharp edges | 57 (81.43) | 29 (58) | 86 (71.67) |
| | | (c) Repetitive motion | 70 (100) | 43 (86) | 113 (94.17) |
| | | (d) Awkward posture | 70 (100) | 43 (86) | 113 (94.17) |
| | | (e) Forceful motion | 25 (35.71) | 21 (42) | 46 (38.33) |
| | | (f) Manual handling | 59 (84.29) | 22 (44) | 81 (67.50) |
| 2. | **Biological** | (a) Rashes/Allergy | 12 (17.14) | 4 (8) | 16 (13.33) |
| | | (b) Skin infection | 12 (17.14) | 29 (58) | 41 (34.17) |
| 3. | **Chemical** | (a) Solvents | 27 (38.57) | 22 (44) | 49 (40.83) |
| | | (b) Chlorine | 24 (34.29) | 15 (30) | 39 (32.50) |
| | | (c) Cleaning compounds | 27 (38.57) | 13 (26) | 40 (33.33) |
| | | (d) Waste anaes-thetic gases | 5 (7.14) | 32 (64) | 37 (30.83) |
| | | (e) Dust | 20 (28.57) | 29 (58) | 49 (40.83) |
| | | (f) Skin burn from acid | 19 (27.14) | 6 (12) | 25 (20.83) |
| 4. | **Physical** | (a) Noise | 30 (42.86) | 42 (84) | 72 (60) |
| | | (b) Radiation | 3 (4.29) | 34 (68) | 37 (30.83) |
| | | (c) Heat | 9 (12.86) | 28 (56) | 37 (30.83) |
| | | (d) Cold | 9 (12.86) | 28 (56) | 37 (30.83) |
| 5. | **Psycho-social hazards** | (a) Lack of Control | 26 (37.14) | 20 (40) | 46 (38.33) |
| | | (b) Fatigue from shift-work | 64 (91.43) | 50 (100) | 114 (95) |
| | | (c) Over work | 17 (24.29) | 9 (18) | 26 (21.67) |
| | | (d) Job pressure | 19 (27.14) | 8 (16) | 27 (22.50) |
| | | (e) Job stress | 15 (21.43) | 5 (10) | 20 (16.67) |
| | | (f) Sleep disorders | 17 (24.29) | 5 (10) | 22 (18.33) |
| | | (g) Long working hours | 46 (65.71) | 44 (88) | 90 (75) |
| | | (h) Boring work | 37 (52.86) | 22 (44) | 59 (49.17) |
| | | (i) Threats to physical security | 12 (17.14) | 6 (12) | 18 (15) |

Figures in parentheses indicate the percentage values

The data in Table 4.14 concluded that on the whole, majority of the nurses (95 per cent and 75 per cent) felt fatigue from shift work and long working hours and very few (15 per cent) nurses reported threats to physical security. Particularly with regard to nurses from Government hospitals, maximum of 91.43 per cent felt fatigue from shift work and a small proportion (17.14 per cent) faced threats to physical security. In case of nurses from private hospitals, all faced fatigue from shift work and very few (10 per cent each) reported problems of job stress and sleep disorders. The results concluded that psycho-social hazards are common among health care personnel (Plates 17-20). Groch (2006) reported that shift workers who took nap, were having more vigour, less fatigue and less sleepiness. So, there should be the provision of nap in the hospitals to eliminate the ill effects of long working hours, job pressure and over work.

## 4.16 Environmental Parameters at Workplace

### *4.16.1 Environmental Conditions during Field Experiments*

Environmental parameters were recorded in areas, viz. patient ward; where nurses do patient care and handling and the duty room; where they sit and work and can take short rest in between the work.

The maximum and minimum temperature were 27.4°C and 14.08°C, 22.3°C and 12.00°C at patient ward and duty room respectively in the Government hospitals while in case of private hospitals, maximum and minimum temperature were 30.12°C and 15.12°C, 25.3°C, and 13.63°C both in patient ward and duty room respectively.

The humidity ranged from 47 to 55 per cent and 42.5 to 52 per cent in patient ward and duty room respectively in Government hospitals, while in private hospitals, humidity was recorded from 48 to 56.65 per cent and 42.25 to 55.5 per cent in patient ward and duty room respectively.

It was observed that illumination was more at patient ward, i.e. 865.5 and 888.25 lux in Government and private hospitals as compared to duty room of both categories of hospitals (806 and 841.75 lux).

**Table 4.15:** Environmental Conditions During Field Experiments

N=11

| Hospitals | Activity Areas | Temperature °C Max | Min | Humidity % Max | Min | Light (lux) | Sound (dB) |
|---|---|---|---|---|---|---|---|
| **Government (n=5)** | Patient ward | 27.40 | 14.08 | 55 | 47 | 865.5 | 71.53 |
| | Duty room | 22.30 | 12.00 | 52 | 42.5 | 806 | 58.9 |
| **Private (n=6)** | Patient ward | 30.12 | 15.12 | 56.65 | 48 | 888.25 | 73.88 |
| | Duty room | 25.30 | 13.63 | 55.5 | 42.25 | 841.75 | 64.63 |

Further, the noise level was recorded as 71.53 and 58.9 dB in patient ward and duty room of Government hospitals, 73.88 and 64.63 dB in patient ward and duty room of the private hospitals. It is clear from Table 4.15 that noise was also high in patient ward as compared to duty room.

### *4.16.2 Report of Nurses Regarding Environmental Parameters at Workplace*

The environmental parameters like light, sound, temperature, humidity and air circulation can affect the performance of nurses. As reported by Gitlin (1998), the design of the structural environment support a person's daily life and allows for the individual to meet physical, psychological and social needs, and promote a sense of well-being and safety.

Report of nurses was taken about surrounding conditions both in patient ward and duty room. Here, patient ward refers to the room where patients are admitted and the duty room is the room where nurses can do their work, can sit and take some rest if possible in between the work. In case of Government hospitals, beds were provided to take rest when there is less engagement of work especially in night shifts, but in case of private hospitals, rarely there was the provision of any bed or proper rest.

**Table 4.16:** Report of Nurses Regarding Environmental Parameters at Workplace

| S. No. | Environmental parameters | Government (n=70) | | Private (n=50) | |
|---|---|---|---|---|---|
| | | Patient ward | Duty room | Patient ward | Duty room |
| 1. | Highly noisy area | 23 (32.86) | 5 (7.14) | 31 (62) | 8 (16) |
| 2. | Poor lighting | 17 (24.29) | 5 (7.14) | 11 (22) | 17 (34) |
| 3. | Comfortable temperature during summer | 9 (12.86) | 3 (4.29) | 13 (26) | 5 (10) |
| 4. | Comfortable temperature during winter | 5 (7.14) | 7 (10) | 6 (12) | 5 (10) |
| 5. | Too high humidity | 11 (8.57) | 5 (7.14) | 11 (22) | 8 (16) |
| 6. | Too low humidity | 4 (10) | 6 (8.57) | 9 (18) | 5 (10) |
| 7. | Poor air circulation | 25 (35.71) | 8 (11.43) | 8 (16) | 5 (10) |
| 8. | Pollution free air | 5 (7.14) | 4 (5.71) | 4 (8) | 5 (10) |
| 9. | Crowded area | 6 (8.57) | 5 (7.14) | 5 (10) | 4 (8) |
| 10. | Overall poor physical environment | 25 (35.71) | 16 (22.86) | 21 (42) | 18 (36) |

*Note*: Figures in parentheses indicate the percentage values.

The nurses who were working in private hospitals have to take rest in their staff or duty room only in head down position as sleeping were not allowed during night shifts.

In Table 4.16 details about different environmental conditions are given and it can be concluded from the data that on an average in Government hospitals, major problems were reported to be poor air circulation and overall poor physical environment in patient wards by 35.71 per cent nurses each. Regarding nurses from private hospitals, again problems were more in patient wards maximum, i.e. 62 per cent from complained of highly noisy area and pollution free air was felt by minimum of 8 per cent nurses. The results were in line with the findings of Lindstrom and Vuori (1984) who reported that disturbance in work performance due to noise was greater especially when estimated noise level was higher. Noise creates annoyance and distracts the mind thus chances of committing errors are high.

## 4.17 Psycho-Social Parameters

### *4.17.1 Sleep, Sleepiness and Related Factors*

Sleep is an important consideration in studying the profile of shift workers especially night shift workers. Nurses as shift worker has to do 12 hours duty during night time as compared to day shift nurses who perform 6 or 8 hours job. So, it becomes imperative to study the sleep related factor in case of night shift workers in particular and rotational shift workers in general.

#### *4.17.1.1 Sleep Time*

The data envisaged in Table 4.17 reveals that majority of the nurses, i.e. 60.83 per cent were sleeping at 10:00 pm in the night followed by 23.33 whose sleeping time was 11:00 pm in the

**Table 4.17:** Sleep, Sleepiness and Related Factors

| *S. No.* | *Factors* | *Time* | *Government (n=70)* | *Private (n=50)* | *Total (N=120)* |
|---|---|---|---|---|---|
| 1. | **Sleep time** | 9:00 pm | 19 (27.14) | — | 19 (15.83) |
| | | 10:00 pm | 33 (47.14) | 40 (80) | 73 (60.83) |
| | | 11:00 pm | 18 (25.71) | 10 (20) | 28 (23.33) |
| 2. | **Time taken for sleep** | <10 min | 39 (55.71) | 20 (40) | 59 (49.17) |
| | | 10-20 min | 14 (20) | 13 (26) | 27 (22.50) |
| | | 20-30 min | 17 (24.29) | 17 (34) | 34 (28.33) |
| 3. | **Sleep off time** | 4:00 am | 2 (2.86) | 5 (10) | 7 (5.83) |
| | | 5:00 am | 59 (84.29) | 30 (60) | 89 (74.17) |
| | | 6:00 am | 9 (12.86) | 15 (30) | 24 (20) |
| 4. | **Feeling of freshness or relaxation in morning** | | 41 (58.57) | 36 (72) | 77 (64.17) |
| 5. | **Fluctuation in bed and rise time** | | 9 (12.86) | 25 (50) | 34 (28.33) |
| 6. | **Fluctuation in bed and rise time on holidays** | | 56 (80) | 40 (80) | 96 (80) |
| 7. | **Sleep duration on holidays** | 4-6 hrs | 5 (7.14) | 12 (24) | 17 (14.17) |
| | | 6-8 hrs | 2 (2.86) | 5 (10) | 7 (5.83) |
| | | >8 hrs | 63 (90) | 33 (66) | 96 (80) |
| 8. | **Bothered by poor sleep quality** | | 17 (24.29) | 5 (10) | 22 (18.33) |

*Note*: Figures in parentheses indicate the percentage values.

night. Data pertaining to sleep time of nurses from Government hospitals reveal that it was 10:00 pm for 47.14 per cent and for nurses from private hospitals also sleep time was 10:00 pm.

*4.17.1.2 Time Taken for Sleep*

Data pertaining to time taken by nurses for sleep is outlined in Table 4.17. It is evident from the table that a large proportion of nurses (49.17 per cent) took less than 10 minutes to sleep followed by 20-30 minutes (28.33 per cent). In case of both Government hospital nurses (55.71 per cent) and nurses from private hospitals (40 per cent), time taken for sleep was 10 minutes or less.

*4.17.1.3 Sleep Off Time*

Majority (74.17 per cent) of nurses were getting up at 5:00 am followed by 6:00 am (20 per cent). It was again revealed from data that sleep off time was 5:00 am for both Governments (84.29 per cent) and private (60 per cent) nurses.

*4.17.1.4 Feeling of Freshness or Relaxation in Morning*

On the whole, 64.17 per cent nurses felt fresh in the morning. Out of that, 58.57 per cent Government hospitals and 72 per cent nurses from private hospitals reported feeling of relaxation.

*4.17.1.5 Fluctuation in Bed and Rise Time*

It is evident from Table 4.17 that a good proportion of nurses (28.33 per cent) reported fluctuation in their bed and rise time and regarding hospitals of both types, 12.86 per cent from Government hospitals and 50 per cent nurses from private hospitals.

*4.17.1.6 Fluctuation in Bed and Rise Time on Holidays*

On the whole, fluctuation on holiday was reported by 80 per cent of nurses. Particularly for nurses from Government hospitals fluctuation was reported by 80 per cent and again 80 per cent for nurses from private hospitals.

*4.17.1.7 Sleep Duration on Holidays*

It is inevitable to see the sleep duration of nurses who were in shift work, as it affects their sleep pattern. The data in Table 4.17 reveal that majority of nurses, i.e. 80 per cent were able to take more than 8 hours sleep followed by 14.17 per cent who had 4-6 hours sleep. In case of nurses from Government hospitals (90 per cent) had more than 8 hours sleep and in private hospitals also. This shows that sleep and sleepiness is not a major problem in Indian nurses as they have good cooperation of doctors.

*4.17.1.8 Bothering by Poor Sleep Quality*

It can be observed from the data that on the whole 18.33 per cent nurses were suffering from poor sleep quality, about 24.29 per cent from Government hospitals and only 10 per cent nurses from private hospitals.

### *4.17.2 Rating of Sleep Quality of Nurses*

It is evident from Figure 4.3 that 15.71 per cent nurses from Government hospitals and 54 per cent from private hospitals had very good sleep quality and none of them had very bad sleep quality.

### *4.17.3 Factors Affecting Sleep Quality at Workplace*

Poor sleep quality adversely affects the quality of life of the person. Depression, pain may be likely sources of sleep impairment. Fatigue, depression and pain interfere with sleep quality by increasing nocturnal awakening and sleep fragmentation Gowda *et al.* (2009).

The factors which can affect the sleep quality of nurses are enlisted in Table 4.18. On the whole, it was observed from the data that cold sleeping area and snoring problem were the most dominant factors as per 47.5 per cent and 39.17 per cent nurses, respectively. However, very few nurses, i.e. 2.5 per cent were sufferers of asthma, which may create disturbances in deep sleep.

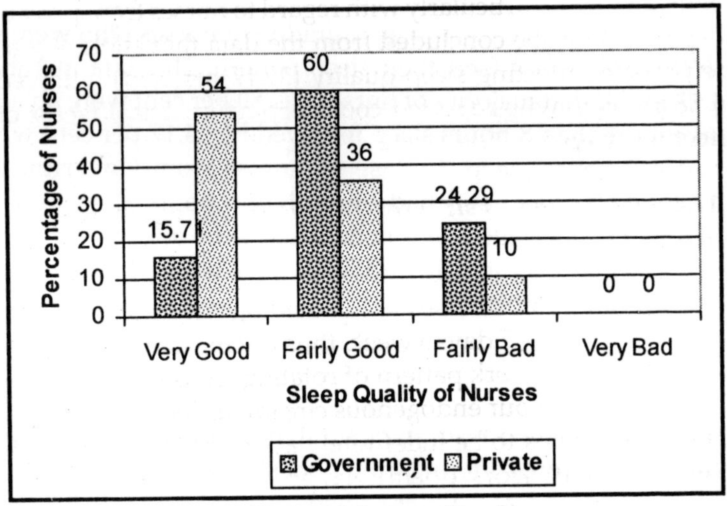


**Fig. 4.3:** Rating of sleep quality of nurses

**Table 4.18:** Factors Affecting Sleep Quality at Workplace

| *S. No.* | *Factors* | *Government (n=70)* | *Private (n=50)* | *Total (N=120)* |
|---|---|---|---|---|
| 1. | Cold sleeping area | 13(18.57) | 44 (88) | 57 (47.50) |
| 2. | Humid | 7 (10) | 16 (32) | 23 (19.17) |
| 3. | Dry | 6 (8.57) | 8 (16) | 14 (11.67) |
| 4. | Noisy | 5 (7.14) | 2 (4) | 7 (5.83) |
| 5. | Uncomfortable bedding | 15 (21.43) | 22 (44) | 37 (30.83) |
| 6. | Indigestion/gas/heartburn | 7 (10) | 15 (30) | 22 (18.33) |
| 7. | Asthma | 2 (2.86) | 1 (2) | 3 (2.50) |
| 8. | Need to urinate | 4 (5.71) | 22 (44) | 26 (21.67) |
| 9. | Cough | 5 (7.14) | 20 (40) | 25 (20.83) |
| 10. | Snoring | 25 (35.71) | 22 (44) | 47 (39.17) |
| 11. | Frightening dreams | 7 (10) | 21 (42) | 28 (23.33) |

*Note*: Figures in parentheses indicate the percentage values.

The data pertaining to factor affecting sleep quality of nurses from Government hospitals (as individually assessed)

reveals that maximum of 35.71 per cent and 21.43 per cent nurses had problem of snoring and uncomfortable bedding which affected their sleep quality and very few nurses, i.e. only 2.86 per cent were sufferers of asthma interfering the sleep quality in night. Particularly with regard to nurses from private hospitals, it can be concluded from the data that snoring was the problem affecting sleep quality (39.17 per cent) followed by 88 per cent who reported cool sleeping area as a factor of affecting sleep.

### 4.17.4 Factors Responsible for Troublesome Sleeping and Awakening

More and more businesses are providing their full range of services 24 h a day, 7 days a week, thus forcing their employees to work either in work pattern of rotating shifts or fixed night shifts. Dictates of our endogenous circadian clock prevent our brains and bodies to be indefinitely adaptable to those work schedules. Shift work operations are thus associated with serious health and social problems for the workers Van (1998). The various factors which are responsible for troublesome sleeping and awakening are enclosed in Table 4.19.

#### *4.17.4.1 Troublesome Sleeping*

It can be observed from the table that majority of the nurses (73.33 per cent) had to go to bathroom resulting in disturbance in sleep, followed by 55.83 per cent who woke up in early morning and 55 per cent woke up in mid-night. A few proportion of nurses (11.67 per cent) had problem of coughing resulted in sleep problems. The data pertaining to trouble sleeping among nurses from government and private hospitals reveal that 17.14 per cent nurses were not able to sleep within 30 minutes for past 1 month, whereas 44 per cent nurses from private hospitals could not sleep within 30 minutes during a week. Further nurses (21.43 per cent from government and 56 per cent from private hospitals) woke up early in the morning during a week followed by wake up in mid-night during a week by 31.43 per cent from Government and 56 per cent nurses from private hospitals.

Results can be supported by the report of Almasi (2006) who concluded that out of 128 nurses, more than 96 per cent had sleep disorders. Among them 0.8 per cent had only sleepiness during the day, 30.4 per cent had only nightly sleeplessness and 68 per cent had both nightly sleeplessness and sleepiness during the day.

#### *4.17.4.2 Trouble Awakening*

It refers to problems related with staying awake and it was concluded from Table 4.19 that majority of the nurses (78.33 per cent) were not able to awake during rest period closely followed by 70.83 per cent and 70 per cent nurses who had problems in awakening while watching television and during sitting and reading. A few proportion (5.83 per cent) were not able to awake and concentrate in the meeting.

The data related to nurses particularly from government hospitals, reveals that maximum of 37.14 per cent nurses and 64 per cent from private hospitals were not able to stay awake in rest period during a week. Further trouble awakening during watching the television was reported by 35.71 per cent and 70 per cent nurses from private hospitals during a week.

Similar study was also conducted by Ohida (2000) who found significant correlation between average hours of sleep and subjective sleep quality, difficulty in getting to sleep and day-time drowsiness. Research further reported that sufficient hours of sleeping are needed for nurses who work in night shifts to ensure good quality of sleep and consequently better services for patients.

#### *4.17.4.3 Use of Supplements to Induce Sleep*

Majority (78.33 per cent) of nurses reported book reading as supplement to induce sleep. Particularly, 41.43 per cent nurses from Government hospitals and 68 per cent from private hospitals were reading books during a week and twice a week respectively.

**Table 4.19:** Factors Responsible for Troublesome Sleeping and Awakening

| S. No | Factors | Government (n=70) | | | Private (n=50) | | | Total |
|---|---|---|---|---|---|---|---|---|
| | | Past 1 month | During a week | Twice a week | Past 1 month | During a week | Twice a week | (N=120) |
| | **[A] Troublesome Sleeping** | | | | | | | |
| 1. | Cannot sleep within 30 min. | 12 (17.14) | 8 (11.43) | 7 (10) | 8 (16) | 22 (44) | — | 57 (47.50) |
| 2. | Wake-up in mid-night | — | 22 (31.43) | — | — | 28 (56) | 16 (32) | 66 (55) |
| 3. | Wake-up in early morning | 4 (5.71) | 15 (21.43) | 4 (5.71) | 16 (32) | 28 (56) | — | 67 (55.83) |
| 4. | Have to go bathroom | 8 (11.43) | 36 (51.43) | — | 14 (28) | 23 (46) | 7 (14) | 88 (73.33) |
| 5. | Cannot breath comfortably | — | — | — | 21 (42) | 23 (46) | — | 44 (36.67) |
| 6. | Coughing | — | 8 (11.43) | — | 2 (4) | 3 (6) | 1 (2) | 14 (11.67) |
| 7. | Snoring loudly | — | 20 (28.57) | -- | 4 (8) | 7 (14) | 1 (2) | 32 (26.67) |
| 8. | Feeling cold | — | 8 (11.43) | — | 5 (10) | 8 (16) | 3 (6) | 24 (20) |
| 9. | Having bad dreams | 4 (5.71) | 6 (8.57) | 6 (8.57) | 4 (8) | 6 (12) | — | 26 (21.67) |
| 10. | Having pain | 4 (5.71) | 6 (8 57) | 14 (20) | 1 (2) | 7 (14) | 5 (10) | 37 (30.83) |
| | **[B] Trouble Awakening** | | | | | | | |
| 1. | As a passenger in the vehicle | 4 (5.71) | 14 (20) | 4 (5.71) | 8 (16) | 35 (70) | 7 (14) | 72 (60) |
| 2. | Working at computer | 4 (5.71) | 4 (5.71) | 2 (2.86) | 3 (6) | 8 (16) | 3 (6) | 24 (20) |
| 3. | Engaging in social activity | 4 (5.71) | — | — | — | 4 (8) | 1 (2) | 9 (7.50) |
| 4. | Eating meals | — | 4 (5.71) | — | — | 4 (8) | 4 (8) | 12 (10) |
| 5. | Sitting and reading | 12 (17.14) | 21 (30) | — | — | 27 (54) | 24 (48) | 84 (70) |
| 6. | Watching T.V. | 10 (14.29) | 25 (35.71) | — | 8 (16) | 35 (70) | 7 (14) | 85 (70.83) |
| 7. | Talking to someone | — | 2 (2.86) | — | — | 23 (46) | 27 (54) | 52 (43.33) |

*(contd.)*

**Table 4.19** *(contd.)*

| S. No | Factors | Government (n=70) | | | Private (n=50) | | | Total |
|---|---|---|---|---|---|---|---|---|
| | | Past 1 month | During a week | Twice a week | Past 1 month | During a week | Twice a week | (N=120) |
| 8. | In the meeting | — | 3 (4.29) | — | — | 4 (8) | — | 7 (5.83) |
| 9. | In rest period | 18 (25.71) | 26 (37.14) | 2 (2.86) | — | 32 (64) | 16 (32) | 94 (78.33) |
| | **[C] Use of Supplements to Induce Sleep** | | | | | | | |
| 1. | Reading books | 6 (8.57) | 29 (41.43) | 6 (8.57) | — | 19 (38) | 34 (68) | 94 (78.33) |
| | **[D] Problems Related with Awakening** | | | | | | | |
| 1. | Headache | 4 (5.71) | 15 (21.43) | — | — | 9 (18) | 8 (16) | 36 (30) |
| 2. | Bodyache | 3 (4.29) | 11 (15.71) | — | — | 20 (40) | — | 34 (28.33) |
| 3. | Fogginess/incordination | — | — | — | 1 (2) | 8 (16) | 6 (12) | 15 (12.50) |
| 4. | Dry mouth | — | — | — | — | 1 (2) | 5 (10) | 6 (5) |
| 5. | Temporarily paralyzed | 1 (1.43) | — | — | — | — | 4 (8) | 5 (4.17) |
| 6. | Increased yawning | — | 14 (20) | 12 (17.14) | — | 14 (28) | 14 (28) | 54 (45) |
| 7. | Drowsiness | — | 6 (8.57) | 10 (14.29) | — | 8 (16) | 5 (10) | 29 (24.17) |
| 8. | Low mood, irritability | 25 (35.71) | — | — | — | 11 (22) | — | 36 (30) |

*Note*: Figures in parentheses indicate the percentage values.

#### *4.17.4.4 Problems Related with Awakening*

The problems as reported by nurses were increased yawning by 45 per cent nurses on the whole and a small proportion (4.17 per cent) of nurses reported temporary feeling of paralysis. In case of government hospitals, maximum of 35.71 per cent nurses felt low mood or irritability and very few nurses from Government (1.43 per cent) reported feeling of being temporarily paralyzed. About 40 per cent from private reported problem of bodyache and only 2 per cent each reported fogginess and dry mouth.

These findings were in line with the results of the study conducted by Perkins (2001) who reported that nurses had more depression and poorer sleep quality, depression and anxiety, depression and sleep quality which resulted in chronic fatigue.

### *4.17.5 Social Consequences of Nursing Job*

Nursing job allows nurses to a number of social problems which are enlisted in Table 4.20, in the form of statements. Responses on each item in the table were scored for never (1), occasionally (2), sometimes (3), fairly often (4) and very often (5). From the individual score, mean score of each item was computed. It is evident from the results that in case of nurses from Government hospitals, highest mean score (2.83) was computed to the statement, i.e. job subjects to potential legal liability followed by they have primary responsibility for childcare duties with mean score of 2.64. The results can be supported by the study of Costa (2001), who indicated that women can be more vulnerable to shift-work in relation to both their more complex circadian and infradian (menstrual) hormonal rhythms and extra demands related to family life. The statement, viz. physical assault during job obtained lowest mean score of 1 indicating that physical insecurity was not the problem of nurses.

In case of private hospitals, nurses gave highest mean score (3.50) to the statement which says they have primary responsibility for child care duties and the statements like job

**Table 4.20:** Social Consequences of Mursing Job

| S. No | Statements | Government (n=70) | | | | | | Private (n=50) | | | | | |
|---|---|---|---|---|---|---|---|---|---|---|---|---|---|
| | | N | O | S | FO | VO | MS | N | O | S | FO | VO | MS |
| 1. | Job exposes to verbal abuses | 30 (42.86) | 3 (4.29) | 25 (35.71) | 12 (17.14) | — | **2.27** | 44 (88) | 4 (8) | 2 (4) | — | — | **1.16** |
| 2. | Job exposes to physical harm | 58 (82.86) | — | 12 (17.14) | -- | — | **1.34** | 44 (88) | 4 (8) | 2 (4) | — | — | **1.16** |
| 3. | Physically assaulted during job | 70 (100) | — | — | — | — | **1** | 44 (88) | 3 (6) | 1 (2) | — | 2 (4) | **1.26** |
| 4. | Job subjects to potential legal liability | 11 (15.71) | 8 (11.43) | 33 (47.14) | 18 (25.71) | — | **2.83** | 28 (56) | 8 (16) | 9 (18) | 5 (10) | — | **1.82** |
| 5. | Shift workers schedule lead to marital strain | 45 (64.29) | 13 (18.57) | 7 (10) | 2 (2.86) | 3 (4.29) | **1.64** | 42 (84) | 7 (14) | 1 (2) | — | — | **1.18** |
| 6. | Struggle between shift work and family life | 46 (65.71) | 19 (27.14) | 5 (7.14) | — | — | **1.41** | 10 (20) | 20 (40) | 17 (34) | 3 (6) | — | **2.26** |
| 7. | Primary responsibility for childcare duties | 20 (28.57) | 12 (17.14) | 20 (28.57) | 9 (12.86) | 9 (12.86) | **2.64** | — | 7 (14) | 17 (34) | 20 (40) | 6 (12) | **3.50** |
| 8. | Primary responsibility for house cleaning duties | 25 (35.71) | 7 (10) | 15 (21.43) | 16 (22.86) | 7 (10)) | **2.61** | 8 (16) | 12 (24) | 17 (34) | 10 (20) | 3 (6) | **2.76** |
| 9. | Spend time at voluntary or religious organization | 46 (65.71) | 18 (25.71) | 3 (4.29) | 3 (4.29) | — | **1.47** | 22 (44) | 16 (32) | 12 (24) | — | — | **1.80** |

N—never (1), O—Occasionally (2), S—Sometimes (3), FO—Fairly often (4), VO—Very often (5), MS—Mean score
*Note*: Figures in parentheses indicate the percentage values.

expose to verbal abuse and job exposes to physical harm scored a least mean score of 1.16. So, nurses from private hospitals again did not face problems related with security.

### *4.17.6 Job Satisfaction Among Nurses*

Satisfactory work ability is sustained and promoted by good physical and mental health and by favourable working condition. Extent of satisfaction derived by nurses from job is presented in the form of statements in Table 4.21.

In order to get meaningful result, a descriptive satisfaction scale was constructed to assess the extent of satisfaction derived. Responses on each item in the scale were scored for DA—Disagree (1), A—Agree (2), SA—Strongly agree (3). From the individual item score, mean score of each item was computed of each nurse. The findings related to frequency distribution, mean score on each statement of the scale are presented in Table 4.21.

The data pertaining to job satisfaction among nurses from Government hospitals, reveal that highest mean score (2.60) was given to the statements like 'I am regular for my work' as reported by 60 per cent nurses, who were strongly satisfied with the statements. The statements such as "loose self-confidence" and "job stress and unrest" were given least mean score of 1.24 for each and 80 per cent and 78.57 per cent nurses were strongly satisfied with the statement.

In case of nurses from private hospitals, it was observed that nurses gave highest mean score to the statement, viz. receive recognition when a job is done well by 66 per cent nurses who were satisfied with the statement, whereas nurses gave a very low mean score (1.10) to the statement "there is job stress and unrest" as reported by 10 per cent who were satisfied with the statement.

The results were in accordance with the findings of Gelsema *et al.* (2005) who indicated that job characteristics, such as demand and control mediated the relationship between work conditions, such as work agreements and rewards and outcomes. It was further reported that organizational and

**Table 4.21:** Job Satisfaction Among Nurses

| S. No | Statements | Government (n=70) | | | | Private (n=50) | | | |
|---|---|---|---|---|---|---|---|---|---|
| | | DS | S | SS | MS | DS | S | SS | MS |
| 1. | Poor work conditions lead to restlessness | 41 (58.57) | 29 (41.43) | — | **1.41** | 16 (32) | 29 (58) | 5 (10) | **1.78** |
| 2. | Job is monotonous in nature | 33 (47.14) | 22 (31.43) | 15 (21.43) | **1.74** | 28 (56) | 10 (20) | 12 (24) | **1.68** |
| 3. | Working hours are not fit | 19 (27.14) | 24 (34.29) | 27 (38.57) | **2.11** | 5 (10) | 28 (56) | 17 (34) | **2.24** |
| 4. | Hardly get time for entertainment | 39 (55.71) | 27 (38.57) | 4 (5.71) | **1.50** | 5 (10) | 31 (62) | 14 (28) | **2.18** |
| 5. | Job requires great concentration | 9 (12.86) | 49 (70) | 12 (17.14) | **2.04** | — | 33 (66) | 17 (34) | **2.34** |
| 6. | Not able to give time to family | 46 (65.71) | 18 (25.71) | 6 (8.57) | **1.42** | 10 (20) | 36 (72) | 4 (8) | **1.88** |
| 7. | Job requires to remember different things | — | 38 (54.29) | 32 (45.71) | **2.45** | 3 (6) | 35 (70) | 12 (24) | **2.18** |
| 8. | Job requires to work fast | — | 36 (51.43) | 34 (48.57) | **2.48** | 5 (10) | 26 (52) | 19 (38) | **2.28** |
| 9. | Job requires to work hard | 6 (8.57) | 30 (42.86) | 34 (48.57) | **2.40** | 5 (10) | 26 (52) | 19 (38) | **2.28** |
| 10. | Lost interest in activities, used to enjoy | 20 (28.57) | 32 (45.71) | 18 (25.71) | **1.97** | 13 (26) | 29 (58) | 8 (16) | **1.90** |
| 11. | Loose self confidence | 56 (80) | 11 (15.71) | 3 (4.29) | **1.24** | 42 (84) | 8 (16) | — | **1.16** |
| 12. | Getting edgy and bad-tempered | 37 (52.86) | 33 (47.14) | — | **1.47** | 19 (38) | 31 (62) | — | **1.62** |
| 13. | Job stress and unrest | 55 (78.57) | 15 (21.43) | — | **1.24** | 45 (90) | 5 (10) | — | **1.1** |
| 14. | Good work environment facilitate to work quickly & energetically | — | 40 (57.14) | 30 (42.86) | **2.42** | — | 29 (58) | 21 (42) | **2.42** |
| 15. | People at work speak softly | 5 (7.14) | 32 (45.71) | 33 (47.14) | **2.40** | 31 (62) | 19 (38) | — | **1.38** |
| 16. | Group members are supportive | 37 (52.86) | 27 (38.57) | 6 (8.57) | **1.55** | 12 (24) | 15 (30) | 23 (46) | **2.22** |
| 17. | Influence over quantity and quality of work that is done | — | 66 (94.29) | 4 (5.71) | **2.05** | — | 37 (74) | 13 (26) | **2.26** |

(contd.)

**Table 4.21** (*contd.*)

| *S. No* | *Statements* | *Government (n=70)* | | | | *Private (n=50)* | | | |
|---|---|---|---|---|---|---|---|---|---|
| | | *DS* | *S* | *SS* | *MS* | *DS* | *S* | *SS* | *MS* |
| 18. | Job helped to raise standard of living | — | 34 (48.57) | 36 (5143) | **2.51** | 19 (38) | 31 (62) | — | **1.62** |
| 19. | Regular for work | — | 28 (40) | 42 (60) | **2.60** | — | 34 (68) | 16 (32) | **2.32** |
| 20. | Better physical and mental health | — | 34 (48.57) | 36 (51.43) | **2.51** | — | 38 (76) | 12 (24) | **2.24** |
| 21. | Feel good about working as nurse at hospital | — | 43 (61.43) | 27 (38.57) | **2.38** | 9 (18) | 28 (56) | 13 (26) | **2.08** |
| 22. | Satisfied with salary | — | 42 (60) | 28 (40) | **2.40** | 26 (52) | 19 (38) | 5 (10) | **1.58** |
| 23. | Job gives sense of accomplishment | 26 (37.14) | 22 (31.43) | 22 (31.43) | **1.94** | 9 (18) | 28 (56) | 13 (26) | **2.08** |
| 24. | Satisfied with the way task is carried out | | 46 (65.71) | 24 (34.29) | **2.34** | — | 23 (46) | 27 (54) | **2.54** |
| 25. | Capable of making professional decisions | 16 (22.86) | 33 (47.14) | 21 (30) | **2.07** | 13 (26) | 15 (30) | 22 (44) | **2.18** |
| 26. | Certainty of promotion/ advancement | 6 (8.57) | 42 (60) | 22 (31.43) | **2.23** | 35 (70) | 15 (30) | — | **1.30** |
| 27. | Use skills from experiences for my job | — | 50 (71.43) | 20 (28.57) | **2.29** | 5 (10) | 38 (76) | 7 (14) | **2.04** |
| 28. | Receive recognition when a job is done well | 25 (35.71) | 40 (57.14) | 5 (7.14) | **1.71** | 17 (34) | 33 (66) | — | **2.66** |

DS—Dissatisfactory (1), S—Satisfactory (2), SS—Strongly satisfactory, (3), MS—Mean Score

*Note*: Figures in parentheses indicate the percentage values

environmental conditions of work can influence job satisfaction and distress among nurses.

From the findings, it can be concluded that however personal factors of the nurses influence the degree of job satisfaction but organizational and environmental factors play a major role in deriving satisfaction from the work.

## 4.18 Physiological Parameters

### *4.18.1 Anthropometric Measurements of the Nurses*

Anthropometric measurements of nurses were taken in sitting position. The scope of this study was limited to measuring those body dimensions that were considered important and useful for the design of table and chair used for daily working of the nurses. On the whole, 16 body dimensions were selected for measurements. The 5th, 95th percentiles along with average values and standard error are presented in Table 4.22. Anthropometric data must be taken into consideration when the adequacy of furniture is considered.

From Table 4.22 it is clear that the mean eye height above seat was 64.46 cm with standard error of ± 0.47 cm. The percentiles were also calculated which were 56.04 cm for 5th and 72.88 cm for 95th percentile.

#### *4.18.1.1 Body Height From Ground*

Body height from ground is useful for designing of total height of the chair. The mean body height of the nurses from ground was 115.77 cm. The 5th and 95th percentiles of body height from ground level were 106.41 and 125.13 cm respectively, with standard error of ±0.52.

#### *4.18.1.2 Body Height Above Seat*

The mean body height above seat with regard to nurses calculated to be 70.15 cm ± 0.44. The 5th percentile was found as 62.25 cm and 95th percentile of body height above seat was 78.05 cm.

**Table 4.22:** Anthropometric Measurements of the Nurses (Sitting Position)

N=120

| *S. No* | *Parameters* | *5th percentile (cm)* | *Mean± SEm* | *95th percentile* |
|---|---|---|---|---|
| 1. | Body height from ground | 106.41 | 115.77 ± 0.52 | 125.13 |
| 2. | Body height above seat | 62.25 | 70.15 ± 0.44 | 78.05 |
| 3. | Eye height from ground | 98.97 | 105.34 ± 0.35 | 111.71 |
| 4. | Eye height above seat | 56.04 | 64.46 ± 0.47 | 72.88 |
| 5. | Shoulder height from ground | 84.85 | 90.03 ± 0.29 | 95.21 |
| 6. | Shoulder height above seat | 47.50 | 59.40 ± 0.66 | 71.28 |
| 7. | Elbow rest height from ground | 52.69 | 68.17 ± 0.86 | 83.65 |
| 8. | Elbow rest height above seat | 19.97 | 22.65 ± 0.15 | 25.32 |
| 9. | Knee height above ground | 44.56 | 46.82 ± 0.13 | 49.08 |
| 10. | Popliteal height | 40.81 | 42.06 ± 0.07 | 43.31 |
| 11. | Buttock popliteal length | 36.07 | 43.13 ± 0.39 | 50.19 |
| 12. | Buttock knee length | 46.24 | 51.82 ± 0.31 | 57.39 |
| 13. | Thigh height | 10.03 | 13.28 ± 0.18 | 16.53 |
| 14. | Hip breadth | 30.47 | 35.49 ± 0.28 | 40.51 |
| 15. | Hand length | 15.15 | 16.8 ± 0.09 | 18.45 |
| 16. | Finger to shoulder length (Horizontal plane) | 57.04 | 62.75 ± 0.32 | 68.46 |

#### *4.18.1.3 Eye Height from Ground*

The mean eye height from ground was 105.34 cm with error of ±0.35. The 5th percentile of eye height from ground came out to be 98.97 and 95th percentile as 111.71 cm.

#### *4.18.1.4 Eye Height Above Seat*

From Table 4.22 it is clear that the mean eye height above seat was 64.46 cm with standard error of ±0.47 cm, the percentiles were also calculated which were 56.04 cm for 5th and 72.88 cm for 95th percentile.

#### *4.18.1.5 Shoulder Height from Ground*

The mean shoulder height of nurses from ground was calculated as 90.03 cm with ±0.29 cm standard error. The 5th and 95th percentiles were found to be 84.85 and 95.21 cm respectively.

*4.18.1.6 Shoulder Height above Seat*

This height was used for calculating the back rest height of the chair. The mean shoulder height above seat was 59.40 with ±0.66 standard error. The 5th percentile came out to be 47.5 cm and 71.28 cm as 95th percentile.

*4.18.1.7 Elbow Rest Height from Ground*

The mean elbow height from ground was 68.17 cm with a error of ± 0.86 cm. The 5th and 95th percentiles of elbow height from ground were 52.69 cm and 83.65 cm respectively. Elbow height is used as reference value for determining the work surface height and in this case it was used for the height of table.

*4.18.1.8 Elbow Rest Height above Seat*

For making appropriate hand rest height of the chair, this height is considered. The percentiles values of elbow height (5th and 95th) of nurses came out to be 19.97 and 25.32 cm respectively with mean as 22.65 cm with standard error of ± 0.15 cm.

*4.18.1.9 Knee Height from Ground*

In case of nurses, the mean knee height above ground was found to be 46.82 cm with standard error of ± 0.13. The 5th percentile of knee height above ground was 44.56 cm and the 95th percentile came out to be 49.08 cm.

*4.18.1.10 Popliteal Height from Ground*

The mean popliteal height above ground was 42.06 cm with standard error of ± 0.07cm. The 5th and 95th percentiles values of popliteal height above ground were 40.81 cm and 43.31 cm respectively. This height is measured for the designing of seat height of the chair.

*4.18.1.11 Buttock Popliteal Length*

It is measured to design seat depth of the chair. The mean buttock popliteal length of nurses was calculated as 43.13 cm with standard error of ± 0.39. The 5th percentile value came out to be 36.07 cm and 95th percentile was 50.19 cm.

*4.18.1.12 Buttock Knee Length*

The mean buttock knee length came out to be 51.82 cm with a error of ± 0.31 cm. However, 5th and 95th percentiles were 46.24 and 57.39 cm respectively. It is used to determine the area for legs between rows of the chair.

*4.18.1.13 Thigh Height*

The mean thigh height of nurses was 13.28 cm with a error of ± 0.18 cm and percentile values (5th and 95th) were found to be 10.03 and 16.53 cm respectively.

*4.18.1.14 Hip Breadth*

The mean hip breadth of nurses came out to be 35.49 cm with standard error of ± 0.28 cm. However, the 5th percentile was come out as 30.47 cm and 95th percentile was 40.51 cm. Hip breadth is used for chair width and arm rest width.

*4.18.1.15 Hand Length*

Hand length is measured for the purpose of designing the hand rest of the chair. The mean hand length of nurses was 16.8 with standard error of ±0.09 cm. The 5th and 95th percentiles of hand length came out to be 15.15 and 18.45 cm.

*4.18.1.16 Finger to Shoulder Length*

It was measured on the horizontal plane in order to obtain the maximum reach of the nurses on the table and it was found to be 62.75±0.32 cm. The 5th and 95th percentiles were calculated as 57.04 and 68.46 cm respectively.

### 4.18.2 Body Mass Index of Nurses

#### 4.18.2.1 Weight (kg)

The mean weight of the nurses was 58.20±0.54 kg. Further it was found that the mean weight of nurses from Government hospitals was 57.62±0.69 kg and 56.96±0.85 kg in case of nurses from private hospitals (Table 4.23).

#### 4.18.2.2 Height (cm)

The mean height of the nurses was 155.33±0.71 followed by mean height of nurses from Government (153.23±0.94) and private hospitals (152.49±1.13).

#### 4.18.2.3 Body Mass Index (kg/m$^2$)

It was found from the findings that a handsome proportion (69.71 per cent) of nurses had normal BMI and only 8.33 per cent belonged to category II. No one fell under grade III category.

Mean BMI of nurses was 24.08±0.33 (23.76±0.43) for nurses from Government hospitals and 23.74±0.51 for nurses from private hospitals). BMI revealed that nurses had good health status. Similar study conducted by Nehme *et al.* (2008) revealed that the workers with BMI above 30 kg/metre square were sleepier than the other.

### 4.18.3 Physiological Cost of Work of Nurses (BP, HR, EER)

Tables 4.24 to 4.26 and Figures 4.4 to 4.6 show the effect of various groups of activities performed by nurses on physiological cost of work. A total of 5 replications were conducted to observe physiological cost of work in terms of Blood Pressure (BP), Heart Rate (HR) and Energy Expenditure Rate (EER).

**Table 4.23:** Body Mass Index of Nurses

| *S. No.* | *Characteristics* | *Government (n=70)* | *Private (n=50)* | *Total (N=120)* |
|---|---|---|---|---|
| 1. | Weight (kg) | | | |
| | (a) 40-50 | 4 (5.71) | 5 (10) | 9 (7.50) |
| | (b) 50-60 | 23 (32.86) | 15 (30) | 38 (31.67) |
| | (c) 60 and above | 43 (61.43) | 30 (60) | 73 (60.83) |
| | **Mean± SEm** | **57.62±0.69** | **56.96±0.85** | **58.20±0.54** |
| 2. | Height (cms) | | | |
| | (a) 140-145 | 8 (11.43) | 6 (12) | 14 (11.67) |
| | (b) 145-150 | 16 (22.86) | 11 (22) | 27 (22.50) |
| | (c) 150-155 | — | — | — |
| | (d) 155-160 | 8 (11.43) | 5 (10) | 13 (10.83) |
| | (e) 160-165 | 38 (54.29) | 28 (56) | 66 (55) |
| | **Mean± SEm** | **153.23±0.94** | **152.49±1.13** | **155.33±0.71** |
| | **5th percentile** | 140.28 | 139.26 | 142.46 |
| | **95th percentile** | 166.18 | 165.72 | 168.20 |
| 3. | Body Mass Index | | | |
| | (a) Grade III > 40 | — | — | — |
| | (b) Grade II 30-40 | 5 (7.14) | 5 (10) | 10 (8.33) |
| | (c) Grade I 25-30 | 19 (27.14) | 8 (16) | 27 (22.50) |
| | (d) Normal < 25 | 46 (65.71) | 37 (74) | 83 (69.17) |
| | **Mean±SEm** | **23.76±0.43** | **23.74±0.51** | **24.08±0.33** |

*Note*: Figures in parentheses indicate the percentage values.

### *4.18.3.1 Physiological Cost of Work of Nurses in Terms of Blood Pressure (mmHg) and Pulse Rate (per min)*

The data regarding average Blood pressure and Pulse rate are presented in Table 4.24 and Figure 4.4.

- In group I activities (giving medicine, dripping, giving injection and weight check-up), the resting mean Blood pressure (B.P. mmHg) was 88.92 which increased up to 96.16 (during activity) with a change in Pulse rate from 78 to 81.75.
- For group II activities (injury and wound care, measuring heart rate and record keeping and filling), mean Blood pressure and Pulse rate (before activity)

were 89.5 mmHg and 76.75 which may increase up to 97.5 mmHg and 81 respectively.

- In case of group III activities (mobility of patients, first aid and emergency and measuring blood pressure), the mean Blood pressure recorded was 88.6 mmHg (before work) and 98.92 mmHg (during work) with a change in mean Pulse rate from 81 to 83.5.

**Table 4.24:** Physiological Cost of Work of Nurses in Terms of Blood Pressure (mmHg) and Pulse Rate (per min)

N=12

| *Activity Profile* | *Resting (mean value)* | | *During work (mean value)* | | *Per cent increase (During work)* | |
|---|---|---|---|---|---|---|
| | *Mean B.P. (mmHg)* | *Pulse rate/min* | *Mean B.P. (mmHg)* | *Pulse rate/min* | *B.P.* | *Pulse rate* |
| Group I (n=4) | 88.92 | 78 | 96.16 | 81.75 | 8.14 | 4.81 |
| Group II (n=4) | 89.5 | 76.75 | 97.5 | 81 | 8.94 | 5.54 |
| Group III (n=4) | 88.6 | 81 | 98.92 | 83.5 | 11.65 | 3.1 |

Thus, it is evident from the data that on the basis of blood pressure and pulse rate, group II and III activities were more tiring as compared to other group of activities.

### *4.18.3.2 Physiological Cost of Work of Nurses in Terms of Heart Rate (beats/minute)*

The results of experiments conducted on various nurses (as per activity profile) were analyzed and presented in Table 4.25 and Figure 4.5 for mean HR and per cent increase in heart rate from its resting level. Work performance leads to an increase in the heart rate. The mean resting Heart rate ranged from 76 to 77 beats/minute for various groups of activities.

- **Group I Activity:** The mean Heart rate at resting level was 76.25 beats/minute, which increased up to 112.88 beats/minute during performance. Whereas, per cent increase in Heart rate was found to be 5.57, which was minimum in case of group I activity.

- **Group II Activity:** For group II activities, it was found that mean HR was 77 beats/minute at resting level, which reached to 115 beats/min during work with per cent increase of 5.84.
- **Group III Activity:** The mean HR before work, during work and recovery period was 76.5, 114.25 and 84.25 beats/min, respectively and per cent increase in Heart rate was 10.13 which was also high.

**Table 4.25:** Physiological Cost of Work of Nurses in Terms of Heart Rate (beats/min)

**N=12**

| *S. No.* | *Activity Profile* | *Mean Heart Rate (beats/min)* | | | *Per cent Increase in HR* |
|---|---|---|---|---|---|
| | | *Resting* | *During Work* | *Recovery* | |
| 1. | Group I (n=4) | 76.25 | 112.875 | 80.5 | 5.57 |
| 2. | Group II (n=4) | 77 | 115 | 81.5 | 5.84 |
| 3. | Group III (n=4) | 76.5 | 114.25 | 84.25 | 10.13 |

$$\text{Per cent increase} = \frac{\text{After activity} - \text{Before activity}}{\text{Before activity}} \times 100$$

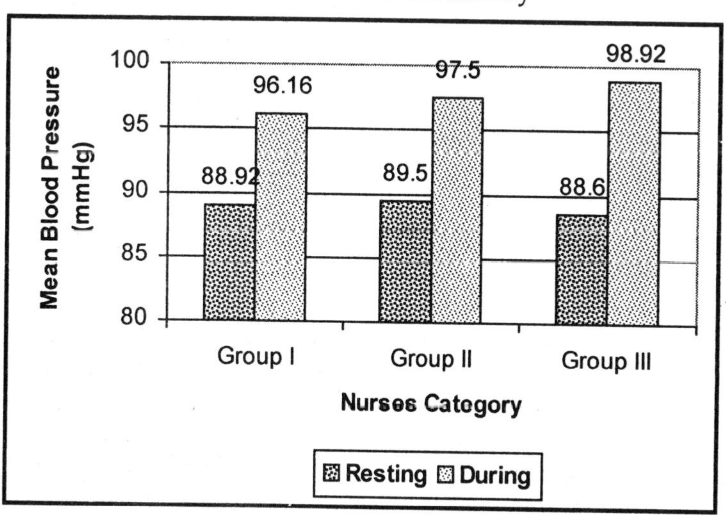


**Fig. 4.4:** Physiological Cost of Work of Nurses in Terms of Blood Pressure (mmHg)

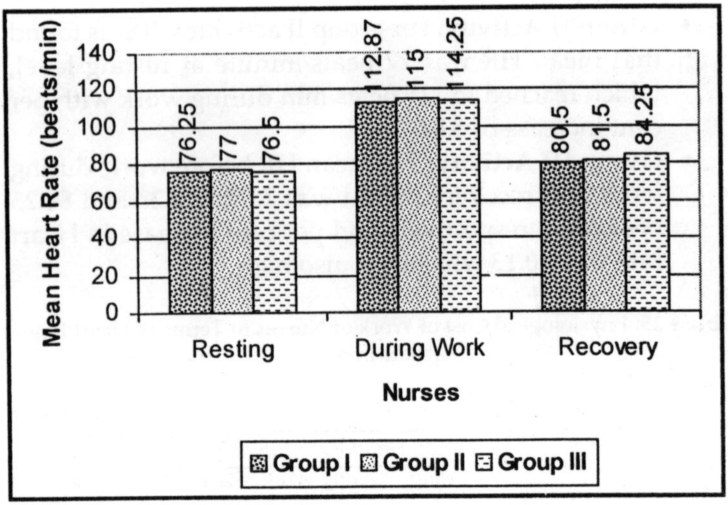


**Fig. 4.5:** Physiological Cost of Work of Nurses in Terms of Heart Rate (beats/minute)

Thus, there was a marked difference in per cent increase in heart rate for various groups of activities. The per cent increase in heart rate was maximum in group III activity, i.e. mobility of patients, first aid and emergency and measuring blood pressure and minimum in group I activity which are giving medicine, dripping, giving injection and weight check-up. Figure 4.5 summarizes the information regarding physiological cost of work in relation to heart rate.

### *4.18.3.3 Physiological Cost of Work in Terms of Energy Expenditure Rate*

- Table 4.26 and Figure 4.6 show the mean Energy Expenditure Rate (EER) kJ/min and increase in EER from its resting level for various groups of activities performed by selected nurse. While performing activities like giving medicine, dripping, giving injection and weight check-up (Group I activity), the Energy expenditure rate before work was 3.40 kJ/min which increased up to 9.23 kJ/min (during work), with per cent increase of 20.

- For group II activity [injury and wound care (dressing)], measuring heart rate, record keeping and filling) EER at resting, work and recovery period was 3.52, 9.57 and 4.24 (kJ/min), respectively with per cent increase of 21.45.
- In case of group III activity, per cent increase in EER found to be 36.05, ranging from 3.44 (before work) to 9.45 (during work).

**Table 4.26:** Physiological Cost of Work of Nurses in Terms of Energy Expenditure Rate (kJ/min)

**N=12**

| *S. No.* | *Activity Profile* | *Energy Expenditure Rate (kJ/min)* | | | *Per cent Increase in EER* |
|---|---|---|---|---|---|
| | | *Before Work* | *During Work* | *After Work* | |
| 1. | Group I (n=4) | 3.41 | 9.23 | 4.08 | 20 |
| 2. | Group II (n=4) | 3.52 | 9.57 | 4.24 | 21.45 |
| 3. | Group III (n=4) | 3.44 | 9.45 | 4.68 | 36.05 |

In the nutshell, it can be concluded that on the basis of energy expenditure, group III activities (mobility of patients, first aid and emergency and measuring blood pressure) were found to be most strenuous activity, however, group I activity (giving medicine, dripping, giving injection and weight check-up) were least exhaustive one.

The reason behind this may be that group 3 activities like mobility of patients, first aid and emergency and measuring blood pressure involve the use of muscles of the nurses for a long time and that too in awkward position which results in increased blood pressure.

### *4.18.4 Rated Perceived Exertion of Nurses*

To study the effect of various groups of activities on the perception of nurses for exertion, they were asked to give ratings on a 10 point scale after completion of task. Table 4.27 and Figure 4.7 envisaged the mean exertion perceived by nurses. It was found that the mean rating of perceived exertion ranged from 3.75 to 4.5 on the basis of verbal expression of fatigue.

It was further found from the study that nurses involved in group III activities felt weak to strong exertion with mean rating of 4.5, followed by somewhat less exertion mean RPE, i.e. 3.75 each in case of group I and II activities.

**Table 4.27:** Rated Perceived Exertion of Nurses

**N=12**

| *Activities* | *RPE Score* | | | | | | | | | | | | |
|---|---|---|---|---|---|---|---|---|---|---|---|---|---|
| | *0.0* | *0.5* | *1.0* | *2.0* | *3.0* | *4.0* | *5.0* | *6.0* | *7.0* | *8.0* | *9.0* | *10.0* | *Mean* |
| **Group I (n=4)** | — | — | — | — | 2 | 1 | 1 | — | — | — | — | — | 3.75 |
| **Group II (n=4)** | — | — | — | 1 | — | 2 | 1 | — | — | — | — | — | 3.75 |
| **Group III (n=4)** | — | — | — | — | 1 | 1 | 1 | 1 | — | — | — | — | 4.5 |

It might be because these activities were performed for short duration however for several times a shift. Lusted *et al.* (1996) also reported that nurses had higher ratings of perceived exertion while performing activities and transferring the materials.

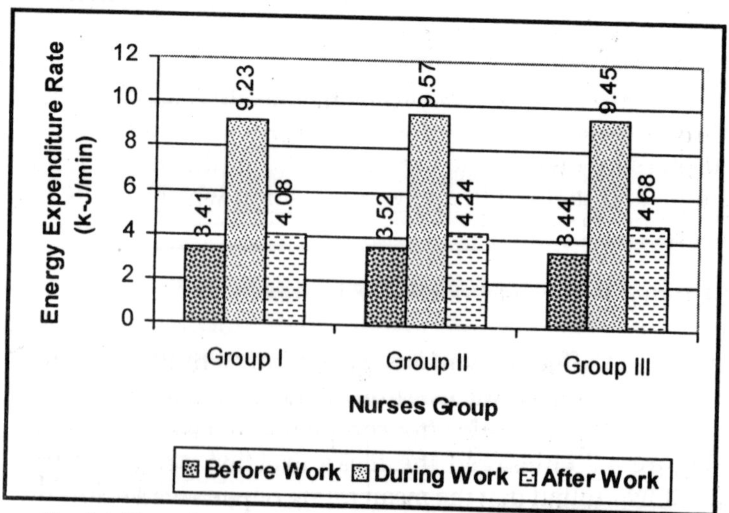


**Fig. 4.6:** Physiological Cost of Work of Nurses in Terms of Energy Expenditure Rate (kJ/min)

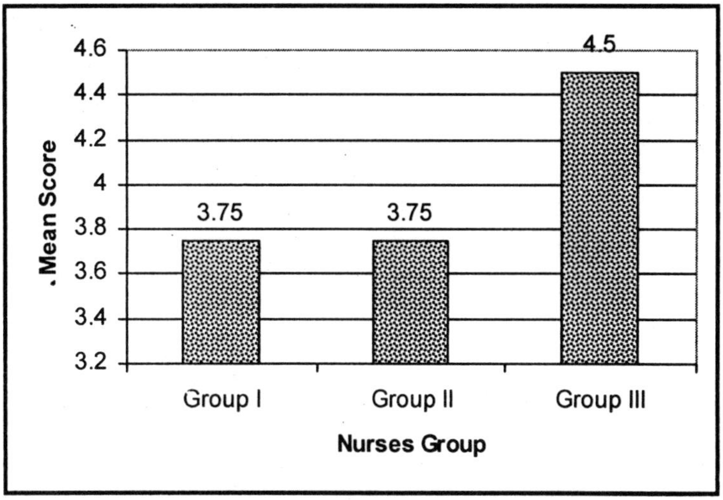


**Fig. 4.7:** Rated Perceived Exertion of Nurses

### *4.18.5 Rapid Entire Body Assessment (REBA) Analysis for Postural Discomfort of Nurses*

Nursing work stresses physically more the musculoskeletal system than the cardio-respiratory system. Musculoskeletal system primarily with the dimensions, compositions and the mass properties of body segments and the work related musculoskeletal disorders caused due to frequent bending, pulling or pushing of muscle, over exertion, adoption of awkward postures used for task completion. Nurses have to work in awkward posture for short time but for several times in a shift. Therefore, this study was an attempt to provide an objective measure of the postural discomfort of nurses with the application of REBA (Rapid Entire Body Assessment). The findings related with objective assessment of postural discomfort are enclosed in Table 4.28 and Figure 4.8. Various postures of neck, trunk and leg in group A (plus load/force), upper arms, lower arms and wrists in group B (plus coupling) along with activity score were observed and analyzed. It was found that a sum total of 37.5 per cent nurses were in AL3 category which interprets high risk level and action is required

**Table 4.28:** REBA Analysis for Postural Assessment of Nurses

**N=120**

| *Activity Profile* | *REBA Action Category* | | | | |
|---|---|---|---|---|---|
| | *$AL_0$* | *$AL_1$* | *$AL_2$* | *$AL_3$* | *$AL_4$* |
| Group I (n=40) | 4(10) | 4 (10) | 8 (20) | 20 (50) | 4 (10) |
| Group II (n=40) | 8 (20) | 9 (22.5) | 7 (17.5) | 15 (37.5) | 1 (2.5) |
| Group III (n=40) | 5(12.5) | 6 (15) | 18 (45) | 10 (25) | 1 (2.5) |

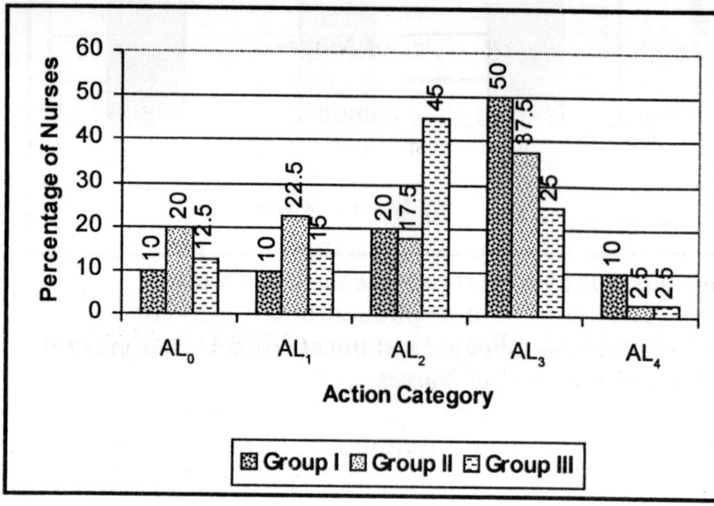


**Fig. 4.8:** REBA Analysis for Postural Assessment of Nurses

now. Again, 7.5 per cent nurses were found in $AL_2$ category indicating medium risk and change is required soon followed by 15.83 per cent nurses in $AL_1$ (low risk and action may be needed in future). In $AL_0$ i.e. 'negligible risk level', aproportion of 14.17 per cent was found and here adopted posture is acceptable. So, no action is required. Only 5 per cent nurses fell into the category of $AL_4$, i.e. very high risk and action necessary now. On the other hand, when activities were analysed separately, it was observed that maximum of 50 per cent nurses performing group I activity were in $AL_3$ category high risk, action necessary now) followed by 45 per cent in activity group III came into zone $AL_2$ (medium risk and change is required soon) and group II (37.5 per cent) in $AL_3$ category. Similar study was conducted by Lusted *et al.* (1996) who reported that nurses are more likely to make a worker's compensation claim for low back symptoms than neck and upper limb symptoms and it is affecting their ability to do their work. The authors found that nurses in one of the units had significantly more reported neck and shoulder symptoms than their counterparts.

### *4.18.6 Spirometry Analysis of Nurses*

Spirometery is the most common of the pulmonary function tests. The spirometery test is performed using a device called a spirometer. Spirometers are widely applied by the healthcare professionals to assess lung function. This medical equipment measures the volume of air inspired and expired by the lungs. Spirometer is a precision differential pressure transducer for the measurements of respiration flow rates. The spirometers record the amount of air and the rate of air that is breathed in and out over a specified time. The output produced by a spirometer is called a kymograph trace. To use spirometer, a person breathes into a mouthpiece. The doctor may ask the person to breathe normally or to take a deep breath and blow the air quickly out of the lungs, like blowing up a balloon. A recording device measures the amount of air inhaled or exhaled and the time taken during each breath. These measurements can help to find out if a person has a lung problem. In the present investigation Pc-based spirometer was used, which is directly connected to the serial port turns any computer into a spirometer that allows user to manage lung function screening in a simple and quick way.

The respiration rate was measured after work performance as post analysis. On the basis of documented history of nurses as age, height, and weight the predicted values of FVC, $FEV_{0.5}$, $FEV_1$, $FEV_1$/FVC per cent and PEF were documented, and post values were measured after test performance. Test results varied from borderline obstacles to severe obstacles.

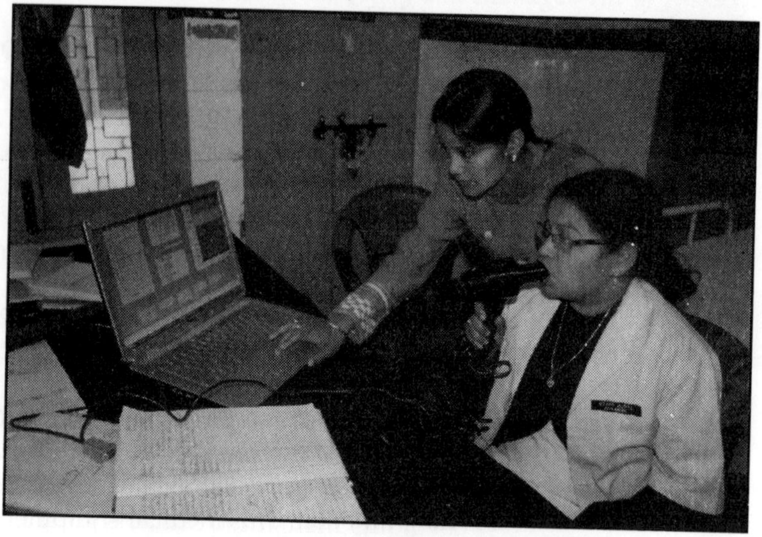

**Plate 21:** Measuring Respiration with Spirometer

**Plate 22:** Measurement of Blood Lactate

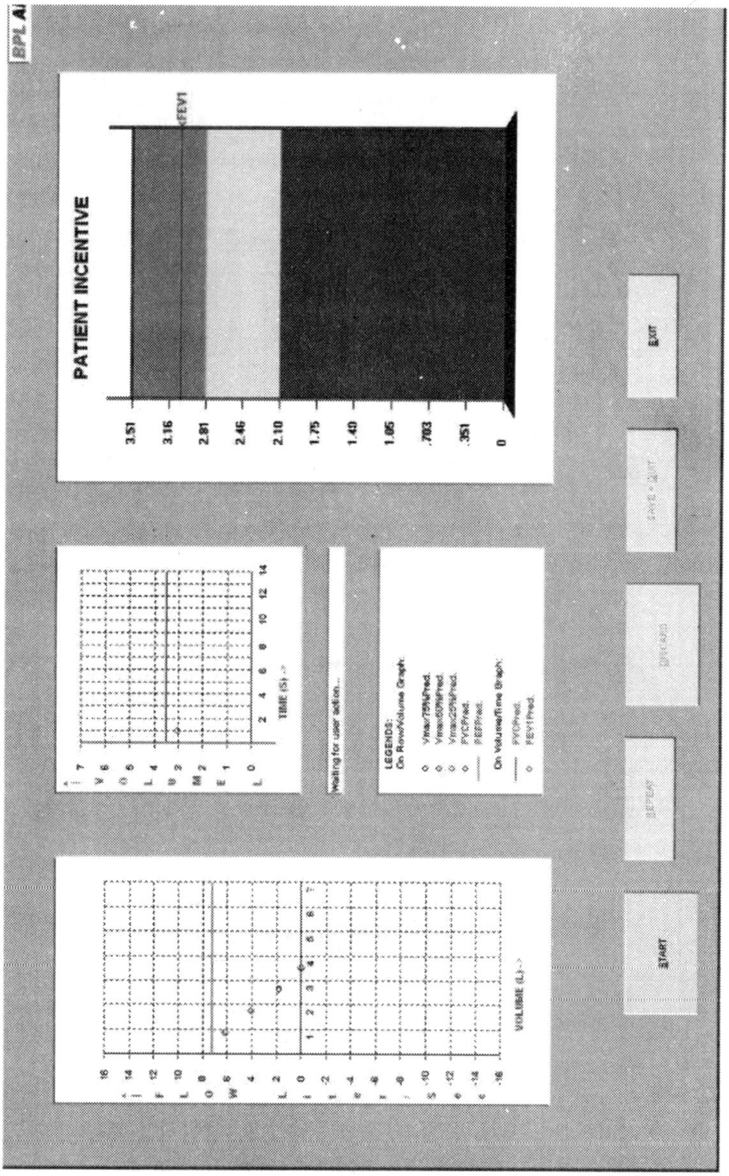


**Fig. 4.9:** Test Protocol for Respiration Rate

FVC TEST REPORT

ID No. :1
Patient Name :POOJA
Age(yrs.) : 27 Sex:F Weight(Kg): 62
Indications
Comments

Report Date: 27-12-2009
Eth. Corr.(%): 80
Height(cm): 149 BSA(m^2): 1.56

FVC GRAPHS

Flow / Volume Graph

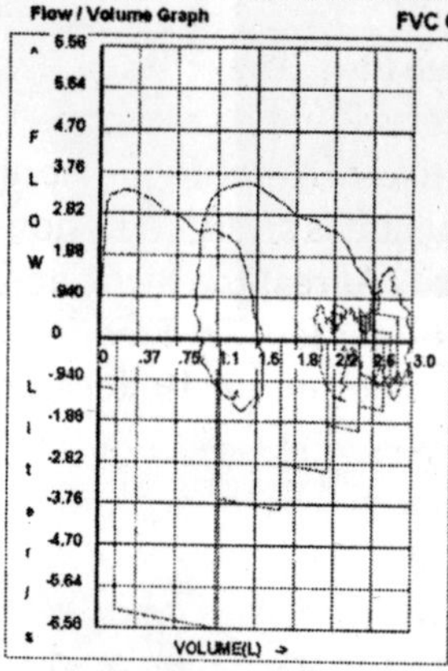


Volume / Time Graph

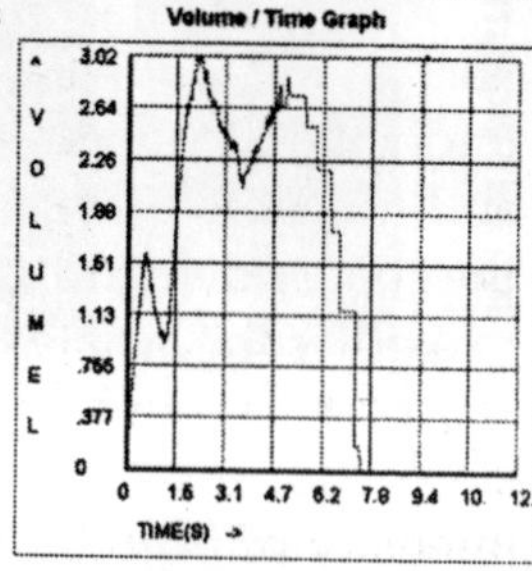


TEST RESULTS

| Date of Test -> | 23/12/2009 | | |
|---|---|---|---|
| Time of Test -> | 08:18:50 | | |
| Parameter (U) | Pred. | Actual | %Pred. |
| FVC (L) | 2.407 | 3.021 | 125.5 |
| FEV0.5 (L) | | 1.416 | |
| FEV1 (L) | 2.088 | 1.069 | 50.71 |
| FEV1/FVC % | 83.97 | 35.03 | 41.72 |
| PEF (L/s) | 5.02 | 3.569 | 71.09 |
| PIF (L/s) | | 6.682 | |
| FEF25-75% (L/s) | 3.092 | 2.38 | 76.97 |
| Vmax25% (L/s) | 4.578 | 2.855 | 62.36 |
| Vmax50% (L/s) | 3.308 | 0.793 | 23.97 |
| Vmax75% (L/s) | 1.6 | 2.458 | 153.6 |
| FET100% (s) | | 2.2 | |

INTERPRETATION: Moderate Obs

This may be clinically co - related.

BPL ARPEMIS

**Fig. 4.10:** Spirometry Analysis (Sample Respondent 1)

For nurses 1, 2, 3, 4, 5, 6, 7, 8, 9, 10, 11, 12, the test report of pulmonary function are given in Appendix III. In majority of nurses pulmonary function faced mild obstacle. The reason behind obstacles in pulmonary function test might be exposure to dust, fumes, anaethetic gases which may cause problems in the functioning of the lung. One result of spirometry analysis is shown in Figure 4.10 and Plate 21.

### *4.18.7 Blood Lactate Analysis of Nurses Involved in Various Group of Activities*

Lactate is known as a fatigue inducing agent. Lactate produced under light to moderate exercise and is removed by liver, heart and non-active skeletal muscle. Aerobic metabolism matches the energy demand and Lactate is shuttled to non-active tissue to oxidise the lactate formed. At rest the lactic acid mechanism is just 'ticking over' so the blood level of lactate is low at about 0.5 to 1.6 mmol/l (millimoles per litre of blood) but as the intensity of exercise increases, the blood level of lactate also rises. Eventually exhaustion occurs at which time the lactate level might be 10 or 20 times the resting level. It is referred to as the 'lactate threshold' at a level of about 3.5-4.0 mmol/l. During intense or prolonged work, lactic acid builds up due to the reason that fatigue occurs.

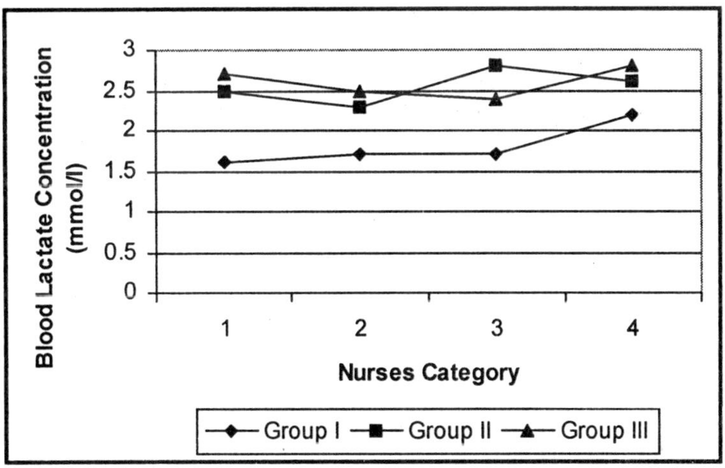


**Fig. 4.11:** Blood Lactate Concentration of Nurses

Data pertaining to blood lactate level is presented in Figure 4.11 and Plate 22. It is evident from the data that mean blood 'ticking over' so the blood level of lactate is low at about 0.5 to 1.6 mmol/l (millimoles per litre of blood) but as the intensity of exercise increases, the blood lactate level ranged from 1.6 mmol/l to 2.2 mmol/l for group I activities, 2.3 mmol/l to 2.6 mmol/l in case of group II activity and regarding group III activity, it was 2.4 mmol/l to 2.8 mmol/l.

It can be concluded from the results that group II and III activities were more tiring as compared to group I as they involved frequent use of muscles for working in standing as well as sitting position.

### 4.19 Testing of Hypothesis

In order to test the hypotheses statistically the null hypothesis as presented below were formulated:

1. $H_0$: Action categories of REBA are independent of activities performed by nurses.
   $H_1$: Action categories of REBA are dependent on activities performed by nurses.

#### *4.19.1 Test of Significance for REBA Analysis*

It was found that action categories of REBA postural analysis technique are independent of various activities performed by nurses.

**Table 4.29:** Test of Significance for REBA Analysis

**N=120**

| *Activity Profile* | *REBA Action Category* | | | | | *Chi-square value* |
|---|---|---|---|---|---|---|
| | $AL_0$ | $AL_1$ | $AL_2$ | $AL_3$ | $AL_4$ | |
| Group I (n=40) | 4 | 4 | 8 | 20 | 4 | 16.59(NS) |
| Group II (n=40) | 8 | 9 | 7 | 15 | 1 | |
| Group III (n=40) | 5 | 6 | 18 | 10 | 1 | |

($\chi^2$ value was calculated after merging some classes of activity profile for which expected frequencies were less than 5)

2. $H_0$: There is no significant difference in mean Blood pressure, mean Heart rate, and Energy expenditure rate during performance of various group of activities by the nurses.

   $H_1$: Significant difference exists in mean Blood pressure, mean Heart rate and Energy expenditure rate during performance of various groups of activities by the nurses.

### *4.19.2 Analysis of Variance for Blood Pressure, HR and EER*

ANOVA technique was applied to compare various activities and mean blood pressure, mean heart rate and mean energy expenditure rate (during activity). The results of ANOVA technique are presented in Table 4.30. The results were found to be significant at P<0.01, indicating average Blood pressure was significantly higher in case of group 3 activities, i.e. 96.16 as compared to other groups. It was again found out that values for mean Heart rate and energy expenditure rate were significant at P<0.01, i.e. these parameters were significantly higher while performing group 3 activities in comparison to other two groups of activity.

**Table 4.30:** Analysis of Variance for Blood Pressure, HR and EER

| *Activities* | *Mean BP (During work)* | *F-value* | *Mean HR (During Work)* | *F-value* | *Mean E.E.R (During Work)* | *F-value* |
|---|---|---|---|---|---|---|
| **Group I (n=4)** | 96.16 | **9.19**** | 112.875 | **5.27*** | 9.23 | **6.07*** |
| **Group II (n=4)** | 97.5 | | 115 | | 9.56 | |
| **Group III (n=4)** | 98.92 | | 114.25 | | 9.45 | |
| | **SEM** | **0.45** | **SEM** | **0.47** | **SEM** | **0.69** |
| | C.D.(1%) | 2.08 | C.D. (5%) | 1.50 | C.D. (5%) | 0.22 |

*Significant at 5% level of significance, ** Significant at 1% level of significance.

3. $H_0$: There is no significant association between sleep quality and performance capacity of nurses.

$H_1$: Significant association exists between sleep quality and performance capacity of nurses.

### 4.19.3 Sleep Quality and Performance Capacity

Chi-square test is applied to see the association between sleep quality and performance. The results are presented in Table 4.31. The results were found to be significant at P<0.05, indicating that performance capacity is dependent on the sleep quality of the nurses. The reason behind this may be that due to inadequate sleep, nurses feel drowsiness and restlessness and thus they are not able to perform better.

**Table 4.31:** Chi-square for Sleep Quality and Performance Capacity

| Performance \ Sleep quality | Very good | Fairly good | Fairly bad | Very bad | Chi-square value |
|---|---|---|---|---|---|
| **Poor** | 1 | 2 | 5 | 0 | **23.94*** |
| **Average** | 22 | 47 | 16 | 0 | |
| **Good** | 15 | 9 | 1 | 0 | |
| **Very good** | 0 | 2 | 0 | 0 | |
| **Excellent** | 0 | 0 | 0 | 0 | |

4. $H_0$: There is no significant association between job satisfaction and working condition, communication skills, coordination within the department, time demand, infrastructure facility available at health care industry.

   $H_1$: Significant association exists between job satisfaction and working condition, communication skills, coordination within the department, time demand, infrastructure facility available at health care industry.

### 4.19.4 Job Satisfaction and Working Condition

The test showed that there was significant association between job satisfaction of nurses and working condition in the health care industry which revealed that job satisfaction is the result of good working condition available at the workplace.

**Table 4.32:** Chi-square Test for Job Satisfaction and Working Condition

| *Working condition* | *Job satisfaction* | | | *Chi-square value* |
|---|---|---|---|---|
| | *Dissatis-factory* | *Satisfactory* | *Strongly satisfactory* | |
| **Poor** | 43 | 11 | 0 | **49.14*** |
| **Average** | 12 | 21 | 1 | |
| **Good** | 2 | 26 | 4 | |

### 4.19.5 *Job Satisfaction and Communication Skills*

The chi-square test showed that there was a significant association between job satisfaction and communication skills, thus, higher job satisfaction is achieved, if communication skills are good. Good communication skills shows that nurses are able to remove the frustration related to job and other factors as a result of poor infrastructural facilities, absence of recognition at work place etc.

**Table 4.33:** Chi-square Test for Job Satisfaction and Communication Skills

| *Communication Skills* | *Job satisfaction* | | | *Chi-square value* |
|---|---|---|---|---|
| | *Dissatis-factory* | *Satisfactory* | *Strongly satisfactory* | |
| **Poor** | 13 | 3 | 0 | **62.40*** |
| **Average** | 11 | 29 | 6 | |
| **Good** | 2 | 23 | 33 | |

### 4.19.6 *Job Satisfaction and Coordination within Department*

The chi-square test showed that there was a significant association between job satisfaction and coordination within department, thus, higher job satisfaction is achieved, if level of coordination among the group members within department as well as outside the department is good.

**Table 4.34:** Chi-square Test for Job Satisfaction and Coordination within Department

| *Coordination within Department* | *Job satisfaction* | | | *Chi-square value* |
|---|---|---|---|---|
| | *Dissatis-factory* | *Satisfactory* | *Strongly satisfactory* | |
| **Poor** | 32 | 5 | 0 | **69.16*** |
| **Average** | 17 | 9 | 7 | |
| **Good** | 0 | 28 | 22 | |

### *4.19.7 Job Satisfaction and Time Demand at Workplace*

Significant association was observed between job satisfaction and time demand. It revealed that very high time demand at workplace results in job dissatisfaction as in this situation they are not able to perform the household duties in good way.

**Table 4.35:** Chi-square Test for Job Satisfaction and Time Demand at Workplace

| *Time demand at workplace* | *Job satisfaction* | | | *Chi-square value* |
|---|---|---|---|---|
| | *Dissatis-factory* | *Satisfactory* | *Strongly satisfactory* | |
| **High** | 17 | 13 | 3 | **35.99*** |
| **Average** | 3 | 27 | 6 | |
| **Low** | 5 | 24 | 22 | |

### *4.19.8 Job Satisfaction and Infrastructure Facility Available at Hospital*

It was revealed that there was a significant association between job satisfaction and infrastructure facility available at the hospitals at 5 per cent level of significance indicating that higher job satisfaction is achieved when infrastructure facilities are good at the hospital. Infrastructure facilities refers to the availability of adequate number of medical equipments and instruments, their proper functioning, availability of latest technology and good expertise to use it, incentives provided by the hospitals to the nurses in terms of monetary gain and other rewards etc. Presence of all these facilities at workplace may result in job satisfaction among nurses.

**Table 4.36:** Chi-square Test for Job Satisfaction and Infrastructure Facility Available at Hospital

| *Infrastructure Facility Available at Hospital* | *Job satisfaction* | | | *Chi-square value* |
|---|---|---|---|---|
| | *Dissatis-factory* | *Satisfactory* | *Strongly satisfactory* | |
| **Poor** | 26 | 11 | 0 | **71.67*** |
| **Average** | 8 | 19 | 5 | |
| **Good** | 0 | 31 | 20 | |

5. $H_0$: Concentration ability and marital strain among nurses are independent of duration of overtime.
   $H_1$: Concentration ability and marital strain among nurses are dependent on duration of overtime.

### *4.19.9 Overtime and Concentration*

Chi-square test between overtime and concentration came out to be non-significant. It indicated that concentration ability is not dependent on overtime. Concentration may depend upon the fatigue level and mood of the nurses.

**Table 4.37:** Chi-square Test for Overtime and Concentration

| *Overtime* | *Concentration* | | | *Chi-square value* |
|---|---|---|---|---|
| | *Good* | *Average* | *Poor* | |
| **4-6 hour** | 5 | 9 | 6 | 4.41 (NS) |
| **6-8 hour** | 4 | 7 | 17 | |

**Table 4.38:** Chi-square Test for Overtime and Marital Strain

| *Overtime* | *Marital strain* | | | | *Chi-square value* |
|---|---|---|---|---|---|
| | *Occasional* | *Sometimes* | *Frequent* | *Very Often* | |
| **4-6 hour** | 13 | 6 | 1 | 0 | 4.22 (NS) |
| **6-8 hour** | 12 | 9 | 4 | 3 | |

### *4.19.10 Overtime and Marital Strain*

It was revealed that marital strain was not dependent on the duration of overtime spent at the hospitals. The reason may be that overtime was not the problem on regular basis. It depends upon the emergencies occurred at the hospital.

## 4.20 Ergonomically Suitable Work Schedule Approaches and Strategies for Nursing Work

- *Short Term Imporovement/Early Intervention*

Early intervention is essential to quick recovery from and long-term prevention of Work Related Musculoskeletal Disorders (WMSDs). WMSDs usually develop gradually as a result of physically stressful and repetitive activities etc. Symptoms such as pain, numbness, and tingling in the upper extremities are often ignored until the condition becomes chronic or permanent injury occurs. Ergonomics is the science of designing jobs, selecting tools, and modifying work methods to suit workers' capabilities and prevent injury. Ergonomics programme strives to reduce worker discomfort and WMSDs. Some improvements can be done within short period of time which may be:

- **Ergonomic Shift Planning** – Shift work is now a major feature of working life across a broad range of industries. Some aspects of shift scheduling may not be feasible, especially because health industry has more female shift workers than in other industries. For example working 3 rotating shifts can be more strenuous for a female nurse with children and other family responsibility. For these nurses patterns of shift schedules are not only strenuous but also dangerous due to travelling at night.
- Shift schedule planned with little thought to ergonomics are a health-and-safety gamble. A day shift

should follow a day shift, a night shift to a day shift, and a night shift to a half day shift. If the shift pattern doesn't balance the demands of work with time for rest and recovery fatigue, accidents, injuries and ill health are all but inevitable.

- Consider the direction of rotation of shifts. It is recommended that shifts rotate forward from day to afternoon to night because circadian rhythms adjust better when moving ahead than back.
- Consider the time at which a shift starts and finishes. Early morning shifts are associated with shorter sleep and greater fatigue. It is advisable to avoid shift start times as early as 5 or 6 a.m. The social customs and desires of the specific work force should be considered as well as the availability of public transportation. The safety on the streets, in terms of crime and violence, is another consideration.
- Provide a rest period of at least 24 hours after each set of night shifts. The more consecutive nights worked, the more rest time should be allowed before the next rotation occurs.
- The features of the shift systems operated can impact on the well-being, performance, and sleep of shift workers. Shift-work environment should be comfortable, safe and free from hazards such as long hours at work.
- Planning of shift schedules should be based on the inputs of nurses.
- Consideration of nurses need for a particular shift and their involvement is important for motivation and acceptance of shift schedule and work. Motivation could improve adaptation of the nurses to awkward hours of night shift.
- Reduction in the duration of shift.
- Introduction of break/nap.
- Rotation of the staff within the different departments of the hospitals.

### *Advantages*

- Flexible time schedule leads to convenience in job performance of nurses.
- Rotation from one department to other helps in gaining better knowledge, better health of the staff.
- Capability of the staff is increased.
- This increase diversity in job performance.
- Reduced monotony.
- Change in the life style.

### *How Nurses Cope with Night Shift*

#### *Napping*

- It is defined as a purposeful, brief sleep period. Naps in the later half of the night shift are superior to earlier naps in terms of sleep quality.
- Night shift work can lead to sleep deprivation, which in turn can threaten the health and safety of both patients and nurses.
- Napping as a strategy can be implemented to improve performance, to reduce fatigue and to increase vigilance in other shift work environments.
- Nurses are trained to provide specialized nursing care, to make rapid decisions, and to perform advanced assessments and motor skills.
- Napping is a strategy to combat sleep loss and fatigue associated with night shift work.
- If you did not have enough sleep, take short naps to minimize the risks. The co-workers should be made aware of your problem, so that they can assist you by rotating your activities and routine work. Monotonous work can cause drowsiness which results in mistakes.
- It is advisable to take short naps of 20 minutes to avoid getting into deep sleep as waking from a deep sleep can make one feel more tired.

- A 120 minutes nap sustained early morning can make performance better than a 60 minute nap.
- Night time napping during a night shift is one of the effective strategies for sleepiness and fatigue.
- Night shifts interfere with circadian rhythms so, adequate day time sleep is recommended.

• ***Intermediate Improvement***

- **Online Ergonomic Training**—All nurses are encouraged to take the online ergonomics training. Online ergonomics training was developed as a resource to assist nurses in setting up their work areas according to good ergonomic guidelines. The online training can help nurses adjust their work stations with step-by-step instructions and guidelines, on their own time. The training takes about 30 minutes to complete.
- **Ergonomics Awareness Training for Nurses**—Ergonomics awareness training covers basic ergonomic principles, teaches the nurses to identify work activities that can lead to injury, and stresses the importance of reporting signs and symptoms of an ergonomic injury early.
- Organization of trainings to the nurses on reduction of occurrence of injuries, accidents, hypertension, postural stress, tiredness and at the same time train them to use latest technology.
- Training on manually handling of scientific instruments, computer, and other gadgets. Manual handling educates nurses on proper methods of lifting, and how to prevent back strain and repetitive strain injury. Discussion topics include handling heavy loads in awkward positions (e.g. above head level), and moving a variety of loads (patients) in numerous situations.
- Trained staff should also be reviewed to judge their knowledge

- Educational packages can be prepared in order to make them aware of the ill effects of extended working hours, overtime.

### *Advantages*

- Trained staff is capable of lowering the accidents rate at their own individual level.
- Increased knowledge and awareness.
- Familiarity with the latest technology.

- ***Long-Term Improvement/Prevention and Intervention Strategies***

Once ergonomic hazards are identified through the systematic worksite evaluation or training, the next step is to devise a strategy to prevent or control these hazards. As with any control strategy, the most effective intervention is the reduction of risk. Following measures can be implemented on long-term basis.

- Use of anthropometric data to design/redesign or modify the furniture. The existing furniture can be replaced with ergonomically designed furniture. Hospitals should procure the ergonomically designed furniture for the nurses who are going to use them in order to increase the productivity.

  Below are the some functionally sound designed furniture useful for hospitals as they reduce the cost of work in terms of fatigue and minimize the time taken to perform the task, and on the other hand they increase the productivity. Large numbers of furniture for different operations of the hospitals are now available with reputed manufacturers of furniture (Plates 23-24). These should be validated by the users and should be made available in the market.

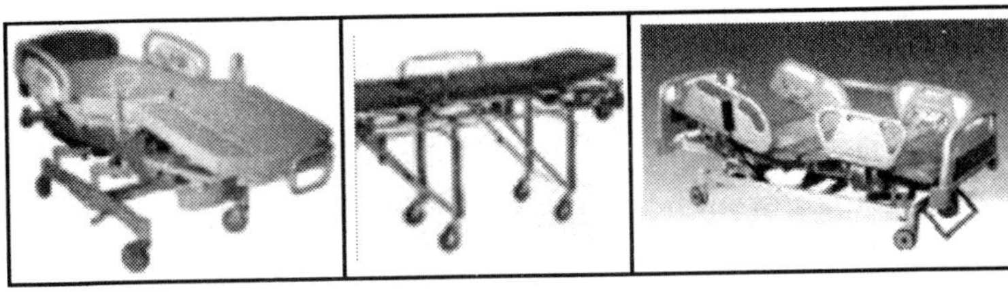

**Hospital Beds**

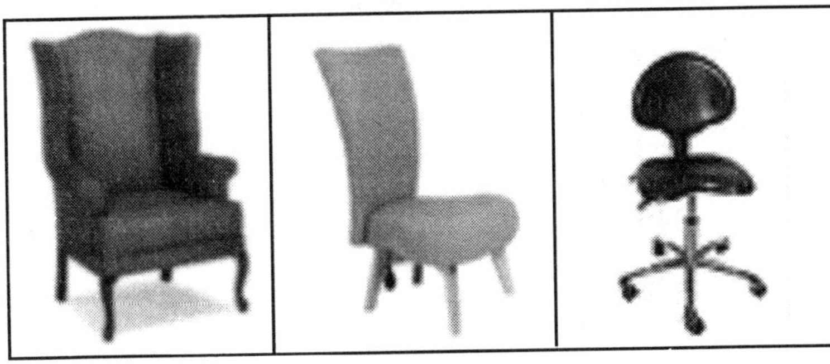

**Hospital Chairs**

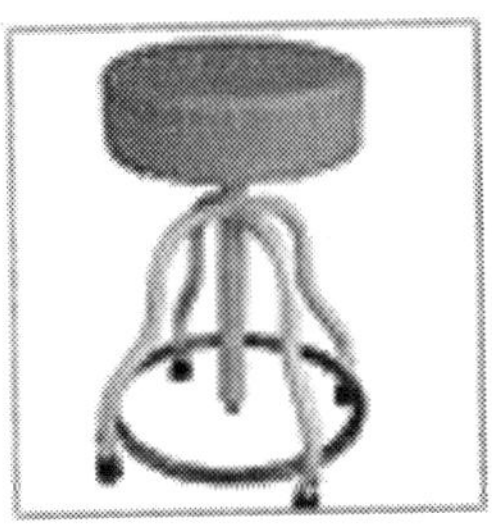

**Hospital Stool**

**Hospital Wheel Chair**

**Hospital Table**

**Plate 23:** Ergonomically Designed Furniture Available in the Market

- Work places and work stations operated by nurses should be ergonomically designed.
- Environmental parameters such as light, humidity, sound, ventilation etc. should be available at the work-place of nurses on ergonomic principles to reduce any hazards or injury.

- ***Minor Infrastructural Facilities and Modification in the Same***
  - Provision of fresh air through exhaust and fans.
  - Tiled flooring.
  - Regular mopping of the floor with use of disinfectants.
  - Use of personal protective equipments by the staff.
  - Provision of adequate number of dustbins.
  - Proper handling of biomedical waste and colour coding of the same as given below—

    (a) **Yellow Bag**—Human anatomical waste as human tissues, organs, body parts. Microbes and biotechnology waste (waste from laboratory cultures, stocks or specimen of microorganisms lie or attenuated vaccines etc.).

    (b) **Blue Bag** – Sharp waste as needles, syringes, scalpels, blades, glasses etc.

    (c) **Red Bag** – Solid wastes as items contaminated with body fluid and blood, catheters, tubings etc.

    (d) **Black Bag** – Discarded medicines and cytotoxic drugs (outdated, contaminated and discarded medicines).

### *Tips for Good Sleep*

The amount of sleep a person gets affects his or her physical health, emotional well-being, mental abilities, productivity and performance.

- Sleep on a set schedule is required to help establish a routine and to make sleep during the day easier. Some people may prefer to get a full period of rest just before the next work shift (as it is with "normal day" work).
- Make time for quiet relaxation before bed to help get better sleep.
- If you do not fall asleep after an hour, read a book or listen to quiet music on the radio for a while.
- Plan your sleep time and sleep off time, keeping a steady schedule, make and keep rules.

- Get a full night's sleep every night.
- Avoid foods or drinks that contain caffeine, as well as any medicine that has a stimulant, prior to bedtime.
- Do not bring your worries to bed with you.
- Do not go to bed hungry, but don't eat a big meal before bedtime.
- Avoid any rigorous exercise within six hours of your bedtime.
- Make your bedroom quiet, dark and a little bit cool.
- Do not work too many nights in a row.
- Develop a good sleeping environment.
- Drinking beverages such as milk.
- Eye shades and ear plugs can be used by those who are comfortable wearing them. Turn telephone volume to off.
- If under stress, relax before going to bed. One possibility of relaxation is light exercise.
- Beware of sleep debt. The less sleep one get the more tired and prone to make mistakes he/she will be.

### *Gastrointestinal Disorders Associated with Shiftwork*

The following problems are more common among rotating shiftworkers and night workers than among day workers.

- Indigestion,
- Heartburn,
- Stomach ache,
- Loss of appetite.

### *Tips for Eating Pattern*

Given the irregularity in type and timing of meals, it is not surprising that the night worker is more likely to have a poorer diet. At night, the loss of appetite often leads to increased snacking on "junk" food rather than eating a full, well-balanced meal. Feelings of fatigue may encourage the consumption of beverages with caffeine (coffee, cola) forces the worker to stay awake.

- Maintain regular eating patterns as much as possible Balanced, varied meals are very important.
- Time meals carefully. Afternoon workers should have the main meal in the middle of the day instead of the middle of the work shift. Night workers should eat lightly throughout the shift and have a moderate breakfast. This way they should not get too hungry while sleeping during the day and digestive discomfort should be minimal.
- Pay careful attention to the type of food eaten. Drink lots of water and eat the usual balance of vegetables, fruit, lean meat, poultry, fish, dairy products, grains and bread. Eat crackers and fruit instead of pop and candy bars during work breaks. Reduce the intake of salt, caffeine, and alcohol. Avoid greasy foods, particularly at night.
- Avoid excessive use of antacids, tranquilizers and sleeping pills. It is healthier to watch what and when you eat, and use relaxation techniques to aid sleep.
- Relax during meals and allow time for digestion.
- Choose light healthy meals before going to bed.
- Herbal tea and warm milk are good before going to sleep.
- In shift work, the sleep pattern is altered thus sleep is less restful and it results in poor performance.

### *Suggestion for Improvement of Night Shift*

- Reduce the number of working hours.
- Provision of more staff.
- Introduction of certain adjustments such as stipulating official rest periods for the night nurses in an attempt to reduce some of the ill effects of night shift.
- The important factor to be recognized is that 12 hour night shift is too long and the absence of variations in activities makes it more monotonous and strenuous. This makes the body to enable to adjust and perform as expected without rest.
- Better communication between day and night nurses.

Management should be encouraged to provide a psychologically supportive environment to the nurses. Rest room should provide tranquility and be conducive to contemplation in an attempt to relieve psychological stressors. Music, reading materials, games provide relaxation to many in the workplace. The comfort of the environment and the furniture used for resting is essential and conducive to complete rest. Those who feel tired can benefit from a separate resting area from the cafeteria or work area.

**Control Strategies**—Risk control strategies include the following, in order of preference:

- **The Organizational Level**—Primarily through the design of shift schedules, education and better facilities. Engineering controls include purchasing equipment that fits the workplace to the worker in order to reduce awkward or static postures, repetitive motions, and use of excessive force.
- **The Individual Level**—Helping workers to get better sleep, a healthier diet, and the reduction of stress. Work practice controls include proper work techniques that improve posture and reduce stress and strain on the extremities. They also involve rotating tasks, stretching, and taking mini-breaks.
- **Stretching**—Stretching is an integral part of reducing the risk of WMSDs. Stretches can be performed before work, at the work station, and on mini-breaks. You should not feel pain while stretching. If you do feel pain which you believe is related to a workplace injury, stop immediately and contact the physician.

### *Recommended Stretching Exercises*

If you are recovering from an injury, consult your physician or occupational therapist before doing the stretches shown in below Figure. Perform each of the following stretches 3-5 times at least twice a day. Hold each stretch for 1-5 seconds, then relax and repeat.

### *NECK*

(1) Turn your head slowly to the left and look over your shoulder; hold; then turn head to centre. Repeat on right side.
(2) Tilt your head slowly to the left, return to centre. Repeat on right side.

### *SHOULDERS*

(1) Slowly raise your shoulders up towards your ears and hold. Slowly bring shoulders down and relax.
(2) Roll your shoulders forward slowly five times, and then backwards five times.
(3) Put your hands up with forearms raised; push your arms back squeezing shoulder blades; hold; then relax (Plate 24).

### *BACK*

(1) Stand and stretch your spine straight while raising hands over head—reach for ceiling. Arch your back slightly while stretching.
(2) While sitting, slowly bend your upper body down between your knees and hold; then slowly roll back up to normal posture (Plate 25).

### *ARMS*

(1) Hold arms out in front of you. Rotate arms so that the back of your hands face each other and hold. Then rotate arms so your palms face up and hold (Plates 26 and 27).

### *WRISTS*

(1) Hold your hands in front of you. Point your fingers up towards ceiling; hold; then lower, pointing fingers towards floor; relax.
(2) Move your hands side to side.

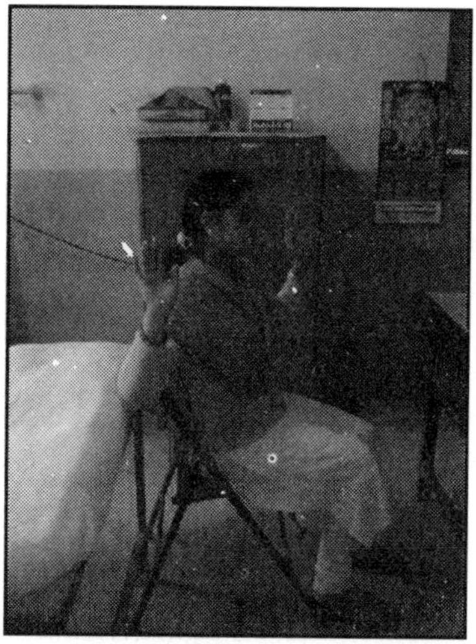

Plate 24: Shoulder Exercise

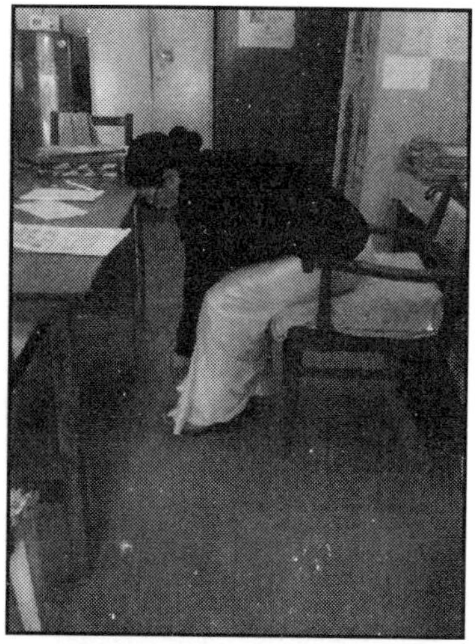

Plate 25: Back Exercise

Plate 26: Exercise for Arms

Plate 27: Exercise for Arms

## *FINGERS AND HANDS*

(1) Make a tight fist with your hand and hold for one second. Then spread fingers as far apart as you can and hold for five seconds. Be sure to bend and stretch

your thumb. Gently shake out hands and arms between sets.

*EYES*

(1) Focus on an object at least 20 feet away.
(2) Cup your hands and place lightly over closed eyes, lean elbows on desk and hold for one minute while breathing deeply. Slowly uncover your eyes.
(3) Close your eyes and slowly roll your eyeballs clockwise all the way around. Repeat counter clock-wise.

*Personal Protective Equipment for Nurses*

- **Gloves** protect hands from infectious materials and protect patients from microorganisms on staff members' hands. Remember that wearing gloves does not replace hand washing or use of antiseptic handrubs.
- **Masks** should be large enough to cover the nose, lower face, jaw and facial hair. Unless the masks are made of fluid-resistant materials, they are not effective in preventing very well. Masks are made from a variety of materials ranging from light weight cotton, gauze or even paper to synthetics, some of which are fluid resistant. Masks made from synthetics can provide some protection from large-particle droplets. It is observed that sometimes the best surgical masks, however, are not designed to provide a tight enough fit to prevent air leakage around the edges. Thus, they do not effectively filter inhaled air and should no longer be recommended for that purpose.
- **Respirators** are specialized types of masks, called particulate respirators, that are recommended for situations in which filtering inhaled air is deemed important (e.g. for the care of a person with pulmonary tuberculosis). They contain multiple layers of filter material and fit the face tightly.

- **Eyewear** includes clear plastic goggles, safety glasses, face shields and visors. Prescription glasses or glasses with plain lenses are acceptable. Masks and eyewear or face shields should be worn when performing any task where an accidental splash into the face is likely (e.g. performing cesarean section or vaginal delivery or when cleaning instruments).
- **Caps** should be large enough to cover all hairs. While caps provide some protection to the patient, their primary purpose is to protect the wearer from blood or body fluid splashes and sprays.
- **Surgical gowns** made of fluid-resistant materials do play a role in keeping blood and other fluids, such as amniotic fluid, off the skin of personnel, particularly in operating, delivery and emergency rooms. If surgical gowns are worn, sleeves should either taper gently towards the wrists or end with elastic or ties around the wrists.
- **Aprons** made of rubber or plastic provide a waterproof barrier along the front of the health worker's body. An apron should be worn when cleaning or during a procedure in which blood or body fluid spills are anticipated (e.g. cesarean section or vaginal delivery). Aprons keep contaminated fluids off the healthcare worker's clothing and skin.
- **Footwear:** Rubber boots or leather shoes provide more protection, but they must be kept clean and free of contamination from blood or other body fluid spills. Shoe covers are unnecessary if clean, sturdy shoes are available for use only in the surgical area.
- **Radiation Protection:** Many endoscopy facilities provide imaging, often for "upper GIs" or barium swallows, and the healthcare workers providing this imaging need to be protected against exposure to radiation. Wear a radiation dosimeter (badge or other) when exposed to radiation; comply with all safety instructions to reduce exposure to a minimum.

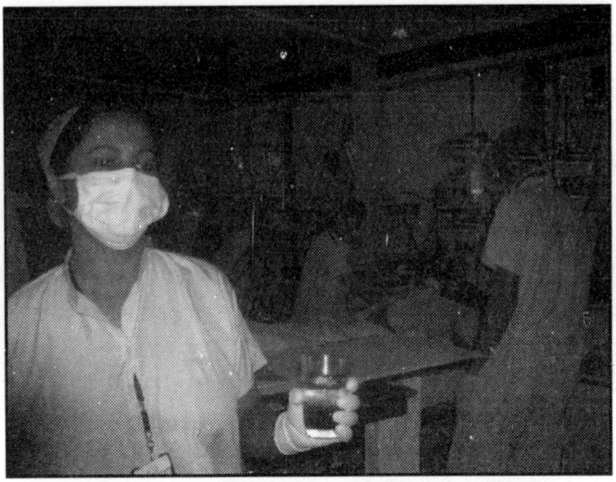

**Plate 28:** Nurses with Personal Protective Equipment

**Plate 29:** Nurses with Personal Protective Equipment

### *Comparison of Hospitals under Study with Model Hospital*

The different hospitals taken under study were compared with the hi-tech model hospital Sir Gangaram Hospital, New Delhi in terms of application of codes and ISO Standards 9001.

**Ergonomically Unsuitable Furniture**

- Fixed height of the stretcher
- Poorly designed
- No additional super features and materials provided

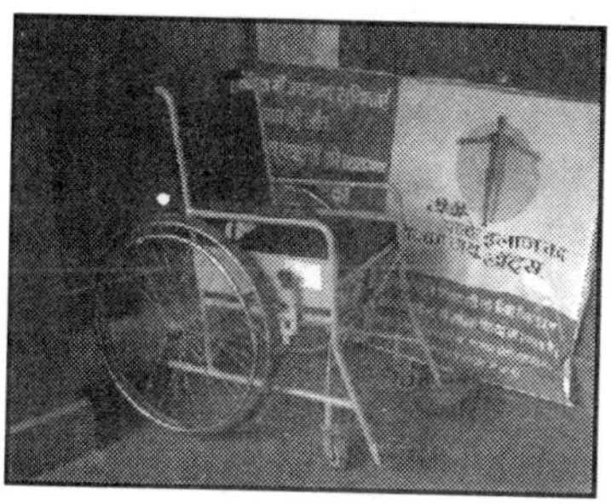

- Large wheels, unproportionate seat
- Poor details of arm and leg rest

**Ergonomically Sound Furniture**

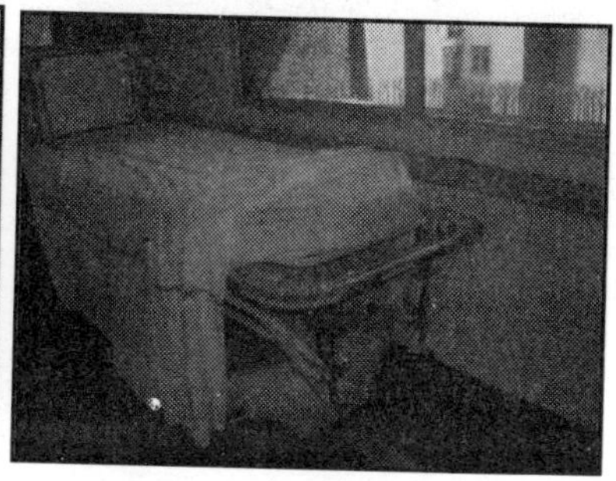

- Adjustable height of stretcher
- Functionally and aesthetically designed
- Additional super features and materials provided

- Functional wheel, Proportionate comfortable seat
- Good details of arm and leg rest

**Plate 30:** Comparison of Hospitals under Study with Model Hospital in Terms of Furniture

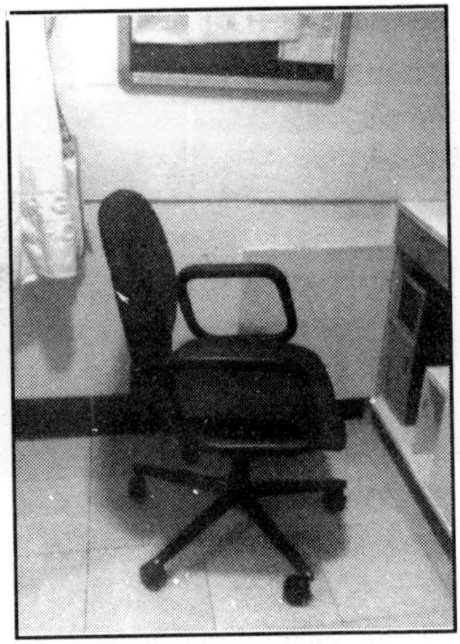

- Ergonomically poorly designed chair at working counter of nurse
- Hi-tech adjustable chair at working counter of nurse

- Wardrobe with unrotating little storage space
- Wardrobes with rotating large storage space with locker facility

**Plate 30** *(contd.)*

- Poorly constructed cupboards at uncomfortable height

- Well constructed built-in cupboards at comfortable height

- Unorganized space for storing belongings of nurses

- Functional storage space for belongings of nurses

- Haphazard waiting counter

- Organized waiting counter

**Plate 30** *(contd.)*

- Details of duty room
- Details of duty room

**Plate 30** (*contd.*)

**Hazardous Working Environment**

**Ergonomically Sound Working Environment**

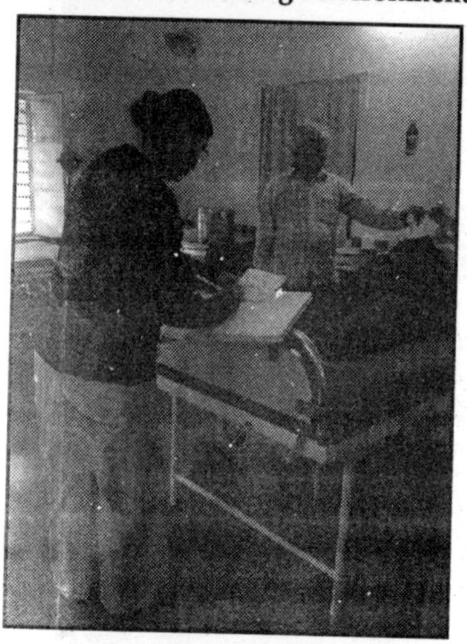

- Absence of functional record counter
- Awkward posture for recording

- Functional record counter
- Good posture for recording

**Plate 31:** Comparison of Hospitals in Terms of Infrastructural Facilities

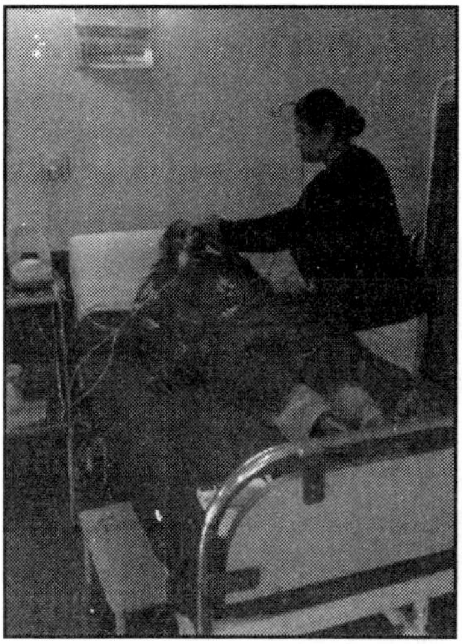

• Poor facilities for patient ward

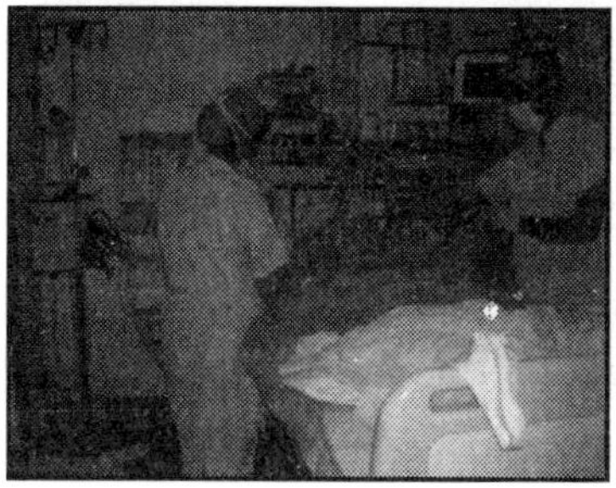

• Hi-tech patient ward

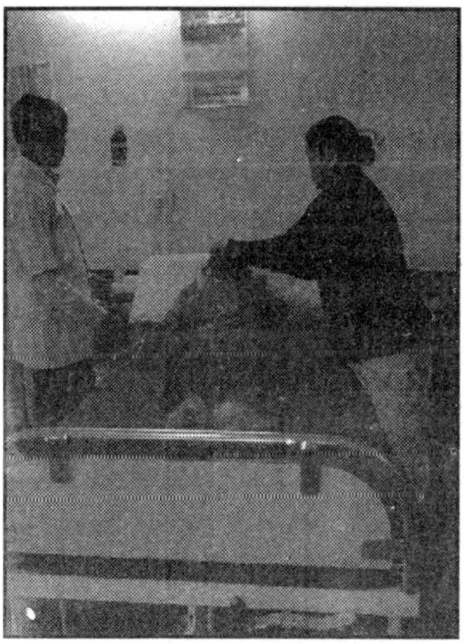

• Absence of constructive facilities for patient comfort

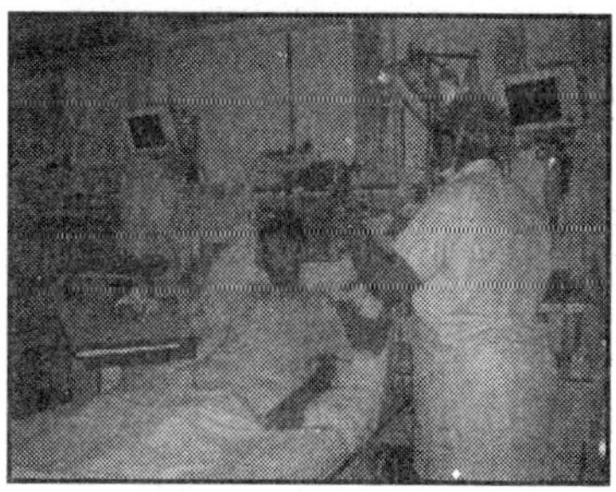

• More constructive facilities for patient comfort

**Plate 31** (*contd.*)

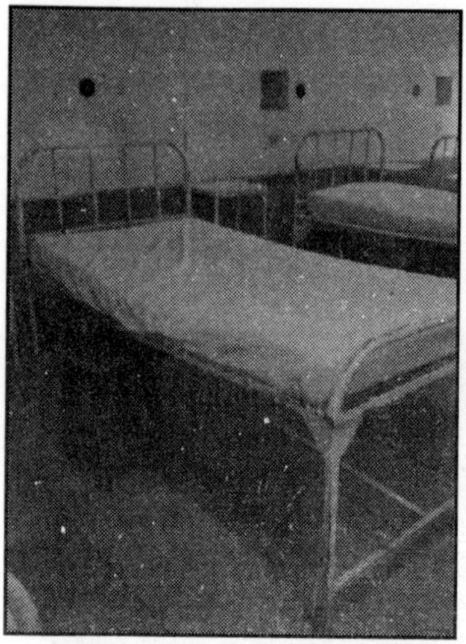

• Poorly designed fixed bed

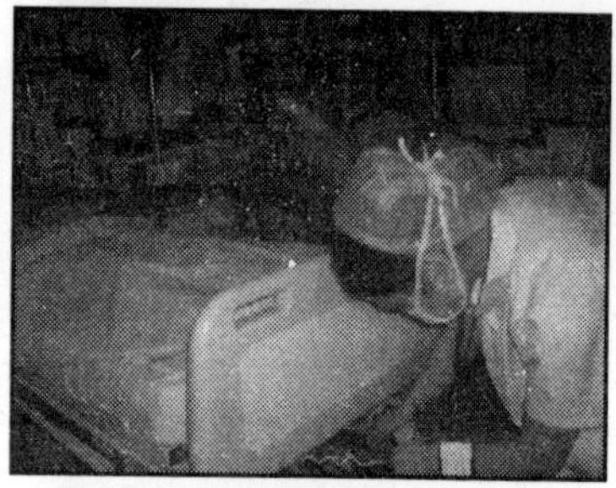

• Hi-tech adjustable bed

• Poorly furnished patient area with no scientific instruments

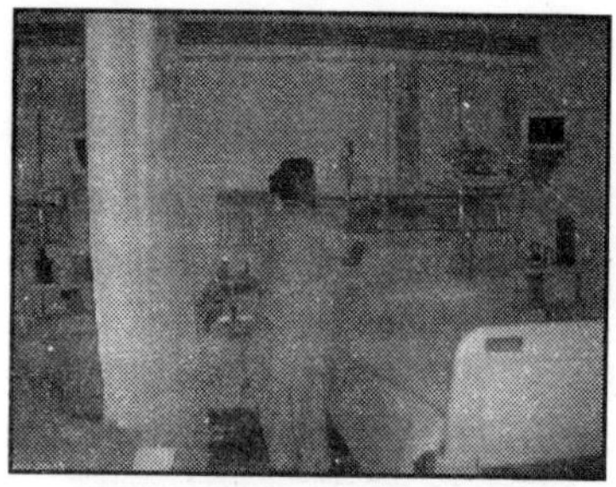

• Well furnished patient area with scientific instruments available

• Unhygienically medicine area

• Hygienically controlled medicine area

**Plate 31** *(contd.)*

- Poorly illuminated
- Well illuminated

- Poorly equipped nurse office
- Nurse without personal protective equipment

- Well equipped nurse office
- Nurse with personal protective equipment

**Plate 30** (*contd.*)

- Poorly designed storage facility
- Poorly lighted storage area

- Well designed storage cupboards
- Well lighted storage area

- Poorly designed and equipped nurse working counter
- Poorly lighted storage area

- Well designed and well equipped nurse working counter
- Well lighted storage area

**Plate 31** *(contd.)*

- Poorly conditioned interior with poor lighting and ventilation

- Well lighted and well ventilated interior

**Plate 31** (*contd.*)

**What Reduces the Psycho-Social and Physiological Stress Among Nurses**

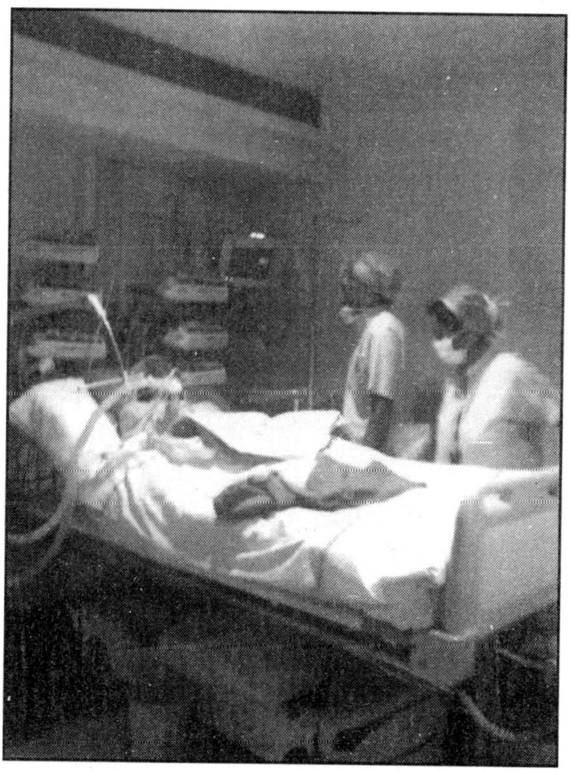

**Plate 32:** Coordinated and Shared Responsibilities of Doctor and Nurse

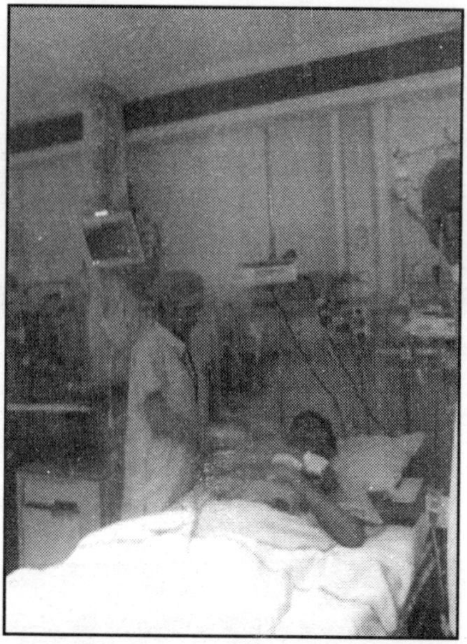

**Plate 33:** Involvement and Coordination of Male and Female Nurse in Patient Care During Night Shift

**Plate 34:** Presence of Hi-Tech Facility Around

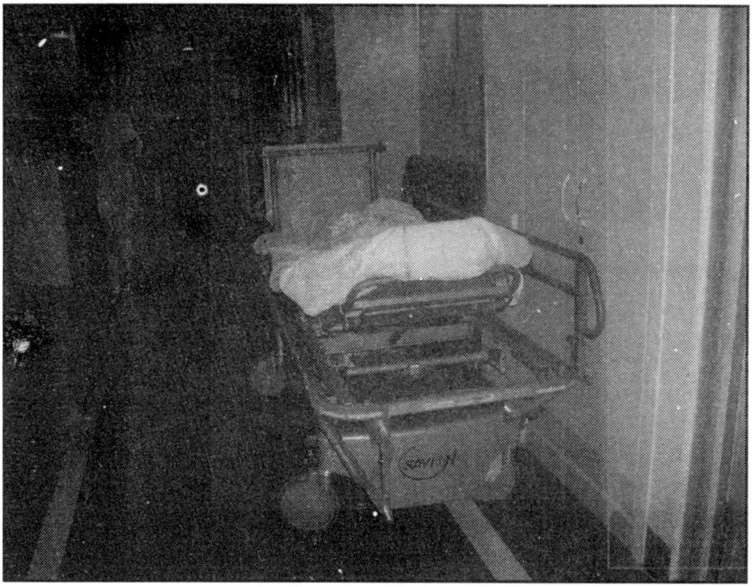

**Plate 35:** Avoidance of Excessive Manually Handling Activities with Introduction of Hi-Tech Furniture

# 5

# Summary and Conclusions

Nursing is a demanding field and involves high accountability, and thus its total workload is considerable. The quality of patient care depends directly on the work of skilful and caring nurses; therefore, the health and work capacity of personnel form a critical factor in the view of the results of the work. The need of professional, skilful nurses will increase as the population ages while the shortage of nurses is the reality already. Nurses are stressed further by inconvenient working hours like extensive working hours, weekend work, evening and night-time work, insufficient breaks during working shifts, and even having to take on two jobs in order to make reasonable pay. Stress experienced in the field of nursing is on the increase even though work related strain in other fields is declining. The growing conflict between demand and the resources available creates an increasing amount of overload. Irregular shift work has an effect on a person's health. For example, the risk of cardiovascular diseases, sleep disturbances and accidents are all increased. Irregular working hours have an impact on a person's mental well-being also, affecting moods and leading to anxiety and strain, even to exhaustion. Working conditions compounded to inconvenient working hours produce joint effects causing still more overload.

Studies have shown that onsets of diseases are caused by disturbances in diurnal rhythms. Factors contributing to shift work related diseases include exposure to example stress, insufficient off-duty time to recover from work and unhealthy ways of life (as to exercise and nutrition) management of fatigue by artificial means (cigarettes, alcohol, medicines, stimulants). Workload measurements conducted in shift work environments in the field of geriatric institutionalized care show that some employees work at levels that drain their functioning capacity perhaps eventually causing problems of fatigue. In nursing differencing from industry, employees take on morning shifts immediately after evening shifts, which causes them a shortage of night time sleep preventing them from having the 7-8 hours requirements.

During the night after an evening shift, the recovery of the autonomous nervous system is deficient and the hormonal load is initially higher in the morning of the next working day than after a morning shift. People adjust to shift systems in their individual ways, but morning shifts immediately following evening shifts may increase the risk of overstrain situations. In multi-shift work schedules, workers need to operate well when on duty, despite sleeping irregular hours. Daytime sleep is often of a shorter length and provides lower restorative values than a full night's sleep. During a night shift, alertness and performance often diminish as time progress. The term shift work describes regular employment outside the normal daytime hours. Night-shift work can cause not only occupational accidents due to severe sleepiness and a resulting reduction in alertness but also can introduce several health problems among these non-day time shift workers. Similarly, in health industry, sleepless nights and irregular sleep of the health care workers especially of nurses have direct and sharp impact on the health and well-being of the patients.

Nursing is the most important component of patient care. The process of restoring patients to normal health depends as much, if not more, on nurses as on doctors or surgeons. The common aspect of all jobs in nursing is that there are always a lot of people; a nurse has to interact with and they are always expected to display a calm, perceptive approach during crises that are only to be expected in hospitals. Long work hours and shift work adversely affect worker's health by increasing exposure to occupational hazards and reducing time for recovery. Research on shift workers, working in different production/service and other industries have been undertaken by different organizations; but not much attention is paid to the industries where workers render their services for the health and care of people. Since ages, the health industry is working in shift pattern, but focus was not given to this area. Due to emergence of multinational companies in India and their shift work has revealed that hospitals are also at risk particularly with regard to nurses who are the worst sufferers of the shift pattern and this area of research has become an important area to be exercised. In order to provide safe working environment to this dedicated group, i.e. nurses, needs several approaches to protect them from any ill effect, thus making them fit to take care of patients.

The objectives were as follow:

- To study the profile of nurses in the field of nursing, i.e. personal and family profile, medical history and selected anthropometric measurements.
- To study the existing infrastructure facilities available in health care industry and handling of the same, i.e. environmental parameters, medical equipments, accessories/supplements/tools and furniture related to care of patients.
- To study the occupational details (type of activities) and associated hazards/accidents/risks/injuries at the place of work.
- To study the physiological and psychosocial cost of nursing work.
- To suggest ergonomically suitable work schedule approaches or strategies for nursing work.

Descriptive-cum-experimental research design was used in this study. Different tools like interview schedule, checklist, job satisfaction scale, experimental table, work sheet for REBA (Rapid Entire Body Assessment), rated perceived exertion scalė, software: BPL ARPEMIS were constructed to collect descriptive data. Scientific instruments like anthropometric rods, lactate instrument, noise level meter, thermohygrometer, spirometer, lux meter, weighing machine were used for collection of experimental data. List of nurses was taken from the concerned hospitals. A total of 120 nurses were selected from the Nainital and Udham Singh Nagar districts of the Uttarakhand State (70 nurses from Government and 50 nurses from private hospitals). The purposive-cum-random sampling technique was chosen to select the sample. The data were collected in two phases: Phase I and Phase II.

**Phase I** – In phase I, information was collected personally with the help of structured interview schedule, checklist, REBA worksheet and scale. Interview schedule was used for collecting data on personal and family profile. Information on medical history, availability of infrastructure facility in health care industry, occupational details of nurses, occupational hazards. Psycho-social cost of nursing work like sleep, sleepiness and related disorders, nutrition and health, and social consequences were gathered with the help of checklist. Postural discomfort while performing different group of activities by the nurses was assessed with the help of REBA technique. Job satisfaction scale was used to find out the satisfaction derived from the nursing job. This data was collected from 120 nurses.

**Phase II** – Experimental data was collected from 12 randomly selected nurses while working and at rest which included parameters like blood pressure, heart rate, respiration rate, and lactate level of the nurses.

All the information received through data sheets were categorized and analyzed using both descriptive (frequency, percentage, average, percentile, standard deviation and weighted mean score) and the experimental analysis (percentage and mean), statistical analysis (Chi-square, ANOVA).

## Results of the Study

The mean age of all the nurses was 39.96 ± 0.77 years whereas, for nurses particularly from Government and private hospitals, mean age was 35.76 ± 1.02 and 33.84 ± 1.16 years respectively. Regarding educational status, majority (54.17 per cent) of them were graduate followed by 37.50 per cent who had education up to intermediate. In case of nurses from Government hospitals, 67.14 per cent nurses were graduate and 48 per cent nurses from private hospitals were educated till intermediate. In total, 60.83 per cent nurses were having nursing diploma majority, i.e 91.43 per cent of them were from Government hospitals. The marital status of nurses showed that 88.33 per cent nurses were married (91.43 per cent from Government hospitals and 84 per cent from private hospitals). Mean income of nurses was found as Rs. 13,674 per month ± 621.31 (Rs. 17,960 per month ± 559.79 in case of Government hospitals and Rs.7,471 per month ± 541.32 in private hospitals).

Regarding type of family of nurses, nuclear family system (65.83 per cent) was more prevalent as compared to joint family (34.17 per cent). About 73.33 per cent nurses were having family composition of 1-4 members followed by family composition of 4-8 members among 26.67 per cent. It was observed that family members of most of the nurses (70 per cent) fell into the age category of more than 30 years. As far as education of family members of nurses was concerned, 38.33 per cent members were educated up to high school followed by 25.83 per cent who were graduate and above and very few (only 5 per cent) were illiterate. Most (70.83 per cent) of the nurses belonged to service class family followed by 29.17 per cent from business class family. Mean family income was Rs. 30,822 per month ± 842.34 (Rs. 33,651±1,128.34 per month for nurses from Government hospitals and Rs. 26,860±1,037.56 per month for nurses from private hospitals).

Medical history of nurses revealed that 40 per cent nurses were suffering from headache, whereas a few (17.50 per cent) nurses were suffering from back pain. In case of nurses from government hospitals, temporary headache due to job was reported by 27.14 per cent nurses and in private hospitals 42 per cent nurses reported temporary back-pain due to job. About chronic illness, most prevalent was anemia among 19.17 per cent nurses on the whole and in Government hospitals, most frequent chronic illness was blood pressure (17.14 per cent) which was continuous due to other sources rather than job and in private hospitals temporary problem of anaemia due to other sources was prevalent among 12 per cent nurses. Most common symptom was tiredness among 44.17 per cent nurses out of which 37.14 per cent nurses from government hospitals reported temporary tiredness from job and 22 per cent nurses from private hospitals. Among psychological problems, fatigue in patient care was felt by 41.67 per cent nurses on the whole. Particularly in government hospitals temporary fatigue in patient care due to job was reported by 38.57 per cent nurses and in private hospitals, 18 per cent nurses reported following, i.e. feeling of increased negativity, irritation from job, greater physical demand and fatigue in patient care which were temporary in nature.

About 33 per cent nurses were receiving medication for illness comprising 47.14 per cent from government hospitals and 14 per cent nurses from private hospitals. Nurses reported type of illness as blood pressure (16.67 per cent), diabetes (12.50 per cent), thyroid (2.5 per cent) and gallstone (1.67 per cent).

Regarding hospitalization faced by the nurses ever in their life, it was found that 11.17 per cent nurses were hospitalized out of which 8.57 per cent nurses were from government hospitals and 16 per cent from private hospitals. Only 1.67 per cent nurses on the whole undergone surgery for gall bladder. Only 7.5 per cent nurses in total were well protected from dangerous substances out of that 12 per cent belonged to government hospitals and 4.29 per cent nurses from private hospitals. The detail about sick leaves taken by nurses during past 6 months revealed that very few (4.17 per cent) nurses had taken 2-3 days sick leaves followed by 2.5 per cent nurses with 1 week leave.

Data regarding caffeine consumption concluded that on the whole 40 per cent nurses consumed tea for 1-2 time per shift followed by 23.33 per cent nurses who had tea for 3-4 time. Coffee was taken by comparatively few nurses (10 per cent). Data related to physical exercise performed by nurses showed that only 18.33 per cent nurses on the whole were performing daily exercise.

Nutritional status of nurses showed that majority (72.5 per cent) of the nurses were able to take full meals daily in which 70 per cent nurses were from government hospitals and 76 per cent from private hospitals. A good proportion of nurses, i.e. 52.86 and 46 per cent from government and private hospitals respectively had fairly good appetite.

Job duration of nurses revealed that majority (52.5 per cent) of nurses worked as nurses for less than 5 years. Particularly in case of government hospitals, it was found that 38.57 per cent nurses were having job experience of more than 15 years, whereas in private hospitals, 90 per cent nurses had job experience of less than 5 years. All the nurses of government and private hospitals were full time permanent employee. Regarding type of job shift, maximum (50.83 per cent) of the nurses were working on rotation of 8 hours job comprised 58.57 per cent nurses from government hospitals and 40 per cent nurses from private hospitals. About 35 per cent nurses had 15 days duration of shift whereas data in a particular category revealed that in government hospitals, 38.57 per cent nurses had a shift for 10 days, whereas in case of nurses from private hospitals, 44 per cent nurses were having shift duration for 15 days. Preference for shift revealed that maximum of the 44.17 per cent nurses preferred 6 hours morning to day shift. Regarding change of shift, 65 per cent nurses changed their shift (95.71 per cent nurses from government hospitals and 22 per cent from private hospitals). As far as frequency of changing the shift was concerned, majority (57.50 per cent) of nurses had no set pattern including 82.86 per cent nurses from government hospitals and 22 per cent from private hospitals. There was change in the shift when call is received from the hospital as reported by 58.33 per cent nurses (87.14 per cent from government and 18 per cent from private hospitals).

Overtime work was reported by 40 per cent nurses on the whole in which majority of nurses belonged to private hospitals (84 per cent). Duration of overtime was 6-8 hours per week as reported by 23.33 per cent in totality. In case of nurses from government hospitals, only 8.57 per cent of nurses worked overtime for 4-6 hour/week, whereas 56 per cent nurses from private hospitals worked for 6-8 hours per week for overtime work. Data regarding dual role of nurses between shift work and family activities showed that 53.33 per cent nurses were facing struggle to do the two jobs, out of which 34.29 per cent nurses from government hospitals and 80 per cent nurses were from private hospitals.

On the whole, 73.33 per cent nurses reduced their work stress with tea and coffee, in which majority (78.57 per cent) of nurses were from government hospitals. With regard to opinion of nurses about themselves, it was found out that 30 per cent nurses each from government and private hospitals searched for social support to reduce their stress.

As far as activities performed by nurses were concerned it was revealed that all the nurses from government hospitals were performing activities like help in medical tests, giving medicine, injury care, measuring blood pressure and heart rate for less than 20 times and for less than 40 minutes whereas in private hospitals, activities like help in medical tests, giving medicine, injury care, measuring blood pressure and heart rate were performed for less than 20 times by all the nurses and for 40-80 minutes by 86 per cent, 72 per cent, 86 per cent and 72 per cent nurses respectively.

The medical equipments which were most frequently used by the nurses both from government as well as private hospitals were heart rate monitor, weighing machine, ECG, ultrasound machine, X-ray machine, instrument sterilizer, paediatric equipment, dental instruments, autoclaves, obstetric labour tables telescope, ophthalmic instruments, orthopedic instruments, endoscopic instruments, ICU bed for less than 20 times and less than 40 minutes duration in a day. In case of handling of medical accessories like medical disposable and dressing bandages, these were used by all the nurses from government hospitals for less than 20 times and less than 40 minutes and among nurses from private hospitals, medicine trolley, dressing trolleys, food service cart, dressing bowl, commode chair were used for less than 20 times and for less than 40 minutes. It was again revealed that chair was used by 38.57 per cent nurses from government hospitals for more than

40 times and all the nurses used it for less than 40 minutes, whereas all nurses from private hospitals used furniture like wheel chair, stool and baby cradle for less than 20 times and for less than 40 minutes.

Regarding comfort or discomfort associated with furniture, 11.67 per cent nurses reported that their furniture is too high to sit comprised 12.86 per cent nurses from government and 10 per cent nurses from private hospitals. Hard textured furniture was felt by 21.67 per cent nurses from government and 34 per cent nurses from private hospitals. Maximum (14.29 per cent) nurses from government hospitals reported their furniture is cushioned. The data pertaining to material used in furniture showed that majority (90.83 per cent) of nurses had wooden furniture. In case of nurses from government hospitals maximum (85.71 per cent) had wooden furniture. Regarding nurses from private hospitals majority (98 per cent) of them possessed wooden furniture. Maximum (47.5 per cent) nurses on the whole reported that their furniture had properly fixed wheels.

Experience in handling medical equipment while performing tasks by nurses from government hospitals revealed that highest mean value was given to blood pressure apparatus and oxygen therapy instrument (2.44 each) by 47.14 per cent and 62.86 per cent nurses respectively thus found as comfortable. Least mean score value (1.71) was calculated for X-ray machine by 50 per cent nurses and was found uncomfortable. Nurses from private hospitals gave highest mean score value (2.94) for blood pressure apparatus which was found to be comfortable by 94 per cent nurses, whereas obstetric labour table telescope was found as uncomfortable with mean score as 2.06 by 26 per cent nurses. Among medical accessories, most comfortable was armoire/wardrobe as reported by 57.14 per cent nurses from government hospitals, while sanitary gloves were found to be uncomfortable by 45 per cent nurses. About 68 per cent nurses from private hospitals gave highest mean score (2.68) to surgical table reported to be comfortable, whereas washbasin stand got the least mean score of 1.42 by 33 per cent of nurses. Most comfortable furniture (mean score 2.57) was hospital stretcher by 57.14 per cent nurses, whereas hospital chair was uncomfortable (mean score 1.69) by 52.86 per cent nurses from government hospitals and in private hospitals stand, racks and hospital stretcher were found to be comfortable (mean score of 2.68) by 68 per cent nurses, whereas hospital bed and chair were somewhat uncomfortable by 68 per cent nurses.

Mechanical hazards as faced by nurses revealed that majority of the nurses (94.17 per cent) had repetitive motion and awkward posture during work schedule consisted of all nurses from government hospitals and 86 per cent nurses from private hospitals. Skin rashes/allergy were reported by 13.33 per cent nurses (17.14 per cent from government and 8 per cent nurses from private hospitals). Most of the nurses (40.83 per cent) got injured with solvents and dust allergy. On the whole, 60 per cent nurses felt noise hazards including 42.86 per cent nurses from government hospitals and 84 per cent nurses from private hospitals. Majority of the nurses (95 per cent) felt fatigue from shift work (91.43 per cent nurses from government and all the nurses from private hospitals).

The maximum temperature ranged from 22.3°C to 27.4°C in patient ward and duty room of government hospitals while in case of private hospitals, the range was 25.3°C to 30.12°C both in patient ward and duty room. The humidity ranged from 42.25 to 55.5 per cent from government to private hospitals. It was observed that illumination was more at patient ward 865.5 lux and 888.25 lux of government and private hospitals as compared to duty room of both categories of hospitals (806 and 847.5 lux). Further, the noise level varied from 58.9 to 73.88 dB in government and private hospitals.

On an average in government hospitals, major problems were poor air circulation and overall poor physical environment in patient wards by 35.71 per cent nurses each. Again problems were more in patient wards of private hospitals in which maximum, i.e. 62 per cent complained of highly noisy area.

Sleep time of majority (60.83 per cent) of the nurses was 10 pm in night and about 49 per cent nurses took 10 minute to sleep. Sleep off time was 5 pm by 74.17 per cent nurses. On the whole, 64.17 per cent nurses felt fresh in the morning, out of that 58.57 per cent nurses from government hospitals and 72 per cent nurses were from private hospitals. About 28 per cent nurses reported fluctuation in their bed and rise time comprised 12.86 per cent from government and 50 per cent nurses from private hospitals. Fluctuation in bed and rise time on holidays was reported by 80 per cent of nurses. Majority of nurses, i.e. 80 per cent were able to take more than 8 hours sleep. It was revealed that 18.33 per cent nurses were disturbed due to poor sleep quality (24.29 per cent nurses from government hospitals and 10 per cent nurses from private hospitals).

Cold sleeping area and snoring problem were the most dominant factors affecting sleep quality of 47.5 per cent and 39.17 per cent nurses respectively. Majority of the nurses (73.33 per cent) have to go to toilet resulting in disturbance in sleep. Trouble sleeping revealed that 17.14 per cent nurses from government hospitals were not able to sleep within 30 minutes for past 1 month, whereas 44 per cent nurses from private hospitals had troubled sleeping during a week.

Troubled awakening concluded that about 78 per cent nurses (37.14 per cent nurses from government and 64 per cent nurses from private hospitals) were not able to stay awake in rest period during a week. Majority (78.33 per cent) of nurses reported book reading as supplement to induce sleep (41.43 per cent nurses from government and 68 per cent from private hospitals during a week and twice a week respectively). The problems as reported by nurses were increased yawning by 45 per cent nurses on the whole. In case of government hospitals, 21.43 per cent nurses felt headache while 40 per cent from private felt bodyache.

Social consequences of nursing job revealed that in case of nurses from government hospitals, highest mean score (2.83) was computed for the statement, i.e. job subjects to potential legal liability. The statement, viz. physical assault during job obtained lowest mean score of 1. In case of private hospitals, nurses gave highest mean score (3.50) to the statement, i.e. they have primary responsibility for childcare duties and the statements like job exposes to verbal abuse and physical harm scored lowest mean.

Job satisfaction among nurses from government hospitals, revealed that highest mean score (2.60) was given to the statements like 'I am regular for my work' as reported by 62 per cent nurses. The statements such as "loose self-confidence" and "job stress and unrest" were given least mean score. In case of nurses from private hospitals, highest mean score was given to the statement, viz. receive recognition when a job was done well and statement "there is job stress and unrest" got lowest mean score (1.10).

Anthropometric measurements of the nurses, it was observed that the mean body height of the nurses from ground and above seat were 115.77 and 70.15 cm respectively. Mean eye height from ground was 105.34 cm and above seat was 64.46 cm. Mean shoulder height of nurses from ground and above seat was calculated as 90.03 and 59.40 cm respectively. The mean elbow rest height from ground and above seat were found as 68.17 cm. 22.65 cm, mean knee height above ground as 46.82 cm, mean popliteal height above ground as 42.06 cm, mean buttock popliteal length as 43.13 cm, mean buttock knee length as 51.82 cm, mean thigh height as 13.28 cm, hip breadth as 35.49 cm, mean hand length of nurses as 16.8 cm, finger to shoulder length as 62.75 cm were found out.

The mean weight of the nurses was 58.20±0.54 kg comprised 57.62±0.69 kg for nurses from government hospitals and 56.96±0.85 kg for nurses from private hospitals. The mean height of the nurses was 155.33±0.72 including 153.23±0.94 cm for nurses from government and 152.49±1.13 cm for nurses in private hospitals. About 69 per cent of nurses had normal BMI and only 8.33 per cent nurses were found in category II.

Per cent increase in blood pressure and pulse rate, heart rate, and energy expenditure was maximum for group III activities. Regarding perceived exertion, nurses involved in group III activities felt weak to strong exertion with mean rating of 4.5 followed by somewhat less mean RPE, i.e. 3.75 each in case of group I and II activities.

A sum total of 37.5 per cent nurses were found in $AL_3$ category which interprets high risk level and action is required now. Again, 7.5 per cent nurses were observed in $AL_2$ category indicating medium risk and change in posture is required soon.

In majority of nurses, the test report of pulmonary function after work was mild obstacles.

Lactate analysis report of nurses showed that group II and III activities were more tiring as compared to group I.

The test of hypothesis showed that action categories of REBA postural analysis technique were independent of various activities performed by nurses. The results of ANOVA technique indicated that average blood pressure, heart rate and energy expenditure rate were significantly higher in case of group III activities as compared to other groups. Significant association was observed between sleep quality and performance capacity, job satisfaction and working condition, job satisfaction and coordination within department, job satisfaction and time demand, job satisfaction and infrastructure facility available at the hospitals.

## Conclusions

On the basis of findings of this investigation, the following conclusions were drawn:

1. The mean age of nurses of government and private hospitals was 35.76 ± 1.02 and 33.84 ± 1.16 years respectively.
2. Most of the nurses (54.17 per cent) were graduate and a large proportion of nurses (60.83 per cent) were having nursing diploma.
3. Majority (88.33 per cent) of nurses were married.
4. Mean income of nurses was Rs. 13,674 per month ± 621.31. Mean family income was Rs. 30,822 per month ± 842.34.
5. Major proportion of nurses (65.83 per cent) belonged to nuclear family system.

6. A higher percentage of nurses belonged to service class family.
7. The most common illness among nurses was headache, anaemia in chronic illness and tiredness were found. Among psychological problems, fatigue in patient care was also felt by the nurses.
8. A small proportion of nurses were receiving medication for illness. The main illness was blood pressure.
9. A small proportion of nurses were hospitalized and only 7.5 per cent nurses were well protected from dangerous substances.
10. Very few nurses took 2-3 days sick leaves in past 6 months.
11. Exercise was performed by a small proportion of nurses.
12. Most of the nurses were able to take full meal daily and at the same time on each shift.
13. A good proportion of nurses had fairly good quality of appetite.
14. Most of the nurses had job experience of less than 5 years. All the nurses were full time permanent employees.
15. About half percentage of nurses were working on rotation of 8 hours job (58.57 per cent nurses from government hospitals and 40 per cent from private hospitals).
16. Maximum, i.e. 35 per cent nurses had 15 days duration of shift. About 65 per cent nurses changed their shift. Out of that, nearly 58 per cent nurses changed their shift when call is received from the hospital.
17. Nearly 40 per cent nurses worked overtime. Duration of overtime was 6-8 hours per week among 23.33 per cent nurses.
18. Half of the nurses faced struggle to do the job due to dual role, out of that, 47.14 per cent nurses from government and all nurses from private hospitals faced struggle.

19. Maximum of nurses spent their personal time with taking tea/coffee and with their family.
20. About 30 per cent nurses each from government and private hospitals searched for social support to reduce their stress.
21. Major activities performed by nurses were help in medical tests, giving medicine, injury care (dressing), measuring B.P. and measuring heart rate.
22. Most frequently used medical equipments were weighing machine, ultrasound machine, X-ray machine, oxygen therapy instrument, sterilizer instrument and B.P. apparatus.
23. Most frequently used medical accessories were glucose drips, dressing bandages, and patient gowns and the mostly used furniture were hospital beds, wheel chair, stool, bed-side table, baby cradle.
24. Very few nurses reported furniture is too high or too low. Hard texture was felt by 21.67 per cent nurses and majority of them had wooden furniture. About 39.17 per cent nurses had heavy furniture.
25. As far as comfortability of handling of medical equipment was concerned, highest mean value was given to BP apparatus and oxygen therapy instrument. Most comfortable medical accessories and furniture were wardrobe and hospital stretcher respectively.
26. Majority of nurses faced mechanical hazards like repetitive motion and awkward posture during work. Skin infection as biological hazard, hazards with solvents and dust, noise as physical hazards and fatigue from shift-work as pycho-social hazards were also faced.
27. Environmental parameters like temperature, humidity, illumination and noise were high in patient ward as compared to duty room of the hospitals.
28. In government as well as private hospitals, major problems regarding environment were present in patient wards which were poor air circulation, overall poor physical environment and highly noisy area.

29. Nearly 49.17 per cent nurses took less than 10 minutes to sleep and a handsome proportion of nurses felt fresh in the morning.
30. About 28.33 per cent reported fluctuation in their bed and rise time. Fluctuation in bed and rise time on holidays was reported by majority of nurses.
31. Most of nurses were able to take more than 8 hours sleep and few nurses were bothered by poor sleep quality.
32. Problems of cold sleeping area and snoring were reported by nurses, which affected their sleep quality at workplace.
33. Trouble sleeping among nurses revealed that these nurses were frequently going to toilet due to above and were not able to sleep with in 30 minutes.
34. Majority of the nurses were not able to awake during rest period, while watching television and during sitting and reading. Nurses reported book reading as supplement to induce sleep.
35. Problems of nurses related with awakening were increased yawning, low mood and irritability and headache.
36. In social consequences of nursing job, highest mean score was computed for statement, i.e. "job subjects to potential legal liability" among nurses from government hospitals and in private hospitals, nurses gave highest mean score to statement, viz. "they have primary responsibility for child care duties".
37. Job satisfaction among nurses from government hospitals, revealed that highest mean score value was given to statement "I am regular for my work", whereas for nurses from private hospitals, highest mean score was calculated for statement, viz. "receive recognition when a job is done well".
38. Mean body height of the nurses from ground and above seat were 115.77 and 70.15 cm respectively, mean shoulder height above seat (59.40 cm), mean elbow rest height above seat (22.65 cm), mean popliteal height

(42.06 cm), mean buttock popliteal length (43.13 cm), hip breadth (35.49 cm), mean hand length (16.8 cm) and mean finger to shoulder length as found as 62.75 cm.

39. The mean weight of the nurses was 58.20 ± 0.54 kg, mean height of the nurses was 155.33 ± 0.71 cm and 69.71 per cent nurses had normal BMI.
40. Per cent increase in blood pressure, heart rate, and energy expenditure was maximum for group III activities. Nurses involved in group III activities felt weak to strong exertion.
41. A total of 37.5 per cent nurses were in $AL_3$ category indicating that they were at high risk level.
42. The test report of pulmonary function was normal among most of the nurses.
43. Lactate analysis showed that group II and III activities were more tiring as compared to group I.
44. Action categories of REBA postural analysis technique are independent of various activities performed by nurses.
45. Test results showed significant difference in mean Blood Pressure, mean Heart Rate and Energy Expenditure Rate during performance of group III activities as compared to Group I and II.
46. Chi-square test showed that performance capacity of nurses was dependent on the sleep quality of the nurses.
47. Tests results revealed that job satisfaction was the result of good working condition available at the workplace.
48. The chi-square test showed that there was a significant association between job satisfaction and communication skills, job satisfaction and coordination within department, job satisfaction and time demand, job satisfaction and infrastructure facility available at the hospitals.

**Implications of the Study**

I. **For Policy Makers:** 24 hours working society require immediate attention and therefore, it is the policy-makers who should be activated. There is a sharp impact of unsociable hours of work on the health and performance of nurses who are partner of 24 hours working society since ages. It is important for the policy-makers of health service organizations that personal, socio-cultural and environmental perspective of the nurses be given due attention. Shift planning should be arranged in such a way that it does not create any physiological and psychological stress. Policies should be worked out for effective napping techniques and to improve the environment. The provision of effective facilities can help the shift workers to cope better.

- Give attention to the work environment. Do not widely separate work stations so that workers at night can remain in contact with one another.
- Provide rest facilities where possible.
- Provide good cafeteria services so a balanced diet can be maintained. The nutritional needs differ between day shifts and other shifts because of circadian rhythms.
- Consider facilities for social activities or recreational opportunities.
- Consider access to quality day-care for shift workers' children.

II. **For Doctors:** Nurses deal with a variety of tasks for long periods, in absence of doctors. Nurse has the supreme role of handling the patients. In such situation, a cooperative hand of doctor to a nurse can help to have any ill effect on the nurses as well as to the care of patients. Therefore, it is recommended that a noticeable sharing of responsibility on the part of doctor will minimize the physiological, psycho-social cost of work of nurses.

III. **For Nurses:** Professional nursing organizations should take the lead in setting the standards that will protect nurses both in and out of the workplace. If they fail to recognize and address sleep deprivation as a serious health issue, nursing shortage will be more acute. Nurse managers/matron has a responsibility to formulate strategies to assist those who find it difficult to work at night. For shift worker (nurses), the research enforces the importance of family support and family involvement in moderating shift work's potentially negative effects. Strategies are needed to assist nurses to promote sleep health within the complex context of their own sleep needs, organizational demands, and domestic responsibilities. Education in stress recognition and reduction techniques is helpful.

## Recommendations to Fill the Research Gaps on Nurses in Night Shift System

Health care industry is one of the biggest industry providing employment to a large portion of the population. Services provided by employee in such health care industries are the rays of hope to the patient community. Better nursing practices are influenced by functional environments and efficient nursing practices and approaches in hospitals have been associated with better care of patients. Worsening nursing shortage, poor working schedule and poor infrastructure facility available in the health care centre required attention at national level. Need is to improve the nursing practices and working environment as a strategy to make the profession more attractive and to retain nurses at the bedside.

Some facts about nursing job in health care industry are as below:

- The variation exist between male and female nurses in terms of physical dimensions, performance capacity, physical strength, social impacts of the jobs, satisfaction derived from job, and the various psychological aspects related to tension, stress management, fatigue, coordination with the authority and the colleagues etc., thus, a study on male and female nurses based on above stated parameters be conducted.

- The impact of *nap* on the performance of nurses of both sexes must be studied with different job rotations.
- Pre and post-training on the performance of nurses (male and female) in different patient handling activities required attention.
- Information on anthropometric measurements of different furniture and work stations should be collected to study mismatches of furniture and workstation with users (male and female nurses and patients). Based on this ergonomically designing of furniture and workstation should be undertaken.
- The problem of musculoskeletal disorders are found very common problems in all occupational industries. Therefore, studies related to musculoskeletal disorders (including cardio vascular and cardio respiratory system, fatigue, workplace morbidity, ECG, risk and injury) should be undertaken in health industry in particular.
- Studies on sleep quality of health care personnel working in different shifts, morningness or eveningness pattern among male and female nurses should be undertaken.
- **Research Kits Like** General Health Questionnaire, Stanford Health Assessment Questionnaire, Generic Job Satisfaction Scale, Self-assessment questionnaire to determine morningness-eveningness in human circadian rhythm, Minnesota satisfaction questionnaire, NIOSH generic job stress questionnaire, Sleep Disorders Inventory, Stanford Sleepiness Scale, Mood Assessment Scale and **NAPS Pittsburg Sleep Quality Index (PSQI) should be exercised in future researches on different issues of male and female nurses.**

# Annexures

*ANNEXURE-1*

## Interview Schedule

---

**SCHEDULE NO** **HOSPITAL-**

***Section – 1***

**(A) Personal and family profile**

(1) Name of the Respondent ____________________

(2) Age (Yrs)

(3) Educational Qualification (Highest education)

(a) High School

(b) Intermediate

(c) Graduate

(d) Nursing diploma

(e) Any other, specify

(4) Marital status-

(a) Married,

(b) Unmarried,

(c) Single, divorced,

(d) Single, widowed

(5) Income (Rs./month) | | | | | |

(6) Type of Family

(a) Nuclear

(b) Joint

(c) Extended

(7) Demographic profile

| Members | Relation with family members | Age (Years) | Education | Occupation | Income (Rs./month) |
|---|---|---|---|---|---|
| | | | | | |

Total income - Rs./month

Family income from all sources_______________

## (B) Medical History/Health Profile

1. State the illness suffered by you during the last one year—

| S. No. Illness | Occurrence | | Type of illness | | | |
|---|---|---|---|---|---|---|
| | Yes | No | Temporary | | Continuous | |
| | | | From job | From other sources | From job | From other sources |
| **Physiological problems** | | | | | | |
| **(a) Common illness** | | | | | | |
| 1. Cough, cold, fever | | | | | | |
| 2. Headache | | | | | | |
| 3. Body-ache | | | | | | |
| 4. Back-pain | | | | | | |
| 5. Skin-rashes, Allergy | | | | | | |
| 6. Wounds | | | | | | |
| 7. Any other | | | | | | |
| **(b) Chronic illness** | | | | | | |
| 1. Diabetes Mellitus | | | | | | |
| 2. Tuberculosis | | | | | | |
| 3. Respiratory diseases | | | | | | |
| 4. BP problem | | | | | | |
| 5. Heart disease | | | | | | |
| 6. Arthiritis | | | | | | |
| 7. Epilepsy | | | | | | |

| | | | | | | |
|---|---|---|---|---|---|---|
| 8. Anaemia | | | | | | |
| 9. Stroke | | | | | | |
| 10. Insomnia | | | | | | |
| 11. Hypertension | | | | | | |
| 12. Gastrointestinal disorders | | | | | | |
| 13. Back problem | | | | | | |
| 14. Ischemia | | | | | | |
| 15. Thyroid | | | | | | |
| 16. Any other | | | | | | |
| **(c) Symptoms** | | | | | | |
| 1. Muscle tightness | | | | | | |
| 2. Hand trembling | | | | | | |
| 3. Excessive perspiration | | | | | | |
| 4. Dizziness | | | | | | |
| 5. Tiredness | | | | | | |
| 6. Difficulty in standing, bending, lifting or other movements | | | | | | |
| 7. Any other | | | | | | |
| **Psychological problems** | | | | | | |
| 1. Increased negativity and Irritation | | | | | | |
| 2. Job strain | | | | | | |
| 3. Greater physical demand | | | | | | |
| 4. More relationship problem | | | | | | |
| 5. Depression | | | | | | |
| 6. Frequent bad mood | | | | | | |
| 7. Inability to concentrate | | | | | | |
| 8. Lack of energy | | | | | | |
| 9. Memory loss | | | | | | |
| 10. Poor communication | | | | | | |
| 11. Arrogant | | | | | | |
| 12. Postural Fatigue | | | | | | |
| 13. Fatigue in patient care | | | | | | |
| 14. Sleep deprivation | | | | | | |

| 15. Work failure | | | | | | |
|---|---|---|---|---|---|---|
| 16. Performance anxiety | | | | | | |
| 17. Fear of crowd | | | | | | |
| 18. Emotional outbursts | | | | | | |
| 19. Anger outbursts | | | | | | |
| 20. Crying spells | | | | | | |
| 21. Work related stress | | | | | | |
| 22. Low self-confidence | | | | | | |
| 23. Frequent absenteeism | | | | | | |
| 24. Low motivation | | | | | | |
| 25. Any other | | | | | | |

2. Are you taking any form of medication at present? Yes/No
3. If yes, mention the illness.________
4. Have you undergone any operation/surgery during last one year. Yes/No
5. If yes, which type of surgery. ___________
6. Any illness which may have originated due to work stress. Yes/No
7. If yes, mention the illness.
8. How many days' leave for ailments did you avail during the past 6 months—
   __________Days,__________Week,___________Month
9. Do you spend time on physical exercise. Yes/No
10. If yes, state the frequency—

| | **20 min** | **30 min** | **1 hour** |
|---|---|---|---|
| Daily | | | |
| Twice a week | | | |
| Thrice a week | | | |

11. On an average working day, do you consume following—

| *Items* | *Frequency* | |
|---|---|---|
| | 1-2 times | 3-4 times |
| Tobacco | | |
| Tea | | |
| Coffee | | |
| Any other | | |

12. Do you take out time for yourself beside work. Yes/No
13. If yes , what do you do—
    (a) Listen to your favourite music to relax
    (b) Just lying on the bed
    (c) Taking tea or coffee
    (d) Indulge in pleasurable activities like go for outings, go for movies
    (e) Spend time with your family
    (f) Cooking
    (g) Reading favourite magazines
    (h) Play
    (i) Yoga
    (j) Watching T.V.
    (k) Any other
14. Score the following statements:

| **Statements** | **Much less than usual** | **Same as usual** | **More than usual** |
|---|---|---|---|
| Score | 1 | 2 | 3 |

(a) Are you able to enjoy normal day-to-day activities?
(b) Do you lose self-confidence in yourself?
(c) Are you getting edgy and bad tempered?
(d) Do you get frightened with crowded places?
(e) Do you feel the inability to relax?
(f) Do you feel losing your balance?
(g) Do you search for social support to reduce your stress?

**(C) Anthropometric Measurements (Sitting position)**

1. Stature height
2. Body weight
3. Body height from ground
4. Body height above seat
5. Eye height from ground
6. Eye height above seat
7. Shoulder height from ground
8. Shoulder height above seat
9. Elbow height from ground
10. Elbow height above seat
11. Knee height above ground
12. Popliteal height above ground
13. Buttock popliteal length
14. Buttock knee length
15. Thigh clearance height
16. Hip breadth
17. Hand length
18. Finger to shoulder length

***Section – 2***

**Report of nurses regarding environmental parameters at workplace**

***(1) Environmental parameters***

1. Highly noisy work area
2. Poor lighting
3. Comfortable temperature during summer
4. Comfortable temperature during winter
5. Too high humidity
6. Too low humidity
7. Poor air circulation
8. Pollution free air
9. Crowded area
10. Overall poor physical environment
11. Any other

### *(2) Medical equipments/Scientific gadgets handled*

| | Equipments | Frequency in time per day | | | Duration in min per day | | |
|---|---|---|---|---|---|---|---|
| | **Scientific gadgets** | **<20** | **20-40** | **>40** | **<40** | **40-80** | **>80** |
| 1. | BP apparatus | | | | | | |
| 2. | Heart rate monitor | | | | | | |
| 3. | Weighing machine | | | | | | |
| 4. | ECG | | | | | | |
| 5. | Ultrasound machine | | | | | | |
| 6. | X-ray machine | | | | | | |
| 7. | Thermometers | | | | | | |
| 8. | Oxygen therapy instrument | | | | | | |
| 9. | First aid kit | | | | | | |
| 10. | Incubator | | | | | | |
| 11. | Instrument sterilizer | | | | | | |
| 12. | Paediatric equipment | | | | | | |
| 13. | Dental instruments | | | | | | |
| 14. | Autoclaves | | | | | | |
| 15. | Obstetric labour tables telescope | | | | | | |
| 16. | Gynaecological instruments | | | | | | |
| 17. | Ophthalmic instruments | | | | | | |
| 18. | Orthopedic instruments | | | | | | |
| 19. | Endoscopic instruments | | | | | | |
| 20. | ICU bed | | | | | | |
| | **Medical accessories** | | | | | | |
| 21. | Medicine trolley | | | | | | |
| 22. | Dressing trolley | | | | | | |
| 23. | Food service cart | | | | | | |
| 24. | Dressing bowl | | | | | | |
| 25. | Instrument trolley | | | | | | |
| 26. | Surgical table | | | | | | |
| 27. | Wash basin stand | | | | | | |
| 28. | Commode Chair | | | | | | |
| 29. | Armoires/Wardrobe | | | | | | |

| Equipments | | Frequency in time per day | | | Duration in min per day | | |
|---|---|---|---|---|---|---|---|
| | **Scientific gadgets** | **<20** | **20-40** | **>40** | **<40** | **40-80** | **>80** |
| 30 | Hearing phone | | | | | | |
| 31. | Sanitory gloves | | | | | | |
| 32. | Glucose drips | | | | | | |
| 33. | Medical disposable | | | | | | |
| 34. | Dressing bandages | | | | | | |
| 35. | Patients' gown | | | | | | |
| 36. | Knifes, blades | | | | | | |
| 37. | Surgical sponges, forceps | | | | | | |
| 38. | Chemicals, glasswares | | | | | | |
| | **Furniture and furnishings** | | | | | | |
| 39 | Hospital beds | | | | | | |
| 40. | Hospital chairs | | | | | | |
| 41. | Hospital stretcher | | | | | | |
| 42. | Wheel chair | | | | | | |
| 43. | Stool | | | | | | |
| 44. | Stands and racks | | | | | | |
| 45. | Hospital bedside table | | | | | | |
| 46. | Baby cradle | | | | | | |

*(3) Furniture details and comfort/discomfort of nurses*

**Dimensional features of furniture**

1. Too high
2. Too low
3. Narrow
4. Too deep

**Structural features of furniture**

1. Hard texture
2. Sharp edges
3. Cushioned

**Material used in furniture**

1. Wooden
2. Metallic
3. Plastic
4. Painted

**Others**

1. Is the furniture heavy rather than lightweight?
2. Is the chair/table/bed sturdy when you put pressure on frame?
3. Are there plastic or rubber gliding tips on the ends of the legs?
4. Are the wheels fixed properly?

*Section – 3*

**Occupational details of nurses**

1. Duration of job. Years____ Months_____
2. Type of job
   a. Full time permanent employee
   b. Part-time permanent employee
   c. Casual
   d. Others
3. Type of job shift
   a. Rotating 6-hours shift
   b. Rotating 8-hours shift
   c. Rotating 12-hours shift
   d. Permanent day shift
   e. Permanent evening shift
   f. Permanent night shift
4. Duration of shift Years_____Months_____Days____
5. If you work on a rotating shift, which pattern would you like to follow—
   (a) 6-hours shift
      1. Morning to day
      2. Day to night
   (b) 12- hours shift
      (1) Morning to day
      (2) Day to night
6. Do you change your shift? Yes/No
7. If yes, give frequency
   (a) 2 times
   (b) More than 2 times
   (c) No set pattern
   (d) Any other

8. Give reasons for changing shift—
   (a) Ill health
   (b) Disturbed mood
   (c) On call from hospital
   (d) Any other
      (i) Do you work over-time? Yes/No
      (ii) If yes, state the duration____hours/week
9. Do you work on any other job? Yes/No
   (a) If yes, state the nature of job_______
   (b) _________hours/week
10. Do you struggle between your shiftwork and family activities? Yes/No
11 Rate your performance
   (a) Poor, (b) Average, (c) Good, (d) Very good (e) Excellent
12. Type of activities performed by nurses—

| Activities | Frequency | | | Duration | | |
|---|---|---|---|---|---|---|
| | <20 | 20-40 | >40 | <40 | 40-80 | >80 |
| 1. Help in medical tests | | | | | | |
| 2. Giving medicine | | | | | | |
| 3. Injury care | | | | | | |
| 4. Measuring B.P. | | | | | | |
| 5. Measuring heart rate | | | | | | |
| 6. Assisting in surgery | | | | | | |
| 7. Dripping | | | | | | |
| 8. Supervision on health and infection control | | | | | | |
| 9. First aid and emergency | | | | | | |
| 10. Record keeping | | | | | | |
| 11. Giving injection | | | | | | |
| 12. Drug administration, care and storage | | | | | | |
| 13. Bathing and toileting | | | | | | |
| 14. Mobility of patients | | | | | | |
| 15. Regular weight check-up | | | | | | |
| 16. Any other, specify | | | | | | |

13. State your experience in handling of various gadgets while performing tasks—

| List of equipments/furniture/ accessories | Handling | | |
|---|---|---|---|
| | C | SC | UC |
| **Medical equipments** | | | |
| B.P. apparatus | | | |
| Heart rate monitor | | | |
| Weighing machine | | | |
| ECG | | | |
| Ultrasound machine | | | |
| X-ray machine | | | |
| Oxygen therapy instruments | | | |
| Incubator | | | |
| Instrument sterilizer | | | |
| Autoclaves | | | |
| Obstetric labour tables telescope | | | |
| Gynaecological instruments | | | |
| Ophthalmic instruments | | | |
| Orthopedic instruments | | | |
| Endoscopic instruments | | | |
| ICU Bed | | | |
| Medical accessories | | | |
| Surgical table | | | |
| Washbasin stand | | | |
| Armoires/wardrobes | | | |
| Sanitary gloves | | | |
| Furniture and furnishings | | | |
| Hospital beds | | | |
| Hospital chair | | | |
| Baby cradle | | | |
| Wheel chair | | | |
| Stool | | | |
| Stands and racks | | | |
| Hospital stretcher | | | |
| Any other (speccify) | | | |

C—Comfortable, SC—Somewhat comfortable, UC—Uncomfortable

*Section–4*

**Occupational hazards/accidents/risks/injuries occurred since last year**

1. Have you ever been hospitalized for any reason? Yes/No
2. Did you have any accident? Yes/No
3. Did your work limited by any reason? Yes/No
4. Did your job cause this disability? Yes/No
5. Have you applied for financial benefits as a result of this disability? Yes/No
6. If yes, did you receive it? Yes/No
7. Are you well protected from exposure to dangerous substances? Yes/No

**Hazard identification checklist**

| Type of hazards | Source of hazard | Frequency of incidence |
|---|---|---|
| Mechanical/ Ergonomics/ Repetitive Strain Injuries (RSI) | Slip<br>Lifting<br>Sharp edges<br>Repetitive motion<br>Awkward posture<br>Forceful motion<br>Manual handling | |
| Biological | Rashes<br>Skin infection<br>Allergy | |
| Chemical | Asbestos | |
| | Solvents | |
| | Chlorine | |
| | Cleaning compounds | |
| | Disinfectants | |
| | Waste anaesthetic gases | |
| | Dust | |
| | Skin burn from acid | |
| Physical | Noise | |
| | Radiation | |
| | Heat | |

| Type of hazards | Source of hazard | Frequency of incidence |
|---|---|---|
| | Cold | |
| Psycho-social | Lack of control | |
| | Fatigue from shift-work | |
| | Over work | |
| | Job pressure | |
| | Job stress | |
| | Sleep disorders | |
| | Long working hours | |
| | Boring work | |
| | Threats to physical security | |

**Checklist**

*Section – 5*

**Psycho-social cost of nursing work**

**(A) Sleep, sleepiness and related disorders—**

(1) At what time usually do you sleep? am/pm

(2) How much time do you take to fall asleep each night?
(a) <10 min., (b) 10- 20 min., (c) 20-30 min.

(3) At what time do you get up during the past month. am/pm

(4) Do you feel fresh/relaxed in the morning? Yes/No

(5) Does your bed-time and rise-time fluctuate from day-to-day? Yes/No

(6) Do you change your bed-time and rise-time on holidays? Yes/No

(7) When there is no night shift or you are free to plan your day, how much sleep do you take?
(a) 4-6 hours sleep
(b) 6-8 hours sleep
(c) >8 hours sleep

(8) Are you bothered by poor sleep quality? Yes/No

(9) If no, how would you rate your sleep quality overall?
(1) Very good, (2) Fairly good,
(3) Fairly bad, (4) Very bad

10. Indicate factors affecting sleep quality at work place—
    (1) Cold sleep area
    (2) Humid
    (3) Dry
    (4) Noisy
    (5) Uncomfortable bedding
    (6) Indigestion/gas/heartburn
    (7) Asthma
    (8) Need to urinate
    (9) Cough
    (10)Snoring
    (11)Frightening dreams/nightmares
11. Does difficulty in staying asleep/falling asleep interfere with day-time functioning—

| S. No | Factors | Past 1 month | During a week | Twice a week |
|---|---|---|---|---|
| **[A]** | **Trouble sleeping** | | | |
| 1. | Cannot sleep within 30 min. | | | |
| 2. | Wake-up in mid-night | | | |
| 3. | Wake-up in early morning | | | |
| 4. | Have to go bathroom | | | |
| 5. | Cannot breath comfortably | | | |
| 6. | Coughing | | | |
| 7. | Snoring loudly | | | |
| 8. | Feeling cold | | | |
| 9. | Having bad dreams | | | |
| 10. | Having pain | | | |
| 11. | Others | | | |
| **[B]** | **Trouble awakening** | | | |
| 1. | As a passenger in the vehicle | | | |
| 2. | Working at computer | | | |
| 3. | Engaging in social activity | | | |
| 4. | Eating meals | | | |
| 5. | Sitting and reading | | | |
| 6. | Watching T.V. | | | |

| S. No | Factors | Past 1 month | During a week | Twice a week |
|---|---|---|---|---|
| 7. | Talking to someone | | | |
| 8. | In the meeting | | | |
| 9. | In rest period | | | |
| **[C]** | **Use of supplements to induce sleep** | | | |
| 1. | Sleeping pills | | | |
| 2. | Reading books | | | |
| 3. | Others | | | |
| **[D]** | **Problems related with awakening** | | | |
| 1. | Headache | | | |
| 2. | Bodyache | | | |
| 3. | Fogginess/incordination | | | |
| 4. | Dry mouth | | | |
| 5. | Experience of being temporarily paralyzed | | | |
| 6. | Increased yawning | | | |
| 7. | Drowsiness | | | |
| 8. | Low mood, irritability, anxiety | | | |

## (B) Nutrition and health

1. Do you take full meals daily? Yes/No
2. Do you take meals at the same time on each shift? Yes/No
3. Do you feel your appetite is poor? Yes/No
4. Do you receive any nutritional counselling for health maintenance? Yes/No
5. How is your appetite during first half hour after having woken in the morning?
   (a) Very poor, (b) Fairly poor,
   (c) Fairly good, (d) Very good

### (C) Social consequences

| Statements | Never | Occasionally | Sometimes | Fairly often | Very often |
|---|---|---|---|---|---|
| Score | 1 | 2 | 3 | 4 | 5 |

1. My job exposes me to verbal abuses and/or confrontations with clients or the general public.
2. My job exposes me to the threat of physical harm or injury.
3. I have been physically assaulted while performing my job.
4. My job personally subjects me to potential legal liability.
5. Shift workers altered sleep schedule lead to marital strain and disruption of social or family life.
6. I have to do struggle between my shift work and family activities.
7. I have primary responsibility for childcare duties.
8. I have primary responsibility for house cleaning duties.
9. I belong to a voluntary or religious organization at which I spend at least 5-10 hours per week.

### (D) Satisfaction scale

(1) DA—Disagree, (2) A—Agree, (3) SA—Strongly agree

1. Work conditions lead to restlessness.
2. My job is monotonous in nature.
3. Working hours are not fit.
4. I hardly get time for entertainment.
5. My job requires a great deal of concentration.
6. I am not able to give time to my family.
7. My job requires me to remember different things.
8. My job requires me to work fast.
9. My job requires me to work hard.
10. I have lost interest in activities that I use to enjoy.
11. I sometimes loose self-confidence in myself.
12. I recently have been getting edgy and bad-tempered.

13. Good work environment facilitate to work quickly and energetically.
14. People at work speak softly.
15. Members of work group are supportive.
16. I have command over quality and quantity of professional work I do.
17. My job helped me to raise standard of living.
18. I am regular for my work.
19. I have less job stress and unrest.
20. I have better mental and physical health.
21. I feel good about working as nurse in this hospital.
22. I am satisfied with salary.
23. My job gives me sense of accomplishment.
24. I am satisfied with the way task is carried out.
25. I feel capable of making decisions about professional things.
26. I am certain about opportunities for promotion and advancement in the future.
27. I use skills from experiences for my job.
28. I receive recognition when a job is done well.

*Section-6* **(experimental)**

1. Name ..............
2. Age ..............

**Hospital—**
**District—**

**Physiological cost of nursing work**

(1) Physical activity and heart rate in performing the activity

| S. No. | Type of activity | Heart rate (beats/min) | | |
|---|---|---|---|---|
| | | Before activity | During activity | After activity |
| | | | | |
| | | | | |
| | | | | |
| | | | | |

(2) Physical activity and blood pressure in performing the activity

| S. No. | Type of activity | Blood Pressure (mmHg) | | Pulse rate (per sec) | |
|---|---|---|---|---|---|
| | | Before activity | During activity | Before activity | During activity |
| | | | | | |
| | | | | | |
| | | | | | |
| | | | | | |

(3) Existing environmental parameters

| S. No | Activity Areas | Temperature | | Humidity | | Noise dB | Light (lux) |
|---|---|---|---|---|---|---|---|
| | | Max | Min | Max | Min | | |
| | | | | | | | |
| | | | | | | | |
| | | | | | | | |

(4) Blood lactate concentration (mmol/L)

| S. No. | Type of activity | Blood lactate level (mmol/L) |
|---|---|---|
| | | After activity |
| | | |
| | | |

(5) Dimension of furniture

| | Chair |
|---|---|
| 1. | Total height |
| 2. | Seat height |
| 3. | Seat depth |
| 4. | Seat widths |
| 5. | Back rest height |
| 6. | Back rest width |
| | **Table** |
| 7. | Total height |
| 8. | Widths/depth |
| 9. | Length |

*ANNEXURE-2*

## Chi-square value for action categories of REBA postural analysis

| Table No. | Chi-square value | Significance |
|---|---|---|
| 1. | 16.59 | NS |

# Analysis of Variance for B.P., H.R. and E.E.R.

## 2. ANOVA for Heart Rate1. ANOVA for Blood Pressure

Table of means

| Group I | Group II | Group III |
|---|---|---|
| 96.1650 | 97.5000 | 98.9175 |

| SOURCE | d.f. | s.s. | m.s. | F-value |
|---|---|---|---|---|
| Treatment | 2 | 15.1484 | 7.5742 | 9.1944** |
| Error | 9 | 7.4140 | 0.8237 | |
| Total | 11 | 22.5625 | | |

GM= 97.5275 SEM=0.4538

**CD at 1%= 2.0827** **CD at 5%= 1.4512** **CV= 0.9306**

## 2. ANOVA for Heart Rate

Table of means

| Group I | Group II | Group III |
|---|---|---|
| 112.8750 | 115.0000 | 114.2500 |

| SOURCE | d.f. | s.s. | m.s. | F-value |
|---|---|---|---|---|
| Treatment | 2.0 | 9.2968 | 4.6484 | 5.2706* |
| Error | 9.0 | 7.9375 | 0.8819 | |
| Total | 11.0 | 17.2343 | | |

GM= 114.0417 SEM=0.4695

CD at 1%= 2.1550 CD at 5%= 1.5015 CV= 0.8234

## 3. ANOVA for EER

Table of means

| Group I | Group II | Group III |
|---|---|---|
| 9.2300 | 9.5674 | 9.4450 |

| SOURCE | d.f. | s.s. | m.s. | F-value |
|---|---|---|---|---|
| Treat | 2.0 | 0.2335 | 0.1167 | 6.0708* |
| Error | 9.0 | 0.1730 | 0.0192 | |
| Total | 11.0 | 0.4066 | | |

GM= 9.4141 SEM=0.0693
**CD at 1% = 0.3182 CD at 5% = 0.2217 CV = 1.4731**

## (4) Chi-square value

| *Table No.* | *Chi-square value* | *Significance* |
|---|---|---|
| 1. | **23.94*** | S |
| 2. | **49.14*** | S |
| 3. | **62.40*** | S |
| 4. | **69.16*** | S |
| 5. | **35.99*** | S |
| 6. | **71.67*** | S |
| 7. | **4.41** | NS |
| 8. | **4.22** | NS |

*ANNEXURE-4*

# Spirometry Analysis (Sample Respondents 2-12)

FVC TEST REPORT

ID No. : 2 — Report Date: 01-01-2010

Patient Name : KAMLA YADAV — Eth. Corr.(%): 80

Age(yrs.) : 40 — Sex:F — Weight(Kg): 60 — Height(cm): 152 — BSA(m^2): 1.56

Indications :

Comments :

Flow / Volume Graph — FVC GRAPHS — Volume / Time Graph

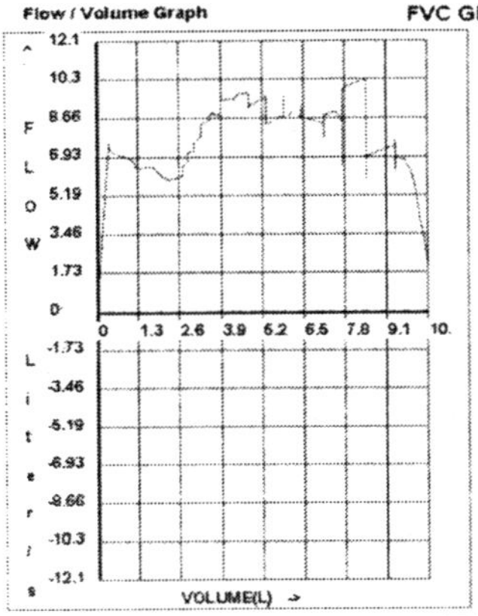


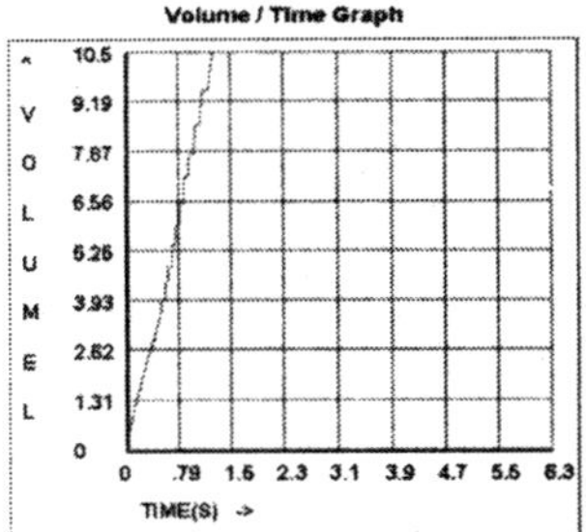


TEST RESULTS

| Date of Test -> | 23/12/2009 | | |
|---|---|---|---|
| Time of Test -> | 12:13:57 | | |
| Parameter (U) | Pred. | Actual | %Pred. |
| FVC (L) | 2.243 | 10.50 | 468.3 |
| FEV0.5 (L) | | 3.343 | |
| FEV1 (L) | 1.923 | 7.803 | 405.7 |
| FEV1/FVC % | 81.5 | 74.29 | 91.16 |
| PEF (L/s) | 4.84 | 12.13 | 250.6 |
| PIF (L/s) | | 0 | |
| FEF25-75% (L/s) | 2.769 | 8.39 | 303.1 |
| Vmax25% (L/s) | 4.396 | 6.82 | 155.1 |
| Vmax50% (L/s) | 3.107 | 9.359 | 301.1 |
| Vmax75% (L/s) | 1.365 | 5.155 | 377.6 |
| FET100% (s) | | 6.1 | |

**INTERPRETATION:** Normal Spirometry

This may be clinically co - related.

**Normal Spirometry**

**BPL ARPEMIS**

**Spirometry analysis (sample respondent 2)**

FVC TEST REPORT

| | | | | |
|---|---|---|---|---|
| ID No. | : 3 | | | Report Date: 01-01-2010 |
| Patient Name | :SHANTI | | | Eth. Corr.(%): 80 |
| Age(yrs.) | : 25 | Sex:F | Weight(Kg): 60 | Height(cm): 156 BSA(m^2): 1.59 |
| Indications | : | | | |
| Comments | : | | | |

FVC GRAPHS

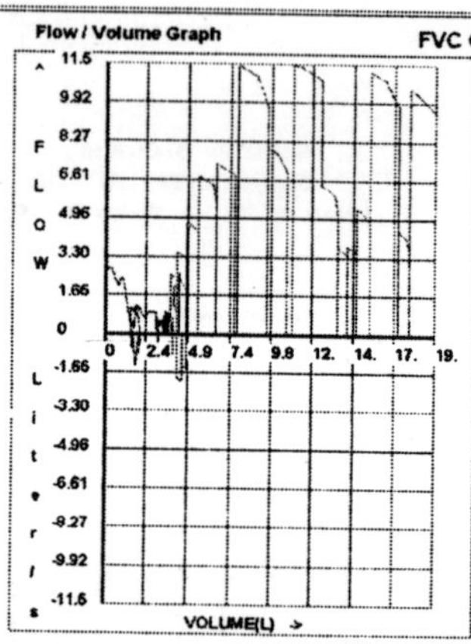


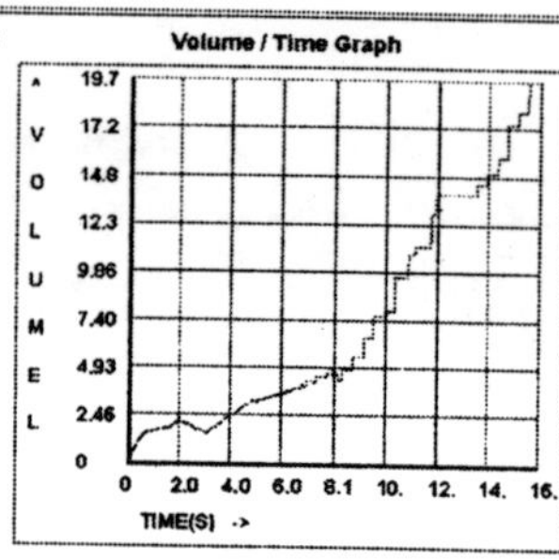


TEST RESULTS

| Date of Test -> | 23/12/2009 | | |
|---|---|---|---|
| Time of Test -> | 14:44:35 | | |
| Parameter (U) | Pred. | Actual | %Pred. |
| FVC (L) | 2.697 | 19.73 | 731.7 |
| FEV0.5 (L) | | 1.201 | |
| FEV1 (L) | 2.35 | 1.67 | 66.80 |
| FEV1/FVC % | 84.35 | 7.957 | 9.433 |
| PEF (L/s) | 5.376 | 11.57 | 215.3 |
| PIF (L/s) | | 2.062 | |
| FEF25-75% (L/s) | 3.216 | 5.113 | 158.9 |
| Vmax25% (L/s) | 4.799 | 4.758 | 99.14 |
| Vmax50% (L/s) | 3.486 | 8.01 | 229.7 |
| Vmax75% (L/s) | 1.698 | 3.807 | 224.2 |
| FET100% (s) | | 16 | |

INTERPRETATION: Mild Obs

This may be clinically co - related.

**Mild Obstacles**

BPL ARPEMIS

Spirometry analysis (sample respondent 3)

FVC TEST REPORT

| | | | |
|---|---|---|---|
| ID No. | : 4 | | Report Date: 01-01-2010 |
| Patient Name | :HEMA BISHT | | Eth. Corr.(%): 80 |
| Age(yrs.) | : 29 Sex:F | Weight(Kg): 65 | Height(cm): 158 BSA(m^2): 1.66 |
| Indications | : | | |
| Comments | : | | |

FVC GRAPHS

Flow / Volume Graph

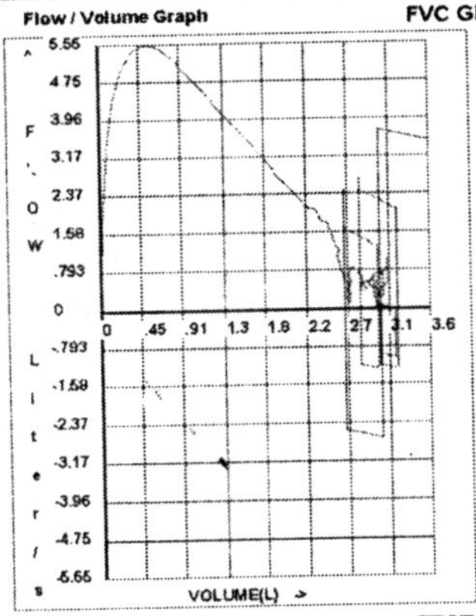


Volume / Time Graph

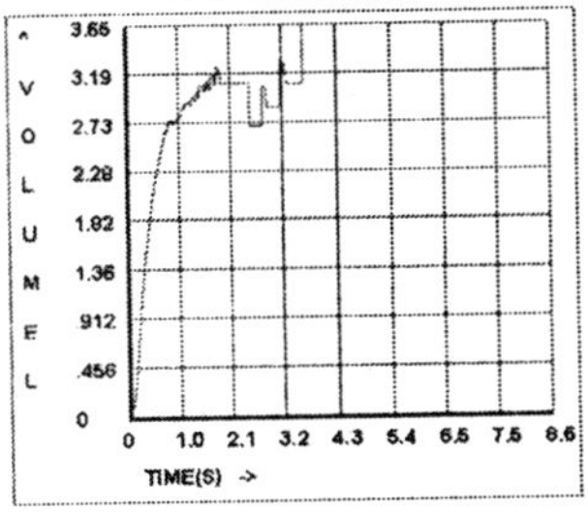


TEST RESULTS

| Date of Test -> | 23/12/2009 | | |
|---|---|---|---|
| Time of Test -> | 14:48:53 | | |
| Parameter (U) | Pred. | Actual | %Pred |
| FVC (L) | 2.684 | 3.652 | 136.0 |
| FEV0 5 (L) | | 1.927 | |
| FEV1 (L) | 2.333 | 2.772 | 118.8 |
| FEV1/FVC % | 83.58 | 75.89 | 90.79 |
| PEF (L/s) | 5.358 | 5.551 | 103.4 |
| PIF (L/s) | | 2.696 | |
| FEF25-75% (L/s) | 3.127 | 2.895 | 92.58 |
| Vmax25% (L/s) | 4.77 | 5.393 | 113.0 |
| Vmax50% (L/s) | 3.445 | 3.251 | 94.36 |
| Vmax75% (L/s) | 1.635 | 0.714 | 43.66 |
| FET100% (s) | | 8.44 | |

INTERPRETATION: Normal Spirometry

This may be clinically co - related.

Normal Spirometry

BPL ARPEMIS

**Spirometry analysis (sample respondent 4)**

FVC TEST REPORT

ID No. : 5
Patient Name : HEMA
Age(yrs.) : 29 Sex:F Weight(Kg): 65
Indications :
Comments :

Report Date: 01-01-2010
Eth. Corr.(%): 80
Height(cm): 156 BSA(m^2): 1.65

FVC GRAPHS

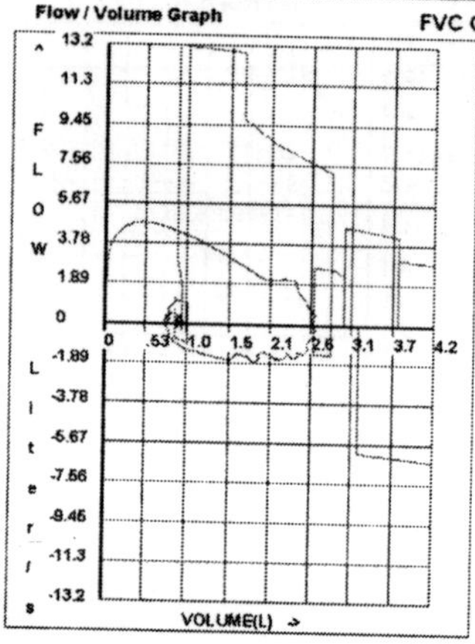


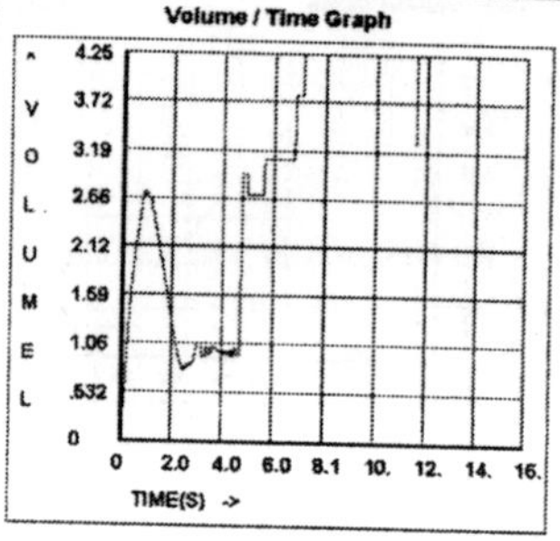


TEST RESULTS

| Date of Test -> | 23/12/2009 | | |
|---|---|---|---|
| Time of Test -> | 14:51:06 | | |
| Parameter (U) | Pred | Actual | %Pred. |
| FVC (L) | 2.613 | 4.269 | 162.9 |
| FEV0.5 (L) | | 1.891 | |
| FEV1 (L) | 2.27 | 2.724 | 120 |
| FEV1/FVC % | 83.59 | 63.96 | 76.52 |
| PEF (L/s) | 5.28 | 13.24 | 250.8 |
| PIF (L/s) | | 6.603 | |
| FEF25-75% (L/s) | 3.107 | 2.832 | 91.14 |
| Vmax25% (L/s) | 4.719 | 4.282 | 90.73 |
| Vmax50% (L/s) | 3.406 | 2.141 | 62.85 |
| Vmax75% (L/s) | 1.618 | 4.6 | 284.3 |
| FET100% (s) | | 11.75 | |

**INTERPRETATION:** **Borderline Obs**

**This may be clinically co - related.**

**Borderline Obstacles**

*BPL* ***ARPEMIS***

**Spirometry analysis (sample respondent 5)**

FVC TEST REPORT

ID No. : 6

Patient Name :REKHA

Age(yrs.) : 28 Sex:F Weight(Kg): 62

Indications :

Comments :

Report Date: 07-01-2010

Eth. Corr.(%): 80

Height(cm): 151 BSA(m^2): 1.58

**FVC GRAPHS**

**Flow / Volume Graph**

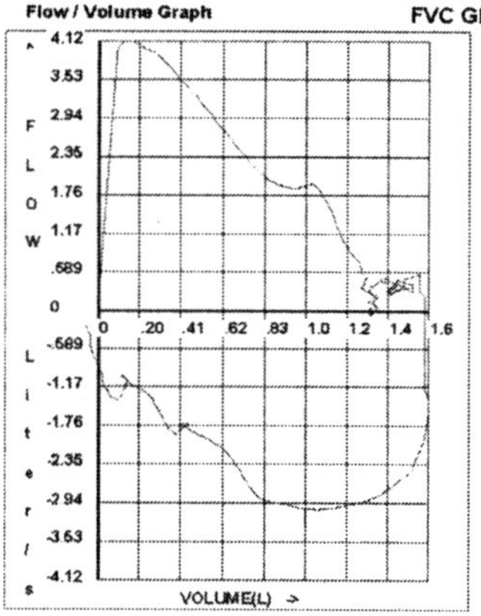


**Volume / Time Graph**

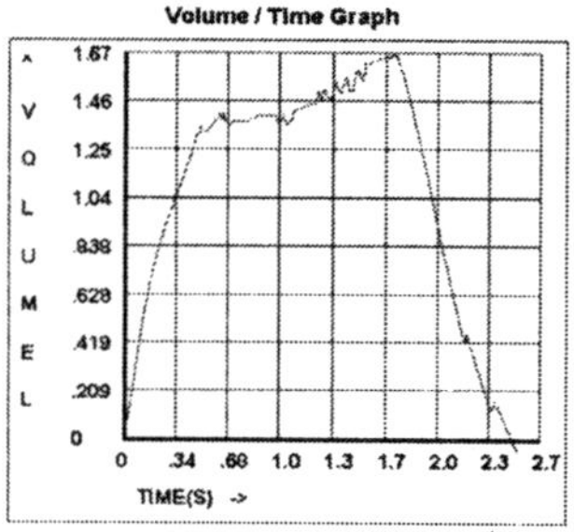


**TEST RESULTS**

| Date of Test -> | 07/01/2010 | | |
|---|---|---|---|
| Time of Test -> | 21:27:26 | | |
| Parameter (U) | Pred. | Actual | %Pred. |
| FVC (L) | 2.457 | 1.677 | 68.25 |
| FEV0.5 (L) | | 1.356 | |
| FEV1 (L) | 2.132 | 1.404 | 65.86 |
| FEV1/FVC % | 83.78 | 83.68 | 99.89 |
| PEF (L/s) | 5.084 | 4.124 | 81.11 |
| PIF (L/s) | | 3.093 | |
| FEF25-75% (L/s) | 3.084 | 2.283 | 74.02 |
| Vmax25% (L/s) | 4.61 | 3.886 | 84.29 |
| Vmax50% (L/s) | 3.328 | 2.22 | 66.70 |
| Vmax75% (L/s) | 1.596 | 1.269 | 79.51 |
| FET100% (s) | | 1.77 | |

**INTERPRETATION: Mild Res Mild Obs Low VC**

**This may be clinically co - related.**

**Mild Obstacles**

***BPL ARPEMIS***

**Spirometry analysis (sample respondent 6)**

FVC TEST REPORT

| | | | |
|---|---|---|---|
| ID No. | 7 | | Report Date: 07-01-2010 |
| Patient Name | M. JANKI | | Eth. Corr.(%): 80 |
| Age(yrs.) | 42 Sex:F | Weight(Kg): 68 | Height(cm): 152 BSA(m^2): 1.65 |
| Indications | | | |
| Comments | | | |

FVC GRAPHS

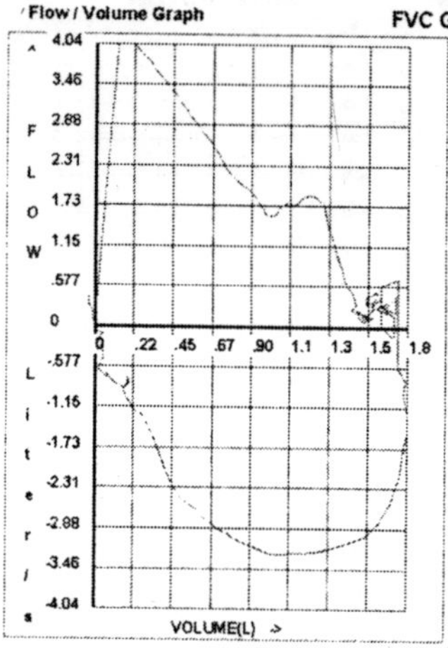


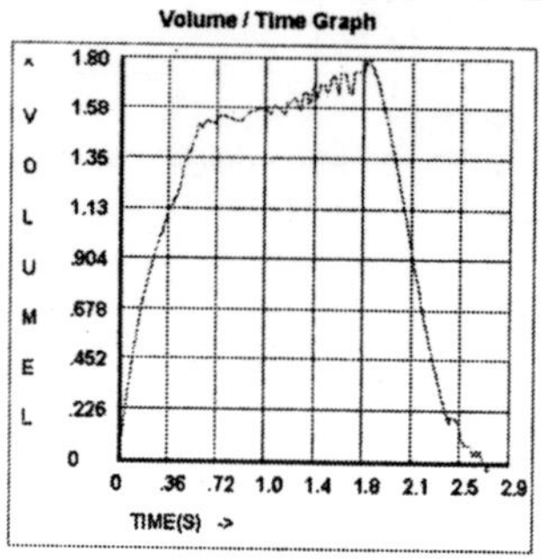


TEST RESULTS

| Date of Test -> | 07/01/2010 | | |
|---|---|---|---|
| Time of Test -> | 21:28:40 | | |
| Parameter (U) | Pred. | Actual | %Pred. |
| FVC (L) | 2 201 | 1.808 | 82.14 |
| FEV0.5 (L) | | 1.344 | |
| FEV1 (L) | 1.883 | 1.57 | 83.37 |
| FEV1/FVC % | 81.12 | 86.84 | 107.0 |
| PEF (L/s) | 4.792 | 4.044 | 84.39 |
| PIF (L/s) | | 3.331 | |
| FEF25-75% (L/s) | 2.714 | 2.153 | 79.32 |
| Vmax25% (L/s) | 4.356 | 3.807 | 87.39 |
| Vmax50% (L/s) | 3.067 | 1.983 | 64.65 |
| Vmax75% (L/s) | 1.325 | 1.903 | 143.6 |
| FET100% (s) | | 1.87 | |

**INTERPRETATION: Normal Spirometry**

This may be clinically co - related.

**Normal Spirometry**

BPL **ARPEMIS**

**Spirometry analysis (sample respondent 7)**

## PULMONARY FUNCTION TEST REPORT

ID No. : 8
Report Date: 07-01-2010
Patient Name :RAJNI PANT
Eth. Corr.(%): 80
Age(yrs.) : 41 Sex:F Weight(Kg): 75 Height(cm): 154 BSA(m^2): 1.73
Indications :
Comments :
History of Smoking : Non - Smoker

**FVC GRAPHS**

**Flow / Volume Graph**

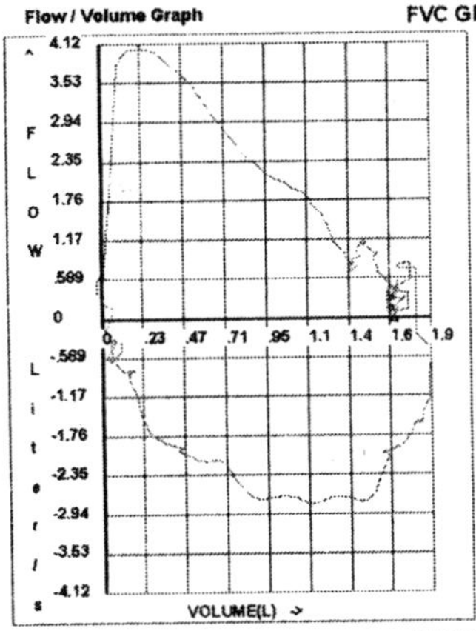


**Volume / Time Graph**

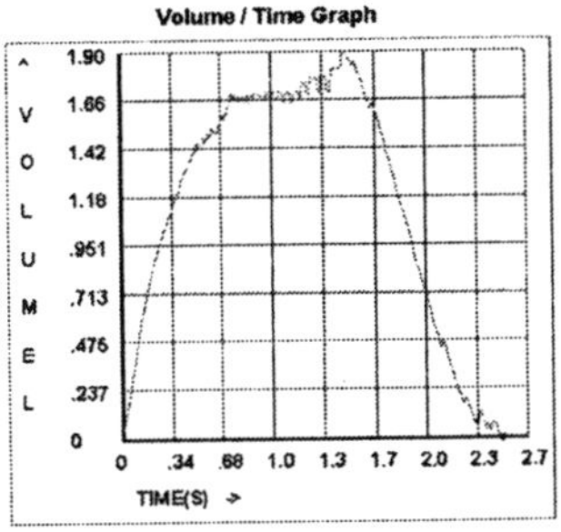


**TEST RESULTS**

Date of Test -> 07/01/2010
Time of Test -> 21:31:16

| Parameter (U) | Pred.# | Actual | %Pred. |
|---|---|---|---|
| FVC (L) | 2.293 | 1.903 | 82.99 |
| FEV0.5 (L) | | 1.404 | |
| FEV1 (L) | 1.966 | 1.713 | 87.13 |
| FEV1/FVC % | 81.31 | 90 | 110.6 |
| PEF (L/s) | 4.904 | 4.124 | 84.09 |
| PIF (L/s) | | 2.856 | |
| FEF25-75% (L/s) | 2.761 | 2.25 | 81.49 |
| Vmax25% (L/s) | 4.427 | 3.965 | 89.56 |
| Vmax50% (L/s) | 3.126 | 2.379 | 76.10 |
| Vmax75% (L/s) | 1.362 | 0.952 | 69.89 |
| FET100% (s) | | 1.51 | |

INTERPRETATION: Normal Spirometry

This may be clinically co - related.

#Predicted Equations : ERS93

**Normal Spirometry**

Page #1/1

BPL ARPEMIS

**Spirometry analysis (sample respondent 8)**

PULMONARY FUNCTION TEST REPORT

ID No. : 9
Patient Name :PUSHPA
Age(yrs.) : 44 Sex:F Weight(Kg): 61 Height(cm): 155 BSA(m^2): 1.6
Indications :
Comments :
History of Smoking : Non - Smoker

Report Date: 07-01-2010
Eth. Corr.(%): 80

FVC GRAPHS

Flow / Volume Graph

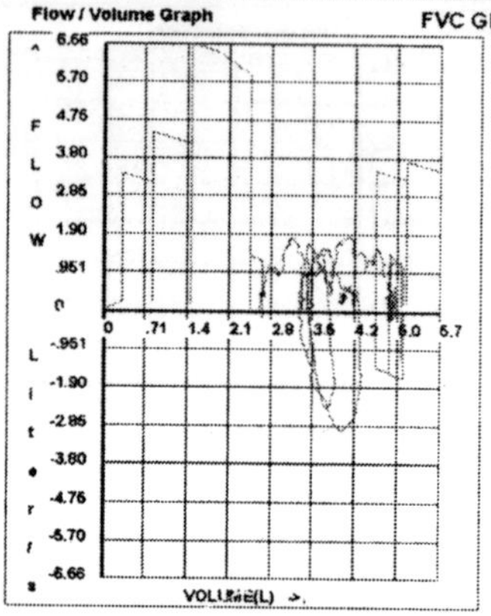


Volume / Time Graph

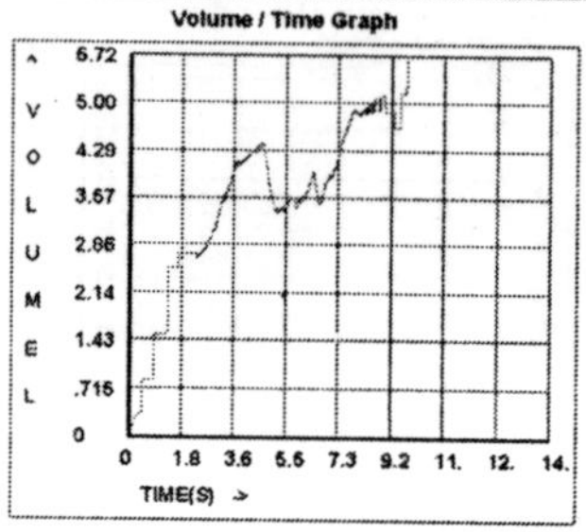


TEST RESULTS

Date of Test -> 07/01/2010
Time of Test -> 21:34:22

| Parameter (U) | Pred.# | Actual | %Pred |
|---|---|---|---|
| FVC (L) | 2.266 | 5.722 | 252.5 |
| FEV0.5 (L) | | 0.845 | |
| FEV1 (L) | 1.939 | 1.511 | 77.96 |
| FEV1/FVC % | 80.74 | 26.40 | 32.70 |
| PEF (L/s) | 4.876 | 6.661 | 136.6 |
| PIF (L/s) | | 3.013 | |
| FEF25-75% (L/s) | 2.699 | 1.269 | 46.92 |
| Vmax25% (L/s) | 4.393 | 4.441 | 101.0 |
| Vmax50% (L/s) | 3.086 | 1.348 | 43.68 |
| Vmax75% (L/s) | 1.31 | 0.634 | 48.39 |
| FET100% (s) | | 14.49 | |

INTERPRETATION: Mild Obs ESA Obs

This may be clinically co - related.

#Predicted Equations ERS93

**Mild Obstacles**

BPL ARPEMIS Page #1/1

**Spirometry analysis (sample respondent 9)**

PULMONARY FUNCTION TEST REPORT

| | | | | |
|---|---|---|---|---|
| ID No. | : 10 | | Report Date: 07-01-2010 | |
| Patient Name | :GEETA | | Eth. Corr.(%): 80 | |
| Age(yrs.) | : 38 Sex:F | Weight(Kg): 56 | Height(cm): 153 | BSA(m^2): 1.52 |
| Indications | : | | | |
| Comments | : | | | |
| History of Smoking | : Non - Smoker | | | |

FVC GRAPHS

Flow / Volume Graph

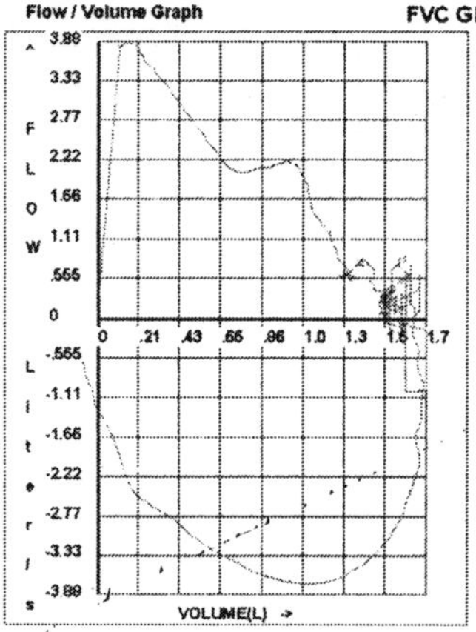


Volume / Time Graph

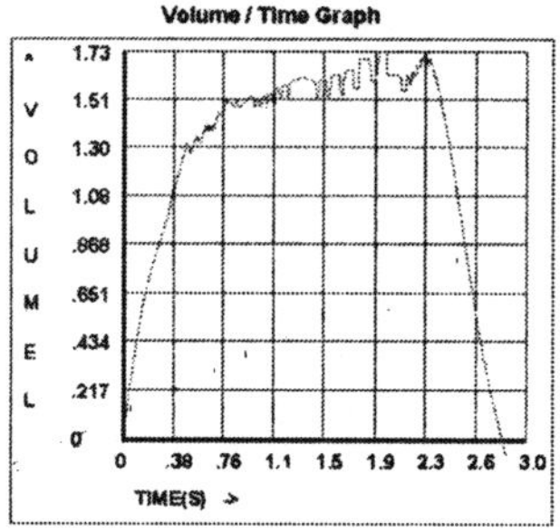


TEST RESULTS

| Date of Test -> | 07/01/2010 | | |
|---|---|---|---|
| Time of Test -> | 21:36:03 | | |
| Parameter (U) | Pred.# | Actual | %Pred. |
| FVC (L) | 2.32 | 1.737 | 74.87 |
| FEV0.5 (L) | | 1.308 | |
| FEV1 (L) | 1.995 | 1.534 | 76.89 |
| FEV1/FVC % | 81.88 | 88.35 | 107.9 |
| PEF (L/s) | 4.932 | 3.886 | 78.79 |
| PIF (L/s) | | 3.727 | |
| FEF25-75% (L/s) | 2.832 | 2.143 | 75.67 |
| Vmax25% (L/s) | 4.461 | 3.331 | 74.66 |
| Vmax50% (L/s) | 3.167 | 2.062 | 65.10 |
| Vmax75% (L/s) | 1.413 | 1.031 | 72.96 |
| FET100% (s) | | 2 | |

INTERPRETATION: Mild Res Mild Obs Low VC

This may be clinically co - related.

#Predicted Equations : ERS93

**Mild Obstacles**

BPL ARPEMIS

Page #1/1

**Spirometry analysis (sample respondent 10)**

PULMONARY FUNCTION TEST REPORT

ID No. : 11 | Report Date: 07-01-2010
Patient Name : KAMLA | Eth. Corr.(%): 80
Age(yrs.) : 34 | Sex: F | Weight(Kg): 49 | Height(cm): 156 | BSA(m^2): 1.46
Indications :
Comments :
History of Smoking : Non - Smoker

FVC GRAPHS

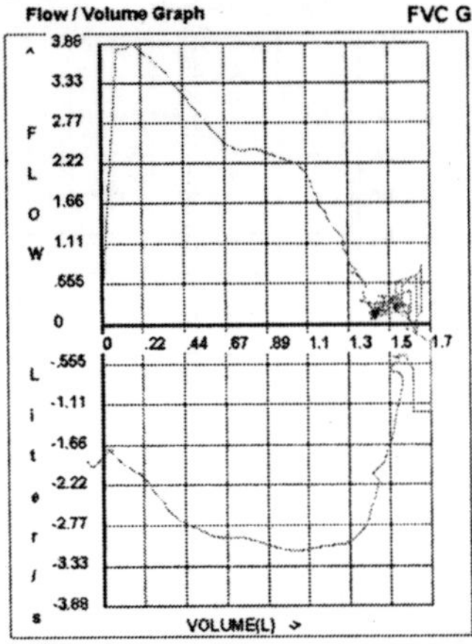


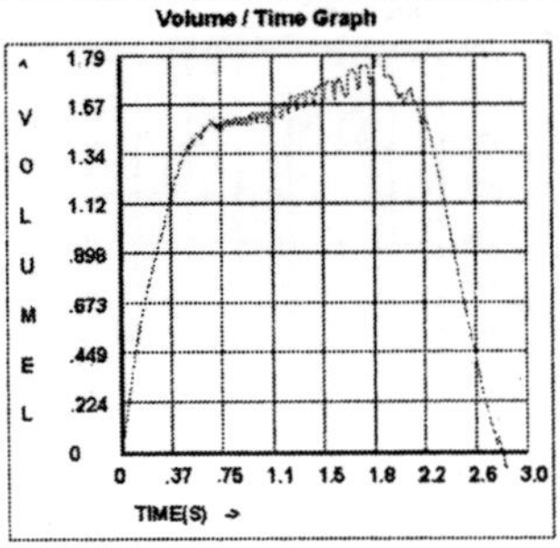


TEST RESULTS

| Date of Test -> | 07/01/2010 | | |
|---|---|---|---|
| Time of Test -> | 21:40:25 | | |
| Parameter (U) | Pred.# | Actual | %Pred. |
| FVC (L) | 2.509 | 1.796 | 71.58 |
| FEV0.6 (L) | | 1.368 | |
| FEV1 (L) | 2.17 | 1.534 | 70.69 |
| FEV1/FVC % | 82.64 | 85.43 | 103.3 |
| PEF (L/s) | 5.16 | 3.886 | 75.31 |
| PIF (L/s) | | 3.172 | |
| FEF25-75% (L/s) | 2.971 | 2.284 | 76.87 |
| Vmax25% (L/s) | 4.619 | 3.489 | 75.63 |
| Vmax50% (L/s) | 3.306 | 2.458 | 74.34 |
| Vmax75% (L/s) | 1.518 | 1.348 | 88.80 |
| FET100% (s) | | 1.96 | |

INTERPRETATION: Mild Res Mild Obs Low VC

This may be clinically co - related.

#Predicted Equations ERS93

**Mild Obstacles**

BPL ARPEMIS

Page #1/1

**Spirometry analysis (sample respondent 11)**

PULMONARY FUNCTION TEST REPORT

ID No. . 12 Report Date: 07-01-2010

Patient Name SHASHI KUMARI Eth. Corr.(%): 80

Age(yrs.) 34 Sex:F Weight(Kg): 47 Height(cm): 149 BSA(m^2): 1.39

Indications

Comments

History of Smoking Non - Smoker

FVC GRAPHS

Flow / Volume Graph

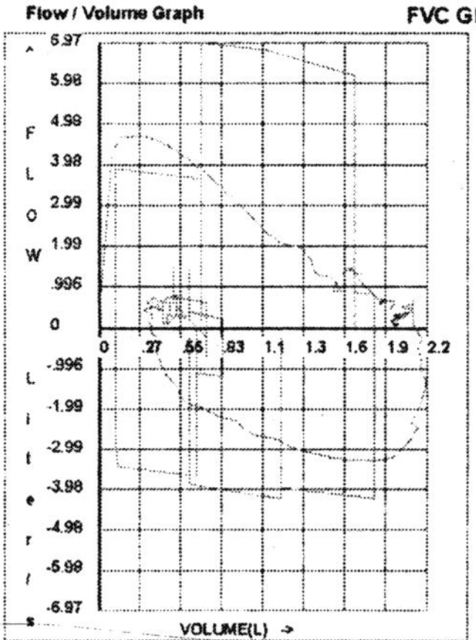


Volume / Time Graph

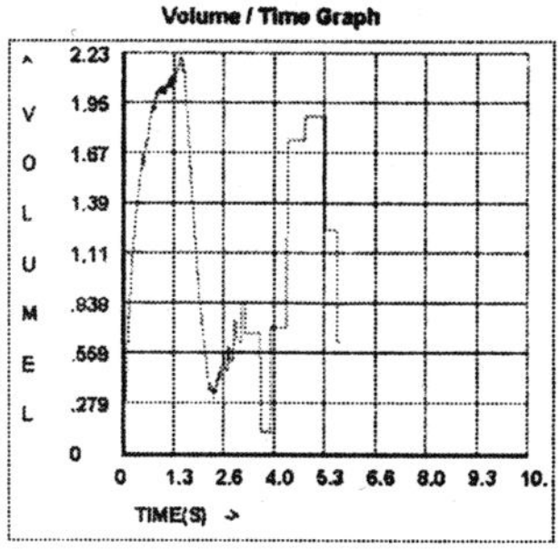


TEST RESULTS

| Date of Test -> | 07/01/2010 | | |
|---|---|---|---|
| Time of Test -> | 21:42:09 | | |
| Parameter (U) | Pred.# | Actual | %Pred. |
| FVC (L) | 2.261 | 2.236 | 98.89 |
| FEV0.5 (L) | | 1.618 | |
| FEV1 (L) | 1.948 | 2.01 | 103.1 |
| FEV1/FVC % | 82.64 | 89.89 | 108.7 |
| PEF (L/s) | 4.862 | 6.979 | 143.8 |
| PIF (L/s) | | 4.205 | |
| FEF25-75% (L/s) | 2.901 | 2.303 | 79.38 |
| Vmax25% (L/s) | 4.438 | 4.52 | 101.8 |
| Vmax50% (L/s) | 3.168 | 2.775 | 87.62 |
| Vmax75% (L/s) | 1.46 | 0.714 | 48.90 |
| FET100% (s) | | 1.54 | |

INTERPRETATION: Normal Spirometry

This may be clinically co - related.

**Normal Spirometry**

#Predicted Equations : ERS93

RPL ARPEMIS Page #1/1

**Spirometry analysis (sample respondent 12)**

# Bibliography


Abdalkader and Hayajneh (2008). Effect of night shift on nurses working in intensive care units at Jordan University Hospital. *European Journal of Scientific Research,* 23(1):70-86. e-reference *http://www.eurojournals.com/ejsr.htm* (Retrieved on 1/Dec/2009)

Abraham, I. ; Siebens, K.; Darras, E. and Dierckx, B. (2006). Work environment and workforce problems: A cross-sectional questionnaire survey of hospital nurses in Belgium. *International Journal of Nursing Studies, 43(6)*: 745-54.

Adalarasu, K. and Balasubramanian, V. (2005). Ergonomic evaluation of chair for computer related works. *International Ergonomics Conference I: 98 (Abstr).*

Almasi, H.; Saberi, H. and Motallebi, M. (2006). Prevalence of sleep disorders in nurses working on rotating shifts. *Journal of Applied Sciences,* 6(3): 644-46.

Anonymous (1986). Lactic acid evaluation in energy contribution. *Br Jnl Sp Med,* 10: 197-201.

Anonymous (2004). Shiftwork practices, Lexington, Mass: Circadian Technologies e-reference. PubMed Result.mht. (Retrieved on 12/Aug/2009).

Araújo, T.; Aquino, E.; Menezes, G.; Oliveira, C. and Aguiar, L. (2003). Work psychosocial aspects and psychological distress among nurses 37(4). *www.revsp@org.usp.br*

Astrila, M. and Wendelin, H. (1974). Comparison of two rating scales in the estimation of perceived exertion in a pulse-conducted exercise test. *Ergonomics,* 17: 577-84.

Beata, P.; Edyta, R.; Jolanta, G. and Agnieszka, B. (2009). Night shift work, melatonin metabolism and breast cancer risk factors ongoing cross-sectional study in nurses in Lonz,

Poland. 19th International Symposium on Shift work and Working Time "Health and Well-being in the 24-h Society"-San Servolo Island, Venezia, Italy, 2-6 Aug 2009. *www.shiftwork2009.it*

Borg, G. (1982). Physiological basis of physical exertion. *Medicine and Science in Sports* 14: 377-81.

Brooks, I. and Swailes, S. (2002). Analysis of the relationship between nurse influences over flexible working and commitment to nursing. *Journal of Advanced Nursing.* 38(2): 117-26. *e-reference. http/www.nectar.northampton.ac.uk/83.* (Retrieved on 26/Nov/2009)

Brown, A. (1998). Turning body times to shift time. *Health Science Centre,* 94: 51-52.

Brown, D.; James, G. and Mills, P. (2006). Occupational differences in job strain and physiological stress: Female nurses and school teachers in Hawaii. Paper presentation in 19th International Symposium on Shift work and Working Time "Health and Well-being in the 24-h Society"-2009. *www.shiftwork2009.it*

Castro, A.B.; Fujishiro, K.; Rue, T.; Paquiz, L.P.; Tagalog, E.A. and Gee, G.C. (2007). Long hours, shift, and overtime: Associations with occupational injury and illness among nurses in the Philippines. 19th International Symposium on Shift work and Working Time "Health and Well-being in the 24-h Society"-San Servolo Island, Venezia, Italy, 2-6 August 2009. *www.shiftwork2009.it*

Chakrabarti, D. (1997). Ergonomics of the design of products, equipments and accessories. *Indian Journal of Indus Med.,* 20(2): 49-63.

Coffey, L.; Skipper, J. and Jung, F. (1998). Nurses and shift work effect on job performance and job related stress. *Journal of Advanced Nursing,* 13(2): 245-54.

Costa, A.; Rotenberg, L.; Griep, R. and Fischer, F. (2008). Recovery from work among nurses: is there an interaction between sleep/rest on the night-shift and domestic work. University of Sao Paulo, Brazil. e-reference. *www.pubmed.gov* (Retrieved on 18/Nov/2009).

Costa, G. (2001). Shift work health consequences. *International Encyclopaedia of Ergonomics and Human Factors*, 2: 1359-61.

Crofts, L. (1999). Challenging shift work: A review of common rostering practices in UK hospitals. *Nursing Progress*, 5. e-reference.*www.rlhleagueofnurses.org.uk/shiftwork/challenge_shiftwork.html* (Retrieved on 12/Nov/2009).

Dewangan, K.N.; Prasanakumar, G.V.; Sujap, L. and Chaudhary, M.D. (2005). Anthropometric dimensions of farm youth of the north eastern region of India. *International Journal of Industrial Ergonomics*, 11: 979-89.

Dhyani, V. (2007). Ergonomic studies on modes of carrying load by hill women. Ph.D. Thesis, GB Pant University of Agriculture and Technology, Pantnagar, India.

Erickson, R. and Grove, W. (2008). Why emotions matter: age, agitation, and burnout among registered nurses. *The Online Journal of Issues in Nursing*, 13(1). *www.nursingworld.org/MainMenuCategories/ANAMarketplace/ANAPeriodicals/OJIN*

Evans, W.A.; Courtney, A.J. and Fak, K.F. (1988). The design of school furniture for Hong Kong school children: An anthropometrics case study. *Applied Ergonomics*, 19: 122-34. e-reference. *www.nursingworld.org* (Retrieved on 18/Nov/2009).

Fanger, P.O. (1979). Local discomfort to the human body caused by non-uniform thermal environments. *Annuals of Occupational Hygiene*, 20: 285-91.

Gamberale, F. (1972). Perceived exertion, heart rate, oxygen uptake and blood lactate levels in different work operation. *Ergonomics*, 15: 545-54.

Gelsema, T.I.; Doef, M.; Maes, S.; Akerboom, S. and Verhoeven, C. (2005). Job stress in the nursing profession: The influence of organizational and environmental conditions and job characteristics. *International Journal of Stress Management*, 12(3): 222-40.

Gitlin, L. (1998). Testing home modification interventions: Issues of theory, measurement, design and implementation. *Annual Review of Gerontology and Geriatrics*, 18: 190-37. e-reference. *www.psycnet.apaorg/index.cfm* (Retrieved on 12/Nov/2009).

Gold, D.R.; Rogacz, S. and Bock, N. (1992). Rotating shift work, sleep, and accidents related to sleepiness in hospital nurses. *Am J Public Health*, 82:1011-14.

Gowda, S.; Goldblum, O.M.; Mccall, W.V. and Feldman, S.R. (2009). Factors affecting sleep quality in patients with psoriasis. *J Am Acad Dermatol*, University of Maryland School of Medicine, Baltimore. e-reference. *www.ncbi.nlm.nih.gov/pubmed* (Retrieved on 15/January/2010)

Grandjean, E. (1980). Fitting the task to the man—an ergonomic approach. Taylor and Francis Ltd., London. 77-81 pp.

Grandjean, E. (ed) (1988). *Fitting the Task to the Man – a textbook of Occupational Ergonomics*. Taylor and Francis Inc., London 35-36 pp.

Groch, J. (2006). Med Page Today, Night-shift nap awakens ER residents and nurses. e-reference. *PubMedresult.mht*. (Retrieved on 3/Nov/2006).

Haghighi, K.S.; Aminian, O.; Pouryaghoub, G. and Yazdi, Z. (2008). Efficacy and hypnotic effects of melatonin in shift-work nurses: double-blind, placebo-controlled crossover trial. *Journal of Circadian Rhythms* 6(10): 1186-1740-3391. *http://www.jcircadianrhythms.com/content/6/1/10*

Harris, C.; Straker, L.; Pollock, C. and Trinidad, S. (2005). Musculo-skeletal outcomes in children using information technology the need for a specific etiological model. *International Journal of Industrial Ergonomics*, 35: 131-38.

Hartel, C. (2000). The consequences and distinctiveness of shift work. *Journal of Occupational and Organizational Psychology*, 42: 168–77.

Hignett and McAtamney (2000). Rapid Entire Body Assessment (REBA). *Applied Ergonomics*, 31 201-205 pp.

Hira, D.S. (1980). An ergonomic apparaisal of educational desks. *Ergonomics* 23(3): 213-21.

Hobbs, B.; Kerk, C.; Kellogg, S. and Hobbs, D. (2007). Night shift and post shift sleepiness. 19th International Symposium on Shift work and Working Time "Health and Well-being in the 24-h Society"—San Servolo Island, Venezia, Italy, 2-6 August 2009. *www.shiftwork2009.it*

ISO 8995 (1989). Principles of visual ergonomics. The lighting of indoor work systems cited in ergonomic design for people at work, pp. 245-48. Van Nostrand, New York.

Kalia, R. (2008). Stress and burnout among NICU nurses. *Journal of Neonatology*. 22(2). *e-reference. www.indianjournals.com/ijor.aspx* (Retrieved on 13/Jan/2009).

Kayis, B. (1991). "Why ergonomic designs in school", cited in V. Popavic and M. Walkar (eds.). Proceedings of the 27th Annual Conference of the Ergonomic Society of Australia, Ergonomic and Human Environment, Coolumn.

Kinzl, J. F.; Knotzer, H.; Traweger, C.; Lederer, W.; Heidegger, T. and Benzer, A. (2005). Influence of working conditions on job satisfaction in anaesthetists. *British Journal of Anaesthesia*. 94(2): 211-15.

Kivimaki, M.; Virtanen, M.; Elovainio, M.; Vaananen, A.; Keltikangas, J. and Vahtera, J. (2006). Prevalent cardiovascular diseases, risk factors and selection out of shift work. *Scand J. Work Environ Health*, 32:204-08.

Klausewitz, W.; Schaefer, W. and Tobias, W. (1986). In: Noise and Radiation Pollution. Fundamentals to Environmental Science. Kalyani Publisher, Ludhiana.133-34 pp.

Kobayashi, F.; Furui, H.; Akamatsu, Y.; Watanabe, T. and Horibe, H. (1997). Influence of changing from a full-day to a half-day work shift before night duty. *International Archives of Occupational and Environmental Health*, 69(2): 83-90.

Korompeli, A.; Sourtzi, P.; Tzavara, C. and Velonakis, E. (2009). Rotating shift-related changes in hormone levels in intensive care unit nurses. *Journal of Advanced Nursing*, 65(6):1274-82.

Kreifeldt, J.G. (1991). Application of ergonomics in product designing. *Proc. International Symposium on Ergonomics*, Occupational Health Safety and Environment, held at 1st Dec.1991, IIT, Bombay, India.

Kubo, T.; Takahashi, M.; Takeyama, H.; Matsumoto, S.; Ebara, T.; Murata, K.; Tachi, N. and Itani, T. (2007). How do the length and timing of nighttime napping have an impact on sleep inertia? 19th International Symposium on Shift work and Working Time "Health and Well-being in the 24-h Society"—San Servolo Island, Venezia, Italy, 2-6 August 2009. *www.shiftwork2009.it*

Kubo, T.; Takeyama, H.; Matsumoto, S.; Ebara, T.; Murata, K.; Tachi, N. and Itani, T. (2007). Impact of nap length, nap timing and sleep quality on sustaining early morning performance. *Industrial Health*, 45: 552–63.

Kudielka, B.M.; Buchtal, J.; Uhde, A. and Wust, S. (2007). Circadian cortisol profiles and psychological self-reports in shift workers with and without recent change in the shift rotation system. *Biological Psychology*, 74(1): 92-103.

Kurumatani, N.; Koda, S.; Nakagiri, S.; Hisashige, A.; Sakai, K.; Saito, Y.; Aoyama, H.; Dejima, M. and Moriyama, T. (1994). The effects of frequently rotating shiftwork on sleep and the family life of hospital nurses. *Ergonomics*, 37(6): 995 – 07.

Landrigan, C.P.; Rothschild, J.M. and Cronin, J.W. (2004). Effect of reducing interns' work hours on serious medical errors in intensive care units. *N Engl J Med*, 351:1838-48.

Lemos, L.C.; Marqueze, E.C.; Nery, M.L. and Moreno, C.R.C. (2007). Association between working hours and complaints of osteomuscular pain in a group of truck drivers. 19th International Symposium on Shiftwork and Working Time "Health and Well-being in the 24-h Society"—San Servolo Island, Venezia, Italy, 2-6 August 2009. *www.shiftwork2009.it*

Lindstrom, K. and Vuori, J. (1984). Relationship between environmental factors, job satisfaction and mental strain in an open-plan drafting office. Cited in *Ergonomics and Health in Modern Offices* edited by E. Grandjean. Taylor and Francis. London and Philadelphia.

Lipkin, J.; Papernik, D.; Plioplys, S. and Plioplys, A. (1998). Chronic fatigue syndrome. *The American Journal of Medicine*, 105(3): 91-93.

Lusted, M.J.; Carrasco, C.L.; Mandryk, J.A. and Healey, S. (1996). Self reported symptoms in the neck and upper limbs in nurses. *Applied Ergonomics* 27(6): 381-87. e-reference. *Content.nejm.org/cgi/content/short/35/18/1838. e-reference* (Retrieved on 12/April/2009).

Pheasant, S.T. (1991). *Ergonomics, Work and Health.* Pp 98-107. Macmillan Press, Hampshire.

Marqueze E. C.; Lemos, L. C.; Nery, M. L.; Soares, N. S.; Lorenzi. G. and Moreno, C.R.C. (2007). Seniority at night work and weight increase among nursing professionals. 19th International Symposium on Shiftwork and Working Time "Health and Well-being in the 24-h Society"—San Servolo Island, Venezia, Italy, 2-6 August 2009. *www.shiftwork2009.it*

Mckennel, A.C. (1971). In: Noise sensitivity performance differential national psychological corporation, Agra. *www.amjmed.com/issues/contents* (Retrieved on 10/Nov/ 2009).

Mckenzie, J. (2001). Circadian Rhythms and Emergency Medicine Practice. *Emergency Medicine Journal,* 21(10): 1250-58.

Mohanty, G. (1980). In: Noise sensitivity and performance differential. 18 pp. National Psychological Corporation; Agra.

Morghen, I.; Turola, M.C.; Forini, E.; Pasquale, P. D.; Zanatta, P. and Matarazzo, T. (2009). Ill-lighting syndrome: Prevalence in shift-work personnel in the anaesthesiology and intensive care department of three Italian hospitals. *Journal of Occupational Medicine and Toxicology,* 4:6 *http:// www.occup-med.com*

Nag, P.K. and Patel, V.G. (1995). Work accident among shift workers in industry in India. *International Journal of Industrial Ergonomics,* 21(3-4): 275-81.

Nehme, P.; Ulhoa, M.; Codarin, M.A.; Moulatlet, E. and Moreno, C.R.C. (2008). Effects of high-carbohydrate and high-protein diet on night security guards' sleepiness. 19th International Symposium on Shiftwork and Working Time "Health and Well-being in the 24-h Society"—San Servolo Island, Venezia, Italy, 2-6 August 2009. *www.shiftwork 2009.it*

Nielsen, K.N.; Garde, A.H. and Diderichsen, F. (2008). The effect of work-time influence on risk factors for cardiovascular disease (CVD). an intervention study. 19th International Symposium on Shiftwork and Working Time

"Health and Well-being in the 24-h Society"—San Servolo Island, Venezia, Italy, 2-6 August 2009. *www.shiftwork 2009.it*

Nielsen, K.N.; Kecklund, G.; Ingre, M.; Skotte, J.; Garde, A. H. and Diderichsen, F. (2008). Individual preferences, work schedule characteristics and intention to leave the workplace. 19th International Symposium on Shiftwork and Working Time "Health and Well-being in the 24-h Society"—San Servolo Island, Venezia, Italy, 2-6 August 2009. *www.shiftwork2009.it*

Norris, B.J. and Wilson, J.R. (1997). Designing safety into products making ergonomics evaluation a part of the design process. The University of Nottingham, Nottingham, U.K.

Noula, A.P.; Yannis, A. and Ioannis, D.K. (2005). Self-rated health, work characteristics and health related behaviours among nurses in Greece: A cross sectional study. *Biomedical central nursing*, 4: 8. *http://creativecommons.org/licenses/by/2.0*

Oginska, H.; Pokorski, J.; Oginski, A.; Kmita, W. and Gondziela, R. (1999). Safety issues and shiftwork. Shiftwork Symposium, Sept. 1999, Germany. proceedings. 32 pp.

Ohida, T.; Kamal, A.; Sone, T.; Ishii, T.; Uchiyama, M.; Minowa, M. and Nozaki, S. (2001). Night-shift work related problems in young female nurses in Japan. *j occup health*, 43: 150–56.

Ohida, T.; Sone, T.; Uchiyama, M. and Ishii, T. (2000). Shift-work and sleep disorders among young female nurses in Japan. *e-reference.* apha.confex.com/apha/128am/techprogram/paper_13679.htm (Retrieved on 31/April/2009).

Pendolf, K.B.; Givoni, B. and Goldman, R. F. (1977). Predicting energy expenditure with loads while standing or walking very slowly. *J Applied Physiology*, 43:4.

Perkins, L. (2001). Occupational hazards: Is the night shift worth the risk? *Emergency Nursing Journal*. 23: 602-09.

Petterson, I.L.; Arnetz, B.B.; Arnetz, J. E. and Horte, L. G. (1995). Work environment, skills utilization and health of Swedish nurses—results from a national questionnaire study. *Psychotherapy and Psychosomatization*, 64:20-31.

Pheasant, S. (1991). *Ergonomics, Work and Health.* 98-107 pp. Macmillan Press, Hampshire.

Pheasant, S.T. (1996). *Body space: Anthropometry, Ergonomics and the Design of Work* (2nd edition), London:Taylor and Francis.

Porter, J.M.; Case, K. and Freer, M.T. (1999). Computer aided design and human models. Cited in: Karwowaski, W. (eds.). *Handbook of Occupational Ergonomics.* CRC Press LLC, Florida, 479-500 pp.

Rauhala, A.; Kivimaki, M.; Fagerstrom, L. Elovainio, M.; Virtanen, M.; Vahtera, J.; Rainio, A.; Ojaniemi, K. and Kinnunen, J. (2007). What degree of work overload is likely to cause increased sickness absenteeism among nurses. Evidence from RAFAEKLA patient classification system. *J Adv Nurs*, 57:286-295

Rivard, C.I.; Dumont, M. and Montplaisir, J. (1989). Sleep disorder symptoms among nurses and nursing aides. *International archives of occupational and environmental health*, 61 (5): 353-58.

Rodgers, S.H. (1980). Ergonomic design for people at work, 245-48 pp. Van Nostrand, New York.

Rogers, E.; Wei-Ting, H.; Linda, D.; Scott, L.; Aiken H. and David, F. (2004). The working hours of hospital staff nurses and patient safety. *Journal of Health Affairs*, 23(4): 202-12.

Ruth, R. and Timothy, H. (1990). A comparison of rotating-shift and permanent night nurses. *International Journal of Nursing Studies*, 27(3): 297-302.

Sahu, S. and Basu, K. (2008). "Individual differences in adaptation to night work rotating at different speed", Proc. of International Conference of HWWE, 39-42 pp.

Sandra, W. (2001). Circadian rhythm, shiftworks and you. *Journal of Royal College of Nursing Australia*, 8(4): 14-21.

Schernhammer, E.; Laden, F.; Speizer, F. and Walter, C. (2003). Night-shift work and risk of colorectal cancer in the nurses' health study. *Journal of the National Cancer Institute*, 95(11):825-28.

Sharma, T.R.; Premi, S.C.L. and Gupta, R.S.R. (1988). Noise pollution and its control measures. Paper presented at workshop on pollution control in Haryana on March 28-29, 1988. CCS Haryana Agricultural University, Hisar.

Shields, M. (2002). Shift work and health. *Health Rep*. 13:11-33.

Smith, C.R.; Rosekind, M. R.; Hurd, S. and Buccino, K. R. (1994). Relationship of day *vs*. night sleep to physician mood and performance. *Ann Emerg Med*, 24: 928-34.

Steele, M.T.; Ma, O.J. and Watson, W.A. (1999). The occupational risk of motor vehicle collisions for emergency medicine residents. *Acad Emerg Med*, 6: 1050-53.

Steenland, K. and Fine, L. (1998). Shift work, shift change and risk of death from heart disease at work. *American Journal of Industrial Medicine*, 29(3): 278-81.

Takahashi, M.; Fukuda, H.; Miki, K.; Haratani, T. and Kurabayashi, L. (1999). Shift work-related problems in 16-h night shift nurses: Effects on subjective symptoms, physical activity, heart rate, and sleep. *Ind Health*, 37(2): 228-36.

Takeyama, H.; Kubol, T. and Itanil, T. (2005). The night time nap strategies for improving night shift work in workplace. *Industrial Health*, 43: 24–29.

Takeyama, H.; Matsumoto, S.; Murata, K.; Ebara, T.; Kubo, T.; Tachi, N. and Itani, T. (2004). Effects of the length and timing of night time naps on task performance and physiological function. *Rev Saude Publica*, 38: 32-7.

Takeyama, H.; Toru, I.; Tachi, N.; Sakamura, O. and Suzumura, H. (2002). Psycho-physiological effects of NAPS during night shifts on morning types and evening types. *J Occup Health*; 44: 89–98.

Tanya, I.; Margot, V.; Stan, M.; Simone, A. and Chris, V. (2005). Job stress in the nursing profession: The influence of organizational and environmental conditions and job characteristics. *International Journal of Stress Management*, 12(3): 222-40.

Thakur, T.C. and Sharma, P. (1998). Ergonomic assessment of various activities performed by women farmers in farm households of hill region of U. P. Report of adhoc. Research Project. I.C.A.R., New Delhi.

Ulbricht, S.; Seibt, R.; Seibt, A. and Hunger, B. (2007). Effects of shift work on the health in employees of the catering trade. 19th International Symposium on Shiftwork and Working Time "Health and Well-being in the 24-h Society"—San Servolo Island, Venezia, Italy, 2-6 August 2009. *www.shiftwork2009.it*

Ulbricht, S.; Seibt, R.; Seibt, A. and Hunger, B. (2008). Correlation between night work and components of health and sleep in employees of the hotel sector and the bakery trade. 19th International Symposium on Shiftwork and Working Time "Health and Well-being in the 24-h Society"—San Servolo Island, Venezia, Italy, 2-6 August 2009. *www.shiftwork2009.it*

Van, R.O. (1998). Sleep and circadian disturbances in shift work: Strategies for their management. *Horm Res, 49(3-4):158-62. www.content.karger.com*

Van, W. P. (1970). Design and Disease. *Applied Ergonomics,* 1: 262-69.

Vannam, R. and Kher, A. (2008). "Effects of night-shift working on human circadian rhythm". Proc. International Conference of Humanizing Work and Work Environment, held on 1-December. IIT India 2008.

Varghese, M.A.; Saha, P.N.; Bhatnagar, A. and Chauhan, M. (1994). Development of data base for occupational workload and physical fitness status of Indian women. DSA project report, SNDT women's university.

Warming, S.; Precht, D.H.; Suadicani, P. and Ebbehoj, N.E. (2009). Musculoskeletal complaints among nurses related to patient handling tasks and psychosocial factors – based on logbook registrations. *Applied Ergonomics,* 40(4): 569-76.

Wickstrom (2001). Healthy Working Hours, Report of the research and development project, 19th International Symposium on Shiftwork and Working Time "Health and Well-being in the 24-h Society"—San Servolo Island, Venezia, Italy, 2-6 August 2009. *www.shiftwork2009.it*

Yamasaki, F.; Schwartz, J.E.; Gerber, L.M.; Warren, K. and Pickering, T.G. (1998). Impact of shift work and race/ ethnicity on the diurnal rhythm of blood pressure and catecholamines. *Hypertension,* 32(3):417-23. *http://www.ncbi.nlm.nih.gov/pubmed/9740605?dopt=Abstract*

Yaung, Y.; Keyserling, W.M. and Chaffin, D.B. (1988). Development of work seat for industrial sewing operations: Results of laboratory study. *Ergonomics* 31(12): 1765-86.

Zieger, A. (2009). Trend: Large, small hospitals differ on safety issues, Fierce healthcare, daily news for healthcare executives. e-reference. *www.fiercehealthcare.com/trend-large-small-hospitals-differ-safety-issues/2009.* (Retrieved on 21/April/2009).

Zverev, Y.P. (2005). The impact of rotating shift work on eating patterns and self-reported health of nurses in Malawi. *Malawi Med Journal,* **16**(2): 37-9. ajol.info/index.php/mmj/article/view/10857

# Index


Absenteeism, 18, 47–48
Accident rate, 31, 33
Accidents
  occupational, 18, 201
  risk of, 31
Activities performed, 111, 113–115
Adjustable chair, 27, 190
Agitation, 22, 40, 63
Alertness, 18, 33, 39, 201
Allergy, 129, 132
Analysis
  descriptive, 53, 83, 86
  postural, 72–73, 83
  regression, 42
  spirometry, 166–167
  statistical, 53, 85–86, 203
Analysis for Postural Discomfort of Nurses, 161
Analysis of Variance for Blood Pressure, 169
ANOVA technique, 169, 212
Anthropometric
  data, 27–29, 150, 178
  dimensions, 29
  kit, 76–77
  measurements, 24, 26, 28, 54, 72, 80, 84, 87, 150–151, 202, 211, 219
Anthropometry, 26, 28–29, 64
Anxiety, 21–22, 36, 50, 63, 70, 145, 200
Appetite, 43, 103, 181, 213
Apron, 187
Arms Plate, 185
Autoclaves, 116, 207
Awakening, 48, 87, 141–142, 145, 215
Awkward posture, 61, 102, 129–130, 161, 192, 209, 214

Baby cradle, 123, 208, 214
Bathrooms, 141
Bed, adjustable, 194
Bed-side table, 214
Beverages, alcoholic, 35–36
Biological clock, 21
Biological hazards, 129, 132, 214
Biomarkers, 48
Blades, squeezing shoulder, 184
Blood lactate analysis, 80, 87, 167–168
Blood pressure, 21, 24, 34–35, 38–39, 47, 58–59, 77, 99, 111, 154–159, 169, 203–205, 207–208, 211–213, 216
  apparatus, 128, 208
  mean, 59
Body dimensions, 29, 150
Body fluid spills, 187
Body height, 65, 150, 211
Body mass index, 38, 62, 87, 154–155

Body weight, 34
Buttock knee length, 69, 153, 211
Buttock popliteal length, 68, 153, 211, 216

Caffeine, 22, 86, 101, 181–182
Cancer, 47
Cardiovascular diseases, 18–19, 21, 39, 62, 200
Chair design, 27
Checklist, 72, 202–203
Chemical Hazards, 132
Chi-square test, 170–171, 173, 203, 216
Chronic illness, 57, 93, 204, 213
Circadian rhythms, 19, 34, 37, 46, 50, 58, 63, 70–71, 107, 175, 177, 217
Cleaning compounds, 132
Coded transmitter, 77
Coding sheets, 83
College of Home Science, 73, 75
Colorectal cancer, 47
Comfortable body temperature, 57
Comfort/discomfort, 86, 123–124
Communication skills, 24, 171, 216
Computer related injuries (CRI), 29
Concentration ability, 24, 173
Conceptual framework, 53–54
Construction and Description of Tools, 71–72
Constructive facilities, 193
Coordination, 24, 44, 171–172, 198, 212, 216, 219
Correlation, 64

Day shift workers, 35, 38
Day time drowsiness, 35
Depression, 19, 21–22, 36, 50, 63, 70, 94, 139, 145
Diabetes, 19, 21, 62, 99, 205
Diagnostic errors, 41
Diastolic pressure, 59
Dimensional features of Furniture, 123
Dimensions of equipment, 28
Discomfort, 30, 61, 123, 208
Display, 17, 201
Dripping, 83, 113, 155, 158–159
Driving, dangerous, 50–51
Driving error, 37
Dual role of nurses, 108
Duty room of government hospitals, 135, 209

Early morning shifts, 175
Elbow rest height, 67, 152, 211, 215
Emergency, 83, 107, 156, 158–159, 174
Energy Expenditure Rate, 24, 60–61, 87, 154, 158–159, 169, 212, 216
Environmental conditions, 17, 42, 87, 134, 136, 150
Environmental parameters, 24, 54, 57, 72–73, 80, 87, 134–135, 179, 202, 214
Ergonomically Suitable Posture, 130
Ergonomics awareness training, 177
Ergonomic shift planning, 174
Ergonomic shift schedules, 49
Evening chronotype, 38–39
Excessive perspiration, 94
Exertion, 70, 159, 161
Experimental data, 80, 85–86, 203
Eye height, 65–66, 150–151
Eyewear, 187

Family profile of nurses, 86, 90, 92
Fatigue, 19, 23, 31–33, 36, 46, 51, 61, 63, 134, 167, 176–178, 200–201, 205, 213–214, 219
  chronic, 36, 145
  effect, 33
  human, 31
  less, 50, 134

level, 78, 173
subjective, 35, 61
symptoms, 36
temporary, 94, 205
worker morning, 33
Feet resting, 65–67, 69
Female nurses, 40, 174, 218–219
Female shift workers, 174
Finger to Shoulder Length, 70, 153
First aid, 83, 156, 158–159
First aid kit, 116
Five-point action level scale, 62
Fluid-resistant materials, 186–187
Forced Expiratory Volume (FEV), 60, 78
Forced Vital Capacity (FVC), 60, 78, 163
forearm, 184
formalization, 18
furniture
cushioned, 124
designed, 178
hard textured, 124, 208
plastic, 124–125

Gallstone, 99, 205
Govind Ballabh Pant University of Agriculture and Technology, 73, 75

Hazards, 54, 64, 128–129, 132–133, 175, 178–179, 214
physical, 132, 214
psycho-social, 133–134
Headache, 93, 204, 210, 213, 215
Health care industry, 24, 26, 53–54, 72, 80, 202–203, 218
Health care professionals, 18, 20
Health problems, 18–19, 45, 201
Heart Rate (HR), 24, 32, 45–46, 59, 61, 70, 73, 77, 111, 116, 154–159, 169, 207, 211–212, 216
measurements, 32, 77
monitor, 77, 116, 207
Higher sleep blood pressure, 35, 38
High-protein, 38
Hip breadth, 69, 153, 211, 216
Horizontal distance, 68–70
Hospitals
academic, 42
categories of, 135, 209
comparison of, 188–189
general, 17
mental, 17
rural, 44
standard, 78
Hospitals activity temperature, 135
Human anatomical waste, 180
Hypertension, 18, 38–39, 62, 177

ICU Bed, 116, 207
Imaging, 187
Index of amount of water vapours, 57
Infrastructure facilities, 24, 53–54, 72, 78, 80, 172, 192, 203, 212, 216
Inhaled air, 186
Injuries
ergonomic, 177
occupational, 33
permanent, 174
work-related, 33
care, 111, 207, 214
musculoskeletal, 23, 33, 129
Insomnia, 20, 70
Instruments, 71, 73, 75–76, 78, 172
dental, 116, 207
endoscopic, 116, 207
ophthalmic, 116, 207
orthopedic, 116, 207
scientific, 80, 177, 194
sterilizer, 116, 207
International Classification of Sleep Disorders (ICSD), 70
Irregular eating pattern, 43, 102
Irritation, 22, 30, 44, 63, 94, 99, 205

Job characteristics, 42–43, 147
  mediation of, 42
Job duration, 58, 104
Job experience, 104, 206, 213
Job performance, 35, 41, 93, 176
Job satisfaction, 22, 24, 30, 42–43, 52, 63, 84, 87, 147, 150, 171–173, 211–212, 215–216
Job satisfaction scale, 72–74, 202–203
  development of, 74
  generic, 219
Job shift, 58, 103–104, 206
Job stress, 18, 134
Joint family system, 90

Knee height, 67–68, 152, 211

Lactate, 61, 167
Lactic acid, 61, 167
Leg rest, 189
Longer sleep times, 35, 38
Lungs, 60, 163, 167

Marital status, 57, 82, 88–89, 204
Marital strain, 24, 63, 173–174
Mean income, 204, 212
Mean shoulder height of nurses, 211
Measurements
  dimensional, 28, 52
  systematic, 26
Medical accessories, 58, 116, 128, 207–208
Medical equipments, 24, 58, 71–72, 80, 86, 111, 116, 125, 172, 202, 207, 214
Medical tests, 111, 207, 214
Melatonin, 21, 37–38, 47, 49
Mid-shoulder landmark, 66–67, 70
Moderate activities, 60–61
Mood Assessment Scale, 219
Morningness scale score, 49
Motivation, 175

Musculoskeletal disorders, 29, 123, 129, 161, 174, 219
Musculoskeletal system, 32, 161

Napping, 176
Night-time napping strategy, 50
Noise hazards, 132, 209
Nurses
  age of, 87–88
  ailments of, 99
  appetite of, 103
  assistants, 40
  critical care, 36
  occupational details, 86, 103, 105
  performance of, 24, 135, 217, 219
  profile of, 24, 86–88, 202
  registered, 42
  shift-work, 37
  shortage of, 39, 200
  skilful, 200
  working counter, 196
Nursing diploma, 82, 88–89, 212
Nursing shortage, 218
Nutritional counselling, 102
nutritional status, 86, 102–103, 206

Obesity, 19, 21, 38, 62
Obstetric labour tables telescope, 116, 128, 207–208
Occupational hazards, 23, 33, 52, 54, 64, 71, 80, 86, 128, 133, 201, 203
Occupational health hazards, 26, 54, 61, 64
Online ergonomics training, 177
Overtime, 42, 52, 58, 63, 102, 107–108, 173–174, 178, 206, 213
  duration of, 24, 58, 63, 108, 173–174
  unplanned, 23, 33
Oxygen therapy instrument, 116, 208, 214

Paediatric equipments, 116, 207
  **pain, 33, 61, 93, 139, 174, 183, 204**

muscle, 45
muscular, 93
osteomuscular, 33–34, 61
Peak Expiratory Flow (PEF), 60, 78, 163
Performance capacity, 63–64, 72, 170, 212, 216, 218
Performing activities, 59–61, 158, 160, 207
Personal Protective Equipment, 180, 188
Physical activities, 34, 45–46, 105
Physiological cost of work, 87, 154, 156–160
Physiological stress, 197
Pittsburg Sleep Quality Index (PSQI), 219
Popliteal height, 67, 152, 211, 215
Postural discomfort of nurses, 87, 161
Postural stresses, 54, 61, 80, 177
Private hospitals, 79–80, 86–94, 99–109, 111, 116, 123–125, 128–129, 132, 134–136, 138–139, 141–142, 145, 147, 154, 203–215
Psychological distress, 40
Psychological problems, 26, 39, 52, 57, 94, 205, 213
Psychological stressors, 183
Psychomotor performance, 19
Pulmonary function, 166
Pulse rate, 31, 155–156, 211

Radiation, 132, 187
Rapid Entire Body Assessment, 24, 62, 87, 161, 168, 202
Rated perceived exertion scale, 202
REBA analysis, 62, 80, 162
Recovery period, 157, 159
Relative humidity, 30, 57, 73
Reliability coefficient, 75–76
Reliability of Scale, establishment of, 75
Repetitive motion, 129, 183, 209, 214
Research design, 53
Research Gaps, 218
Research Kits, 219
Respiration rate, 59, 73, 163, 165, 203
Rest height, 27, 152
Resting area, 78
Rhythms, 46
Right eye, 65–66
Risks
increased, 19, 21, 47
injury, 32
medium, 162, 212
multivariate, 106
occupational, 24
relative, 47
Rotating shift
cycle, 43
nurses, 41

Satisfaction scale, 74, 82
Scientific Equipments, 122
Score sheet, 75
Scoring, 62
Seat height, 27, 152
Seat pan, 27
Selection of variables, 53
Self-opinion of nurses, 109
Self-reported risk factors, 48
Sharp waste, 180
Shift
8-hour, 46
16-hour, 46
afternoon, 31–32, 128
continuous, 71
duration of, 58, 103, 105, 175, 206
environment, 175
extended, 46
first, 31
half-day, 44–45
irregular, 200
Japanese, 35–36
job, 89
planning, 217

roster, 71
rotating, 37, 41, 141, 174
rotational, 46
schedules, 46, 64, 174–175, 183
working non-day, 33
Shoulder, 184
exercise Plate, 185
height, 66–67, 151–152, 215
length, 70, 153, 211, 216
Significant differences, statistically, 49
Skin infection, 129, 214
Sleep, 18–20, 35–36, 38–39, 44–46, 50–51, 63, 70–71, 73, 87, 137–142, 175–176, 180–182, 201, 210, 215
better, 180, 183
daytime, 18, 201
deprivation, 19, 176, 218
disorders, 19–20, 35–37, 52, 63, 72, 134, 142
disturbances, 19, 34, 37, 39, 200
duration, 34, 44, 139
good, 36, 142
health, 51, 218
inertia, 50–51
irregular, 19, 201
length, 48
patterns, 34, 139, 182
poor, 34, 139, 210, 215
problems, 20, 23, 26, 141
subjective, 34 ~~36,~~ 142
sufficient, 24, 40
worse subjective, 34, 39
Sleepless nights, 19, 201
Sleep Onset Latency (SOL), 37
Snoring, 141, 215
Social consequences, 63, 72–73, 84, 203, 215
Social problems, 141, 145
Social support, 109, 207, 214
Solid wastes, 180
Spirometer, 59, 78, 163–164, 202
Spirometry analysis of nurses, 80, 87, 163
Standard Deviation, 84
Standard Error (SE), 84, 88, 92, 150–153
Stanford Sleepiness Scale, 219
Statements Responses Score, 83
Storage spaces, rotating large storage space, 190
Stress, 18, 21, 30, 39, 41, 52, 57, 63–64, 108–109, 177, 181, 183, 200, 207, 214
chronic, 48
occupational, 21
psychological, 64, 217
hormone, 21
management, 219
recognition, 218
responses, 20
tips to reduce, 108–109
Stressor, 21
Stress theory, 21
Stretchers, 123, 189
adjustable height, 189
Subjective symptoms, 45–46
Swedish nurses, 18

Three-shift systems, 35–36, 46
Thyroid, 93, 99, 205
Thyroid-stimulating hormone, 49
Thyroxine, 49
Time
demand~~, 43~~, 172
nap, 49–51, 71, 77
sleep, 37, 201
Tiredness, 22, 44, 63, 94, 177, 205, 213

Uncomfortable bedding, 141
Uncomfortable height, 191
University hospital, 45, 79
Upper arm, 161
Use of Furniture, 123–124

Vaginal delivery, 187
Ventilation, 179, 197
Vertical distance, 65–67

Wakefulness, 19–20, 37
Ward nurses, 25, 53–54, 57–64, 72–74, 76, 78–80, 82–85
  female, 75
  non-sample, 76
  occupational details of, 71, 74, 80
  responses of, 75, 82
Wardrobe, 190, 214
Waste, 180
  biological, 129
  biomedical, 180
  biotechnology, 180
  pathological, 129
Waste anesthetic gases, 132
Weighing machine, 76, 116, 202, 207, 214
  portable, 76
Weight checkup, 83, 155, 158–159
Work agreements, 42, 147
Work conditions, 18, 42, 147
  direct influence of, 42
  environmental, 42
Work-related problems, 45–46
Work shifts, 31, 35, 38, 42, 180, 182
Workstations, 219
Work stress, 86, 108, 207
Wound care, 83, 155, 159

X-ray machine, 116, 125, 132, 207–208, 214

Yawning, 145, 210, 215
Yellow Bag, 180